ZEN

AND THE

PSYCHOLOGY OF

TRANSFORMATION

ZEN

AND THE

PSYCHOLOGY OF

TRANSFORMATION

The Supreme Doctrine

HUBERT BENOIT

FOREWORD BY
ALDOUS HUXLEY

Inner Traditions International
Rochester, Vermont

Inner Traditions International
One Park Street
Rochester, Vermont 05767
www.InnerTraditions.com

Revised edition published in 1990

First published in French under the title *La Doctrine Suprême*
First quality paperback edition published in 1984 by Inner Traditions
     International under the title *The Supreme Doctrine*
Published by arrangement with Pantheon Books

Library of Congress Cataloging-in-Publication Data

Benoit, Hubert.
     [Doctrine suprême. English]
     Zen and the psychology of transformation : the supreme doctrine / Hubert
Benoit ; foreword by Aldous Huxley.
          p.   cm.
     Translation of: La doctrine suprême.
     Reprint. Originally published: New York : Pantheon Books, 1955.
     ISBN 0-89281-272-9
     1. Zen Buddhism—Psychology.   I. Title.
[BQ9268.6B4613   1990]
294.3'375—dc20   90–30217
                                                          CIP

Printed and bound in the United States

10   9   8

CONTENTS

CONTENTS

FOREWORD

PHILOSOPHY in the Orient is never pure speculation, but always some form of transcendental pragmatism. Its truths, like those of modern physics, are to be tested operationally. Consider, for example, the basic doctrine of Vedanta, of Mahayana Buddhism, of Taoism, of Zen. '*Tat tvam asi*—thou art That.' 'Tao is the root to which we may return, and so become again That which, in fact, we have always been.' 'Samsara and Nirvana, Mind and individual minds, sentient beings and the Buddha, are one.' Nothing could be more enormously metaphysical than such affirmations; but, at the same time, nothing could be less theoretical, idealistic, Pickwickian. They are known to be true because, in a super-Jamesian way, they work, because there is something that can be done with them. The doing of this something modifies the doer's relations with reality as a whole. But knowledge is in the knower according to the mode of the knower. When transcendental pragmatists apply the operational test to their metaphysical hypotheses, the mode of their existence changes, and they know everything, including the proposition, 'thou art That', in an entirely new and illuminating way.

The author of this book is a psychiatrist, and his thoughts about the *Philosophia Perennis* in general and about Zen in particular are those of a man professionally concerned with the treatment of troubled minds. The difference between Eastern philosophy, in its therapeutic aspects, and most of the systems of psychotherapy current in the modern West may be summarised in a few sentences.

The aim of Western psychiatry is to help the troubled individual to adjust himself to the society of less troubled individuals—individuals who are observed to be well adjusted to one another and the local institutions, but about whose adjustment to the fundamental Order of Things no enquiry is made. Counselling, analysis, and other methods of therapy are used to bring these troubled and maladjusted persons back to a normality, which is defined, for lack of any better criterion, in statistical terms. To be normal is to be a member of the majority party—or in totalitarian societies, such as Calvinist Geneva, Nazi Germany, Communist Russia, of the party which happens to be in power. For the exponents of the transcendental pragmatisms of the Orient, statistical normality is of little or no interest. History and anthropology make it abundantly clear that societies composed of individuals who think, feel, believe and act according to the most preposterous conventions can survive for long periods of time. Statistical normality is perfectly compatible with a high degree of folly and wickedness.

But there is another kind of normality—a normality of perfect functioning, a normality of actualised potentialities, a normality of nature in fullest flower. This normality has nothing to do with the observed behaviour of the greatest number—for the greatest number live, and have always lived, with their potentialities unrealised, their nature denied its full development. In so far as he is a psychotherapist, the Oriental philosopher tries to help statistically normal individuals to become normal in the other, more fundamental sense of the word. He begins by pointing out to those who think themselves sane that, in fact, they are mad, but that they do not have to remain so if they don't want to. Even a man who is perfectly adjusted to a deranged society can prepare himself, if he so desires, to become adjusted to the Nature of Things, as it manifests itself in the universe at large and in his own mind-body. This preparation must be carried out on two levels simultaneously. On the psycho-physical level, there must be a letting go of the ego's frantic clutch on the mind-body, a breaking of its bad habits of interfering with the otherwise infallible workings of the entelechy, of obstructing the flow of life and grace and inspiration. At the same time, on the intellectual level, there must be a constant self-reminder that our all too human likes and dislikes are not absolutes, that *yin* and *yang*, negative and positive, are reconciled in the Tao, that 'One is the denial of all denials', that 'the eye with which we see God (if and when we see him) is the same as the eye with which God sees us', and that it is the eye to which, in Matthew Arnold's words

each moment in its race,
Crowd as we will its neutral space,

Is but a quiet watershed,
Whence, equally, the seas of life and death are fed.

This process of intellectual and psycho-physical adjustment to the
Nature of Things is necessary; but it cannot, of itself, result in the
normalisation (in the non-statistical sense) of the deranged individual. It will, however, prepare the way for that revolutionary
event. That, when it comes, is the work not of the personal self,
but of that great Not-Self, of which our personality is a partial and
distorted manifestation. 'God and God's will,' says Eckhart, 'are
one; I and my will are two.' However, I can always use my will to
will myself out of my own light, to prevent my ego from interfering
with God's will and eclipsing the Godhead manifested by that will.
In theological. language, we are helpless without grace, but grace
cannot help us unless we choose to co-operate with it.

In the pages which follow, Dr. Benoit has discussed the 'supreme
doctrine' of Zen Buddhism in the light of Western psychological
theory and Western psychiatric practice—and in the process he
has offered a searching criticism of Western psychology and
Western psychotherapy as they appear in the light of Zen. This
is a book that should be read by everyone who aspires to know
who he is and what he can do to acquire such self-knowledge.

ALDOUS HUXLEY.

AUTHOR'S PREFACE

THIS book contains a certain number of basic ideas that seek to improve our understanding of the state of man. I assume, therefore, that anyone will admit that he has still something to learn on this subject. This is not a jest. Man needs, in order to live his daily life, to be inwardly as if he had settled or eliminated the great questions that concern his state. Most men never reflect on their state because they are convinced explicitly or implicitly, that they understand it. Ask, for example, different men why they desire to exist, what is the reason for what one calls the 'instinct of self-preservation'. One will tell you: 'It is so because it is so; why look for a problem where none exists?' This man depends on the belief that there is no such question. Another will say to you: 'I desire to exist because God wishes it so; He wishes that I desire to exist so that I may, in the course of my life, save my soul and perform all the good deeds that He expects of His creature.' This man depends on an explicit belief; if you press him further, if you ask him why God wishes him to save his soul, etc., he will end by telling you that human reason cannot and is not called upon to understand the real basis of such things. In saying which he approaches the agnostic who will tell you that the wise man ought to resign himself always to remaining ignorant of ultimate reality, and that, after all, life is not so disagreeable despite this ignorance. Every man, whether he admits it or not, lives by a personal system of metaphysics that he believes to be true; this practical system of metaphysics implies positive beliefs, which the man in question calls his principles, his scale of values, and a negative belief, belief in the impossibility for man to know the ultimate reality of anything. Man in general has faith in his system of metaphysics, explicit or implicit; that is to say, he is sure that he has nothing to learn in this domain. It is where he is most ignorant that he has the greatest assurance, because it is therein that he has the greatest need of assurance.

Since I write on the problems that concern the state of man I should expect some difficulty in encountering a man who will read my words with an open mind. If I were writing on pre-Columbian civilisation or on some technical subject my reader would assuredly admit my right to instruct him. But it is concerning the most intimate part of himself that I write, and it is highly probable that he will rebel and that he will close his mind, saying of me, 'All the same I hope you are not going to teach me my own business.'

But I am not able to give anything in the domain of which I speak if it is not admitted that there is still something to learn therein. The reader to whom I address myself in writing this book must admit that his understanding of the state of man is capable of improvement; he should be good enough to assume also—while waiting for proof—that my understanding therein is greater than his and that, therefore, I am capable of teaching him; finally, and this is certainly the most difficult part, let him not adopt the attitude of resignation according to which the ultimate reality of things must always escape him, and let him accept, as a hypothesis, the possibility of that which Zen calls *Satori*, that is to say the possibility of a modification of the internal functioning of Man which will secure him at last the enjoyment of his absolute essence.

If, then, these three ideas are admitted: the possibility of improving the understanding of the state of man, the possibility that I may be able to help to this end, the possibility for man to arrive at a radical alteration of his natural state; then perhaps the time spent reading this book will not be wasted. 'But,' it may be argued, 'perhaps the book will enable one to accept these ideas that are not now admitted?' This, however, is not possible; a man can influence another man in the emotional domain, he can lead him to various sentiments and to various ideas that result from such sentiments, but he cannot influence him in the domain of pure intellect, the only domain in which to-day we enjoy freedom. I can lay bare pure intellectual points of view that were latent; they were there, asleep, and I shall have awakened them; but nothing of pure intellectuality can be 'introduced' within the reader; if, for example, the reading of my book seems to bring to birth a definite acceptance of the idea that 'Satori' is possible, it will be in the degree in which such acceptance already existed, more or less dormant, within the reader. In order that the reading of my book may have a chance of being helpful it is certainly not necessary to admit with force and clarity the three ideas that I have mentioned—although it is necessary to admit them a little at least. But above all it is necessary to avoid a hostile attitude *a priori*; if the attitude were hostile I could not convince, and anyhow I would not even make the attempt; metaphysical ideas do not belong to the domain of that which can be demonstrated; each one of us accepts them only to the degree in which he understands intuitively that they explain in us phenomena otherwise inexplicable.

All that I have just written deals with the fundamental misunderstanding that we have to avoid. There are a certain number of misunderstandings of less importance which we should now consider.

Very little will be gained from this book regarding it as a 'digest' that seeks to explain to you 'what you should know concerning Zen'. To begin with it is impossible to conceive of a 'vulgarised' treatment of such subjects; no book will give a rapid initiation in Zen. And then, as a matter of fact, my book is written for those who have already thought much on Oriental and far-Eastern metaphysics, who have read the essential among what is available on the subject, and who seek to obtain an understanding adapted to their occidental outlook. My supposed reader should have read particularly *The Zen Doctrine of No-Mind* of Dr. D. T. Suzuki, or, at least, the preceding works of the same author. I do not pretend that my endeavours conform to a Zen 'orthodoxy'. The ideas that I put forth therein have come to me in espousing the Zen point of view as I have understood it through the medium of the books that set it forth; that is all. Moreover it is impossible here to speak of 'orthodoxy' because there is nothing systematised in Zen; Zen compares all teaching with a finger that points at the moon, and it puts us unceasingly on guard against the mistake of placing the accent of Reality on this finger which is only a means and which, in itself, has no importance.

Nor do I call myself an 'adept of Zen'; Zen is not a church in which, or outside which, one can be; it is a universal point of view, offered to all, imposed on none; it is not a *party* to which one can *belong*, to which one *owes allegiance*. I can help myself from the

Zen point of view, in my search for the truth, without dressing myself up in a Chinese or a Japanese robe, either in fact or in metaphor. In the domain of pure thought labels disappear and there is no dilemma as between East and West. I am an Occidental in the sense that I have an occidental manner of thinking, but this does not hinder me from meeting the Orientals on the intellectual plane and participating in their understanding of the state of man in general. I do not need to burn the Gospels in order to read Hui-neng.

It is because I have an occidental manner of thinking that I have written this book in the way that I have written it. Zen, as Dr. Suzuki says, 'detests every kind of intellectuality'; the Zen Masters do not make dissertations in reply to the questions that they are asked; more often they reply with a phrase that is disconcerting, or by a silence, or by repeating the question asked, or by blows with a stick. It seems that, in order to enlighten an Occidental, dissertations are, within a certain measure that is strictly limited, necessary. Doubtless the ultimate, the real point of view, cannot be expressed in words, and the master would injure the pupil if he allowed him to forget that the whole problem lies precisely in jumping the ditch which separates truth which can be expressed from real knowledge. But the Occidental needs a discursive explanation to lead him by the hand to the edge of the ditch. For example, Zen says, 'There is nothing complicated that Man needs to do; it is enough that he see directly into his own nature.' Personally I have had to reflect for years before beginning to be able to see how this advice could find practical application, concretely, in our inner life. And I think that many of my brothers in the West are in the same case.

If the style of my book is, in one sense, occidental, it differs nevertheless, by the very nature of the Zen point of view, from that strictly ordered architecture which appeals to our 'Cartesian' training. Within each paragraph there is indeed a logical disposition; but it is by no means the same as regards the chapters as a whole, as regards the book as a whole. Again and again breaks intervene, which interrupt the pleasant flow of logic; the chapters follow one another in a certain order, but it would make little difference if they were arranged in almost any other manner. From one chapter to another, certain phrases, if one gave them their literal meaning, may seem to contradict one another. The Western reader should be warned of that; if he begins his reading expecting to find a convincing demonstration correctly carried through from *alpha* to *omega* he will try to make the book accord with this preconceived framework; in this he will fail rapidly and he will abandon the task.

This difficulty depends, I repeat, on the very nature of the Zen point of view. In the teaching of most other doctrines the point of view aimed at comprises a certain invariable angle of vision; if I regard a complex object from a single angle I perceive its projected image on the plane surface of my retina, and this projection is made up of lines and surfaces that are in regular relation. But Zen attaches no importance to theory as such, to the angle from which it studies the volume of Reality. It is this Reality alone which interests it, and it experiences no embarrassment in moving round this complex object in order to obtain every sort of information from which an informal synthesis may result in our mind. Worshipping no formal conception, it is free to wander among all the formal ideas imaginable without worrying itself about their apparent contradictions; this utilisation, without attachment, of conceptions allows Zen to possess its ideas without being possessed by them. Therefore the Zen point of view does not consist in a certain angle of vision, but comprises all possible angles. My reader should realise that no synthetic understanding is deemed to pass from my mind to his by means of this text which might attempt to embody it; this synthesis should occur in his mind, by a means proper to himself, as it occurs in my mind by a means proper to me; no one on Earth can do this work for us. My text offers only the elements suitable for this synthesis; the discursive method, based on logic that is continuous or interrupted, in which these elements are presented, should be accepted for what it is, without demanding the harmonious and formal architecture which would only be an imitation of a true intellectual synthesis based on the depths of the 'being'.

My special thanks go to my friend, Mr. Terence Gray, for his translation of my book; he has solved perfectly the very difficult task of giving a faithful rendering of my thoughts.

Chapter One

ON THE GENERAL SENSE OF ZEN THOUGHT

MAN has always reflected upon his condition, has thought that he is not as he would like to be, has defined more or less accurately the faults of his manner of functioning, has made in fact his 'auto-criticism'. This work of criticism, sometimes rough-and-ready, attains at other times on the contrary, and in a number of directions, a very high degree of depth and subtlety. The undesirable aspects of the natural [1] man's inward functioning are often very accurately recognised and described.

With regard of this wealth of diagnosis one is struck by the poverty of therapeutic effect. The schools which have taught and which continue to teach the subject of Man, after having demonstrated what does not go right in the case of the natural man, and why that does not go right, necessarily come to the question 'How are we to remedy this state of affairs?' And there begins the confusion and the poverty of doctrines. At this point nearly all the doctrines go astray, sometimes wildly, sometimes, subtly, except the doctrine of Zen (and even here it is necessary to specify 'some masters of Zen').

It is not to be denied that in other teachings some men have been able to obtain their realisation. But a clear explanation of the matter and a clear refutation of the false methods is only to be found in pure Zen.

The essential error of all the false methods lies in the fact that the proposed remedy does not reach the root-cause of the natural man's misery. Critical analysis of man's condition does not go deep enough into the determining cause of his inner phenomena;

[1] The expression 'the natural man' in this book describes man as he is before the condition known as satori.

I

it does not follow the links of this chain down to the original phenomenon. It stops too quickly at the symptoms. The searcher who does not see further than such and such a symptom, whose analytic thought, exhausted, stops there, evidently is not able to conceive a remedy for the whole situation except as a development, concerted and artificial, of another symptom radically opposed to the symptom that is incriminated. For example: a man arrives at the conclusion that his misery is the result of his manifestations of anger, conceit, sensuality, etc., and he will think that the cure should consist in applying himself to produce manifestations of gentleness, humility, asceticism, etc. Or perhaps another man, more intelligent this one, will come to the conclusion that his misery is a result of his mental agitation, and he will think that the cure should consist in applying himself, by such and such exercises, to the task of tranquillising his mind. One such doctrine will say to us, 'Your misery is due to the fact that you are always desiring something, to your attachment to what you possess', and this will result, according to the degree of intelligence of the master, in the advice to give away all your possessions, or to learn to detach yourself inwardly from the belongings that you continue to own outwardly. Another such doctrine will see the key to the man's misery in his lack of self-mastery, and will prescribe 'Yoga', methods aimed at progressive training of the body, or of feelings, or of the attitude towards others, or of knowledge, or of attention.

All that is, from the Zen point of view, just animal-training and leads to one kind of servitude or another (with the illusory and exalting impression of attaining freedom). At the back of all that there is the following simple-minded reasoning: 'Things are going badly with me in such and such a way; very well, from now on I am going to do exactly the opposite.' This way of regarding the problem, starting from a *form* that is judged to be bad, encloses the searcher within the limits of a domain that is *formal*, and, as a result deprives him of all possibility of re-establishing his consciousness beyond all form; when I am enclosed within the limits of the plane of dualism no reversal of method will deliver me from the dualistic illusion and restore me to Unity. It is perfectly analogous to the problem of 'Achilles and the Tortoise'; the manner of posing the problem encloses it within the very limits that it is necessary to overstep, and as a result, renders it insoluble.

2

The penetrating thought of Zen cuts through all our phenomena without stopping to consider their particularities. It knows
that in reality nothing is wrong with us and that we suffer because
we do not understand that everything works perfectly, because in
consequence we believe falsely that all is not well and that it is
necessary to put something right. To say that all the trouble
derives from the fact that man has an illusory belief that he lacks
something would be an absurd statement also, since the 'lack' of
which it speaks is unreal and because an illusory belief, for that
reason unreal, could not be the cause of anything whatever.
Besides, if I look carefully, I do not find positively in myself this
belief that I lack something (how could there be positively present
the illusory belief in an absence?); what I can state is that my
inward phenomena behave as if this belief were there; but, if my
phenomena behave in this manner, it is not on account of the
presence of this belief, it is because the direct intellectual intuition
that nothing is lacking sleeps in the depths of my consciousness,
that this has not yet been awakened therein; it is there, for I lack
nothing and certainly not that, but it is asleep and cannot manifest
itself. All my apparent 'trouble' derives from the sleep of my faith
in the perfect Reality; I have, awakened in me, nothing but
'beliefs' in what is communicated to me by my senses and my
mind working on the dualistic plane (beliefs in the non-existence
of a Perfect Reality that is One); and these beliefs are illusory
formations, without reality, consequences of the sleep of my faith.
I am a 'man of little faith', more exactly without any faith, or, still
better, of sleeping faith, who does not believe in anything he does
not see on the formal plane. (This idea of faith, present but asleep,
enables us to understand the need that we experience, for our
deliverance, of a Master to awaken us, of a teaching, of a revelation; for sleep connotes precisely the deprivation of that which
can awaken.)

*In short everything appears to be wrong in me because the fundamental
idea that everything is perfectly, eternally and totally positive, is asleep in
the centre of my being, because it is not awakened, living and active therein.*
There at last we touch upon the first painful phenomenon, that
from which all the rest of our painful phenomena derive. The
sleep of our faith in the Perfect Reality that is One (outside which
nothing 'is') is the primary phenomenon from which the whole of

the entangled chain depends; it is the causal phenomenon; and no therapy of illusory human suffering can be effective if it be applied anywhere but there.

To the question 'What must I do to free myself?' Zen replies: 'There is nothing you need do since you have never been enslaved and since there is nothing in reality from which you can free yourself.' This reply can be misunderstood and may seem discouraging because it contains an ambiguity inherent in the word 'do'. Where the natural man is concerned the action required resolves itself dualistically, into conception and action, and it is to the action, to the execution of his conception that the man applies the word 'do'. In this sense Zen is right, there is nothing for us to 'do'; everything will settle itself spontaneously and harmoniously as regards our 'doing' precisely when we cease to set ourselves to modify it in any manner and when we strive only to awaken our sleeping faith, that is to say when we strive to conceive the primordial idea that we have to conceive. This complete idea, spherical as it were and immobile, evidently does not lead to any particular action, it has no special dynamism, it is this central purity of Non-Action through which will pass, untroubled, the spontaneous dynamism of real natural life. Also one can and one should say that to awaken and to nourish this conception is not 'doing' anything in the sense that this word must necessarily have for the natural man, and even that this awakening in the domain of thought is revealed in daily life by a reduction (tending towards cessation) of all the useless operations to which man subjects himself in connexion with his inner phenomena.

Evidently it is possible to maintain that to work in order to conceive an idea is to 'do' something. But considering the sense that this word has for the natural man, it is better, in order to avoid a dangerous misunderstanding, to talk as Zen talks and to show that work that can do away with human distress is work of pure intellect which does not imply that one 'does' anything in particular in his inner life and which implies, on the contrary, that one ceases to wish to modify it in any way.

Let us look at the question more closely still. Work which awakens faith in the unique and perfect Reality which is our 'being' falls into two movements. In a preliminary movement our discursive thought conceives all the ideas needed in order that we may theoretically understand the existence in us of this faith which is asleep, and in the possibility of its awakening, and that only this awakening can put an end to our illusory sufferings. During this preliminary movement the work effected can be described as 'doing' something. But this theoretical understanding, supposing it to have been obtained, changes nothing as yet in our painful condition: it must now be transformed into an understanding that is lived, experienced by the whole of our organism, an understanding both theoretical and practical, both abstract and concrete; only then will our faith be awakened. But this transformation, this passing beyond 'form', could not be the result of any deliberate work 'done' by the natural man who is entirely blind to that which is not 'formal'. There is no 'path' towards deliverance, and that is evident since we have never really been in servitude and we continue not to be so; there is nowhere to 'go', there is nothing to 'do'. Man has nothing directly to do in order to experience his liberty that is total and infinitely happy. What he has to do is indirect and negative; what he has to understand, by means of work, is the deceptive illusion of all the 'paths' that he can seek out for himself and try to follow. When his persevering efforts shall have brought him the perfectly clear understanding that *all* that he can 'do' to free himself is useless, when he has definitely stripped of its value the very idea of all imaginable 'paths', then 'satori' will burst forth, a real vision that there is no 'path' because there is nowhere to go, because, from all eternity, he was at the unique and fundamental centre of everything.

So the 'deliverance', so-called, which is the disappearance of the illusion of being in servitude, succeeds chronologically an inner operation but is not in reality caused by it. This inward formal operation cannot be the cause of that which precedes all form and consequently precedes *it*; it is only the instrument through which the First Cause operates.

In fact the famous narrow gate does not exist in the strict sense of the word, any more than the path on to which it might open; unless one might wish so to call the understanding that there is no path, that there is no gate, that there is nowhere to go because there is no need to go anywhere. That is the great secret, and at the same time the great indication, that the Zen masters reveal to us.

5

Chapter Two

'GOOD' AND 'EVIL'

W E know that Traditional Metaphysics represent the creation of the universe as the result of the interplay, concomitant and conciliatory, of two forces that oppose and complete one another. Creation results, then, from the interplay of three forces: a positive force, a negative force, and a conciliatory force.

This 'Law of Three' can be symbolised by a triangle; the two lower angles of the triangle represent the two inferior principles

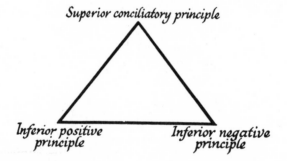

Superior conciliatory principle

Inferior positive principle

Inferior negative principle

of creation, positive and negative; the apex represents the Superior or Conciliatory Principle.

The two inferior principles are, according to Chinese wisdom, the two great cosmic forces of the *Yang* (positive, masculine, dry, hot) and of the *Yin* (negative, feminine, damp, cold) they are also the *Red Dragon* and the *Green Dragon*, whose unceasing struggle is the creative motive power of the 'Ten Thousand Things'.

The diagram of the *T'ai-ki* comprises a black part, the Yin, another which is white, the Yang, of strictly equal extent, and a circle that surrounds them both, which is the Tao (Superior

Conciliatory Principle). The black part contains a white spot, and the white part a black spot, to show that no element of the created world is absolutely positive or absolutely negative. The primordial dualism Yang-Yin includes all the oppositions that we are able to imagine: summer-winter, day-night, movement-immobility, beauty-ugliness, truth-error, construction-destruction, life-death, etc. . . .

This last opposition is particularly stressed in one of the Hindu aspects of the Triad of which we treat: under the authority of

Diagram of the T'ai-ki

Brahma, the Supreme Principle, creation is the simultaneous work of Vishnu, the 'Preserver of Beings', and of Šiva, the 'Destroyer of Beings'.

The creation of the universe, such as we perceive it, unfolds in time; that is to say that the interplay of the two inferior principles is temporal. But these two principles themselves could not be considered as temporal, since they could not be subjected to the limitations which result from their interplay; they are intermediaries, placed between the Superior Principle and the created universe which is the manifestation of this Principle. Universal creation unfolds, then, in time, but is itself an intemporal process to which one can neither attribute nor deny beginning and end, since these words have no sense outside the limits of time. The most modern scientific theories here approach Mataphysics and attribute to the concrete universe neither beginning nor end.

It is very necessary to understand all this in order to free oneself completely from the infantile conception according to which

7

a Creator, imagined anthropomorphically, has at one moment launched the universal movement. My body, for example, was not created only on the day on which I was conceived; it is being un-ceasingly created; at every moment of each year of my life my body is the seat of the birth and death of the cells which compose it, and it is this balanced struggle within me between the Yang and the Yin which goes on creating me up to the time of my death.

In this intemporal Triad which unceasingly creates our tem-poral world one sees the perfect equality of the two inferior principles. Their collaboration being necessary for the appearance of the mass of phenomena, in the appearance of any phenomenon, however small it may be, it is impossible to assign a superiority, either qualitative or quantitative, to either one or the other of these two principles. In one such phenomenon we can see the Yang predominating, in another such the Yin, but the two Dragons balance one another exactly in the spatial and temporal totality of the universe. Also the triangle which symbolises the creative Triad in Traditional Metaphysics has always been an isosceles triangle whose base is strictly horizontal.

The equality of the two inferior principles necessarily carries with it the equality of their manifestations regarded in the abstract. Šiva being the equal of Vishnu, why should life be superior to death? What we are saying here is quite evident from the abstract point of view from which we are now looking. From this point of view why should we see the slightest superiority in construction over destruction, in affirmation over negation, in pleasure over suffering, in love over hate, etc.?

If we now leave aside pure intellectual thought, theoretical, abstract, and if we come down to our concrete psychology, we note two things; first of all our innate partiality for the positive manifestations, life, construction, goodness, beauty, truth; this is easily explained since this partiality is the translation by the intellect of an affective preference, and since this is the logical result of the will to live which is inherent in man. But we notice also something that is less readily explicable: when a metaphysician imagines a man who has attained 'realisation', freed from all irrational determinism, inwardly free and so living according to Reason, identified with the Supreme Principle and perfectly

8

attached to the cosmic order, freed from an irrational need to live and from the preference that follows for life as against death, when a metaphysician imagines this man, he experiences an incontestible intuition that his actions are loving and constructive, and not based on hatred and destruction. We would not say that the man who has attained 'realisation' is loving and devoted to construction, for this man has gone beyond the dualistic sentiments of the ordinary man; but we are not able to see his actions otherwise than as loving and constructive. Why should the partiality that has disappeared from the mind of the man who has attained 'realisation' seem to have to persist in his demeanour? We must answer this question if we would completely understand the problem of 'Good' and 'Evil'.

Many philosophers have thought correctly enough in order to criticise our affective way of looking at Good and Evil and to deny it an absolute value—but often for the benefit of a system which, refuting this attitude in all that is erroneous, denies also all it has that is correct, and, taking man beyond a Good and an Evil that have been abolished, this system leaves him disorientated in the practical conduct of his life or hands him over to a morality that has been turned upside down. The difficulty is not in criticising our affective conception of Good and Evil, but in doing it in a way that will integrate it, without destroying it, in an understanding in which everything is conciliated.

Let us examine first of all, briefly, wherein lies the error that man habitually commits in face of this problem. Man perceives, outside himself and within, positive phenomena and negative phenomena, constructive and destructive. By virtue of his will to live he necessarily prefers construction to destruction. Being an animal endowed with an abstract intellect, generalising, he rises to the conception of construction in general and of destruction in general, that is to say to the conception of the two inferior principles, positive and negative. At this stage of thought the affective preference becomes an intellectual partiality, and the man thinks that the positive aspect of the world is 'good', that it is the only legitimate one, and that he ought to eliminate more and more completely the negative aspect which is 'evil'. Whence the nostalgia for a 'paradise' imagined as destitute of any negative aspect. At this imperfect stage of thought man comprehends the existence of the two inferior principles, but not that of the Superior Principle which conciliates them; also he perceives only the antagonistic character of the two Dragons, not their complementary aspect; he sees the two Dragons in combat, he does not see them collaborating in this struggle; also he necessarily experiences the absurd desire to see, at last, the 'Yes' triumph definitely over the 'No'. Distinguishing, for example, in himself the constructive impulses, which he calls 'qualities', and the destructive impulses, which he calls 'faults', he thinks that his true evolution should consist in eliminating entirely his 'faults', so that he may be animated only by the 'qualities'. Just as he has imagined 'paradise' so he imagines the 'saint', a man actuated by nothing but a perfect positivity, and he sets about copying this model. At best this mode of action will achieve a kind of training of the conditioned reflexes in which the negative impulses will be inhibited in the interests of the positive; but it is evident that such an evolution is incompatible with intemporal realisation, which presupposes the conciliatory synthesis of the positive and negative poles, and the fact that these two poles, without ceasing to oppose one another, can finally collaborate harmoniously.

The conception of the two inferior principles, when the idea of the Superior Principle is lacking, necessarily leads the man to bestow on these two inferior principles a nature at once absolute and personal, that is to say to *idolise* them. The positive principle becomes 'God' and the negative 'Devil'. When the apex of the triangle of the Triad is lacking the base of the triangle cannot remain horizontal; it swings a quarter of a turn: the inferior positive angle becomes 'God' and rises up to the zenith ('paradise'); the inferior negative angle becomes 'Devil' and falls to the nadir ('hell'). 'God' is conceived as a perfect anthropomorphic positivity, he is just, good, beautiful, affirming, constructive. 'Satan' is conceived as a perfect anthropomorphic negativity, he is unjust, wicked, ugly, negating, destructive. Since this dualism of the principles contradicts the intuition that man has, in other respects, of a Unique Principle which unifies everything, the existence of 'Evil', of 'Satan', opposed to 'God', poses to man a problem that is practically insoluble and forces him into philosophical acrobatics. Among these acrobatics, there is an idea which we will see presently is well-founded, the idea that 'God' wills the existence of the 'Devil' and not the other way round, an idea which confers an evident primacy on 'God' in regard to the 'Devil'; but nothing in this dualistic perspective can explain why 'God' has need to desire the existence of the 'Devil' while remaining perfectly free.

Let us note the close relationship which exists between this dualistic conception 'God-Devil' and the *aesthetic* sense which distinguishes the human animal from the other animals. The aesthetic sense consists in perceiving the dualism, affirmation — negation, in 'form'. 'Satan' is deformed, that is to say of negative form, form in the process of decomposition, tending towards the formless. Man has an affective preference for formation (construction) as against deformation (destruction). The form of a beautiful human body is that which corresponds to the apogee of its construction, at the moment at which it is at the maximum distance from the formless and has not yet begun to return thereto. It is not astonishing that every morality should be in reality a system of aesthetics of subtle forms ('make a fine gesture', 'you have ugly propensities', etc.).

This dualistic conception 'Good-Evil', without the idea of the Superior Conciliating Principle, is that at which man's mind arrives spontaneously, naturally, in the absence of a metaphysical initiation. It is incomplete, and in so far as it is incomplete it is erroneous; but it is interesting to see now the truth that it contains within its limitations. If the intellectual partiality in favour of 'Good', due to ignorance, is erroneous, the innate affective preference of man for 'Good' should not be called erroneous since it exists on the irrational affective plane on which no element is either according to Reason nor against it; and this preference has certainly a cause, a *raison d'être*, that our rational intellect ought not to reject *a priori*, but which, on the contrary, it ought to strive to understand.

Let us pose the question as well as we can. While the two inferior principles, conceived by pure intellect, are strictly equal in their complementary antagonism, why, regarded from the practical affective point of view, do they appear unequal, the positive principle appearing indisputably superior to the negative principle? If, setting out the triangle of the Triad, we call the inferior angles 'Relative Yes' and 'Relative No', why, when we wish to name the superior angle, do we feel obliged to call it 'Absolute Yes' and not 'Absolute No'? If the inferior angles are 'relative love' and 'relative hate' why can the superior angle only be conceived as 'Absolute Love' and not as 'Absolute Hate'? Why must the word 'creation', although creation comports as much destruction as construction, necessarily evoke in our mind the idea of construction and not at all the idea of destruction?

In order to make it clear how all this happens we will cite a very simple mechanical phenomenon. I throw a stone: two forces are in play, an active force which comes from my arm, a passive force (force of inertia) which belongs to the stone. These two forces are antagonistic, and they are complementary; their collaboration is necessary in order that the stone may describe its trajectory; without the active force of my arm the stone would not move; without the force of inertia belonging to the mass of the stone it would not describe any trajectory on leaving my hand; if I have to throw stones of different masses the stone that I will throw farthest will be that one whose force of inertia will balance most nearly the active force of my arm. Let us compare these two forces: neither of the two is the cause of the other; the mass of the stone exists independently of the force of my arm, and reciprocally; looked at in this manner neither is of a nature superior to the other. *But the play of the active force causes the play of the passive force*; if the play of my arm is action the play of the inertia of the stone is reaction. And what is true of these two forces in this minor phenomenon is equally true at all stages of universal creation. The two inferior principles, positive and negative, conceived in the abstract or existing apart from their interplay, are not the cause of one another; they derive, independently of one another, from a Primary Cause in the eyes of which they are strictly equal. But as soon as we envisage them in action we observe that the play of the active force causes the play of the passive force (it is in this that 'God' desires the existence of the 'Devil' and not the other way round). In so far as the two inferior principles interact and create, the positive principle sets in motion the play of the negative principle, and it then possesses in that respect an indisputable superiority over this negative principle. The primacy of the active force over the passive force does not consist in a chronological precedence (it is at the same moment that reaction and action occur), but in a causal precedence; one could express that by saying that the instantaneous current by means of which the Superior Principle activates the two inferior principles reaches the negative principle in passing by the positive. In this way we can understand that the two inferior principles, equal noumenally, are unequal phenomenally, the positive being superior to the negative. If the force that moves the sister of charity is strictly equal to that which moves the assassin, the helping of orphans represents an undeniable superiority over assassination; but let us note at the same time that it is the concrete charitable action which possesses an incontestable superiority over the concrete murder, while the two acts, regarded in the abstract, are equal since, so regarded, they are no longer anything but the symbolic representatives of equal positive and negative forces.

Arrived at this point we can understand that every constructive phenomenon manifests the play of the active force (action) and that every destructive phenomenon manifests the play of the passive force (reaction). It is for this reason that the man who has attained 'realisation' is as constructive, at every moment, as circumstances allow him; this man in fact is freed from conditioned reflexes: he no longer reacts, he is active; being active he is constructive.

Such and such a destructive demeanour on the part of the 'wicked' man can seem to show initiative, can appear to result from the play of an active destructive force. In fact this 'wicked' man acts in the first place in order to affirm himself (construction); it is by virtue of associations inaccurately forged in ignorance, that the act, necessarily begun in order to construct, results predominantly in destruction. If the stone that I wish to pick up is too heavy it is not the stone that is raised but I that am dragged down; my initial active force has none the less been directed towards lifting.

The man that has attained 'realisation', as we have seen, does 'good': but we note that this 'good' is a simple consequence of the inner process which has led the Divine Reason of this man to a constant activity in the process of realising his triple synthesis. This 'good' is a simple consequence of a liberating understanding integrated in the total being: and this understanding has done away with all belief in the illusory pre-eminence of the positive inferior principle or principle of 'Good'. *This man no longer does anything but 'good' but precisely because he no longer idolises it and does not devote more attachment to it than to 'evil'.* His demeanour is not that of a man who has trained himself to be a 'saint'; the demeanour of the 'saint', fixed, systematised, can cause ultimately more destruction than construction. The demeanour of the man that has achieved 'realisation' attains ultimately more construction than destruction (without this being in any degree a goal for this man) because it proceeds from a pure activity and he adapts himself to circumstances in a manner that is continually readjusted and fresh.

In short true morality is a direct result of intemporal realisation. The way of liberation could not be 'moral'. All morality, before satori, is premature and is opposed, on account of its restraints, to the attainment of satori. This does not mean to say that the man who strives for his liberation should endeavour to check his affective preference for 'good'. He accepts this preference with the same comprehensive intellectual neutrality with which he accepts the whole of his inner life; but he knows how to abstain from falsely transmuting this anodyne emotional preference into an intellectual partiality which would be in opposition to the establishment of his inner peace.

All that we understand here does not result in a condemnation of 'spiritual' or 'idealist' doctrines, which exalt virtue, goodness, love, etc., in the eyes of men of goodwill; that again would be an absurd intellectual partiality; man thinks and acts according to his lights. We state merely that these doctrines could not, by themselves, lead to the attainment of satori. If such a man desires, as he too has the right to desire, to attain satori, he must by his understanding, go beyond every doctrine which comprises a theoretical partiality in face of the Yang and the Yin. Zen proclaims: 'The Perfect Way knows no difficulty except that it denies itself any preference. . . . A difference of a tenth of an inch and Heaven and Earth are thereby separated.'

Chapter Three

THE IDOLATRY OF 'SALVATION'

ONE of the errors which most surely hinder man's intemporal realisation is that of seeing in this realisation a compulsive character. In many 'spiritual' systems, religious or otherwise, man has the 'duty' of achieving his 'salvation'; he denies all value to that which is temporal and concentrates all the reality imaginable on the 'salvation'. It is evident, however, that there is again here a form of idolatry, since realisation, seen thus as something which excludes other things, is then only one thing among others, limited and formal, and that it is regarded at once as alone 'sacred' and immeasurably superior to all the rest. All the determining, enslaving reality which man attributed to this or that 'temporal' enterprise is crystallised now on the enterprise of 'salvation', and this enterprise becomes the most determining, the most enslaving that can be imagined. Since realisation signifies liberation one arrives at the absurd paradox that man is subjected to the coercive duty to be free. Man's distress is concentrated then on this question of his salvation; he trembles at the thought that he may die before having attained his deliverance. Such a grave error of understanding necessarily entails anxiety, inner agitation, a feeling of unworthiness, an egotistical crispation on oneself-as-a-distinct-being, that is to say, it prevents inner pacification, reconciliation with oneself, disinterestedness towards oneself-as-a-distinct-being, the diminution of emotion— in short all the inner atmosphere of relaxation which governs the release of satori.

The man who deceives himself thus, however, can think again and better. There is no duty except in relation to an authority which imposes it. The believer of this or that religion will say that 'God' is the authority which imposes on him the obligation of salvation. But who then is this 'God' who while imposing something on me, is separate from me and has need of my action? Everything, then, is not included in his perfect harmony?

The same error is found among certain men sufficiently evolved intellectually no longer to believe in a personal God. They seem at least no longer to believe in him. If one looks more closely one perceives that they believe in him still. They imagine their satori, and themselves after their satori, and that is their personal God, a coercive idol, disquieting, implacable. They *must* realise themselves, they *must* liberate themselves, they are terrified at the thought of not being able to get there, and they are elated by any inner phenomenon which gives them hope. There is 'spiritual ambition' in all this which is necessarily accompanied by the absurd idea of the Superman that they should become, with a demand for this becoming, and distress.

This error entails, in a fatally logical manner, the need to teach others. Our attitude towards others is modelled on our attitude towards ourselves. If I believe that I *must* achieve my 'salvation' I cannot avoid believing that I *must* lead others to do the same. If the relative truth that I possess is associated in me with a duty to live this truth—duty depending on an idolatry, conscious or otherwise—the thought necessarily comes to me that it is my duty to communicate my truth to others. At the most this results in the Inquisition and the Dragonnades; at the least those innumerable sects, great and small, which throughout the whole of History, have striven to influence the mind of men who never questioned them, of men who asked nothing of them.

The refutation of this error that we are here studying is perfectly expounded in Zen, and as far as we know, nowhere perfectly but there. Zen tells man that he is free now, that no chain exists which he needs to throw off; he has only the illusion of chains. Man will enjoy his freedom as soon as he ceases to believe that he needs to free himself, as soon as he throws from his shoulders the terrible duty of salvation. Zen demonstrates the nullity of all belief in a personal God, and the deplorable constraint that necessarily flows from this belief. It says: 'Do not put any head above your own'; it says also: 'Search not for the truth; only cease to cherish opinions.'

Why then, some will say, should man strive to attain satori?

16

To put such a question is to suppose absurdly that man cannot struggle towards satori except under the compulsion of a duty. Satori represents the end of this distress which is actually at the centre of one's whole psychic life and in which one's joys are only truces; is it intelligent to ask me why I strive to obtain this complete and final relief? If anyone persists in asking I reply: 'Because my life will be so much more agreeable afterwards.' And, if my understanding is right, I am not afraid that death may come, today or tomorrow, to interrupt my efforts before their attainment. Since the problem of my suffering ends with me why should I worry myself because I am unable to resolve it?

A clear understanding, on the other hand, neither forbids the teaching of others nor obliges one to undertake it; such a prohibition would represent an obligation as erroneous as the first. But the man who has understood that his own realisation is not in any manner his duty contents himself with replying, if asked, that if he takes the initiative of speaking it will be only to propose such ideas with discretion, without experiencing any need of being understood. He is like a man who, possessing good food in excess, opens his door; if a passer by notices this food and comes in to eat it, well and good; if another does not come in, that is equally satisfactory. Our emotions, our desires and our fears, have no place in a true understanding.

Chapter Four

THE EXISTENTIALISM OF ZEN

A MAN declares: 'My life is insipid and monotonous; I do not call that *living*; at most it is *existing*.' Everyone understands what this man means to say, which proves that everyone carries in himself the idea of this distinction. At the same time, everyone feels that 'living' is superior to 'existing'; and this opinion is so clear, so categoric, in the mind of man, that he comes to regard to 'exist' as nothing, and to 'live' as everything. The distinction between the two terms is such that often it demolishes itself; one ends by saying 'existence' for 'life' and *vice versa*. 'Life' appears so uniquely important to man that it annexes the word 'existence' stripped of all its own meaning.

Among the complex mass of phenomena which make up a human being, which are those that proceed from living and which from existing? We find there the distinction between the animal kingdom and the vegetable kingdom. Animal and vegetable are not two creatures entirely different; the animal has everything that the vegetable has (vegetative life) and something more (life of communication). Inside the vegetable and the animal, within the limit constituted by their form, phenomena occur, intimate movements (circulation of sap or of blood, breathing, birth and death of cells, anabolism and catabolism). But, whereas the vegetable is fixed to the soil and has no movement of its whole self in relation to the soil, the animal is mobile in relation to the soil and can make all sorts of movements that one describes by the word 'action'.

However, when man places living so much above existing the frontier of this preferential distinction does not lie between their vegetative phenomena and their actions; it lies within the domain of action, and in the following manner: among my actions some have for object the service of my vegetative life (to eat, to repose,

18

to perform the sexual act by pure animal desire); these actions affirm me (that is to say maintain my creation) in so far as I am an organism in all respects similar to all the other animals, in so far as I live from the point of view of the universe, as a cosmic cog-wheel, in so far as I am 'universal'. But every day, besides these actions, I perform others which do not serve my vegetative life, which often even impede it, and whose aim is to make me appear different from every other man, that is to say to affirm me as distinct from every other man, as a particular man.

Between these two kinds of action lies the frontier which we are studying. My egotistical state, which carries the fiction of my personal divinity, makes me regard as senseless my vegetative life and all the actions by which I serve this life (it is this *ensemble* which constitutes in my eyes the contemptible notion of existing) and leads me to see sense only in those actions which distinguish me (there in my eyes, is the precious, estimable notion of living). I do not count in my own eyes in so far as I am a universal man; I only count in so far as I am the individual 'I'. According to my fiction of personal divinity, to found the sense of my life on my vegetative phenomena and the actions which serve them is absurd, while to found this sense on actions which tend to affirm me as separate is sensible. This view is profoundly rooted in the mind of man.

It is evident to anyone who thinks about it impartially that it is this opinion which is absurd. It assumes implicitly that my particular organism is the centre of the cosmos (only the centre of a sphere is unique in its kind within this sphere; every other point is at the same distance from the centre as an indefinite number of other points). But only the First Cause of the cosmos constitutes this centre; and my particular organism is manifestly not this First Cause. My organism is a link in the immense chain of cosmic cause and effect, and I can only perceive its real sense by considering it in its real place, in its real connexion with all the rest, that is to say by considering it from the point of view of the Universe, in my capacity as universal man and not particular man, in so far as I am similar to all other men and not in so far as I am different.

Man achieves existence, but only (as he thinks) because existing is a necessary condition for living. He eats, he rests, but he does so uniquely because he cannot otherwise affirm himself egotistically, as distinct; he only performs commonplace actions, common to all, in order to do something that no one but he will ever do, he exists in order to live. Basing, thus, the idea of existing on the idea of living he runs counter to the real order of things since he bases the real on the illusory. And so the equilibrium of the ordinary egotistical man is always unstable; this man is comparable with a pyramid standing on its apex.

Zen literature contains, among many others, a remarkable little parable:

'Once upon a time there was a man standing on a high hill. Three travellers, passing in the distance, noticed him and began to argue about him. One said: "He has probably lost his favourite animal." Another said: "No, he is probably looking for his friend." The third said: "He is up there only in order to enjoy the fresh air." The three travellers could not agree and continued to argue right up to the moment when they arrived at the top of the hill. One of them asked: "O friend, standing on this hill, have you not lost your favourite animal?" "No, Sir, I have not lost him." The other asked: "Have you not lost your friend?" "No, Sir, I have not lost my friend either." The third traveller asked: "Are you not here in order to enjoy the fresh air?" "No, Sir." "What then are you doing here, since you answer 'No' to all our questions?" The man on the hill replied: "I am just standing." '

Reading this, the natural man will think in general that 'to be just standing' has no meaning. 'This man on the hill is an idiot,' he will say to himself, 'since he is *doing* nothing' (that is to say, since he is not seeking there any egotistical affirmation. One remembers the ironical phrase of Rimbaud: *'L'action, ce cher point du monde!'*)

'Exist' comes from *ex sistere*, 'to stand outside of', outside the immanent and transcendent Principle of all that exists; existing is the manifestation which emanates (centrifugal impulse) from the Original Being. To exist is dualist, it is positive through 'sistere' and negative through 'ex'. Therefore man feels himself to be therein both well and ill: he possesses something there and he lacks something. The situation in the state of existence necessarily comports, then, a tendency to complete itself, to fill up the void, to neutralise 'ex' by obtaining the consciousness of the Principle from which existing man emanates. But the human intellect develops progressively in such a manner that it is capable of procuring for itself the illusory, and always provisional, appeasement of the egotistical affirmation before being able to feel the fullness of the 'sistere', that is to say before being able to feel that, emanation of the Principle, he is bound to the Principle by a direct filiation which confers on him the very nature of the Principle with its infinite prerogatives. When his intellect arrives at the stage of development at which man can be conscious of his identity with the Principle, this man has already firmly crystallised in his mentality the fascination of the egotistical affirmation; turned towards this affirmation which is the ersatz of the 'sistere' and which, because ersatz, cannot neutralise the 'ex', he turns his back on the 'ex', on the temporal limitation, and thus finds himself in a heart-rending dualism; he is torn between the 'ex', which is behind him and which he cannot destroy, and an illusory 'sistere' which seems to be in front of him in the semblance of the egotistical affirmation and which he never succeeds in seizing.

If man accepted the relative reality of existence, he would feel identified with the Principle from which he emanates. But egotistical man does not accept the relative reality of existence; his mentality, despising and rejecting existence, rushes towards the illusory egotistical affirmation of 'acting' as a distinct being, playing, in regard to this mirage which emanates from him, the rôle, usurped but flattering, of Principle. He thus seeks inner peace in a way that renders it unobtainable. In order to find inner peace, man should reconsider everything, realise the nullity of all his 'opinions', of all his judgements of the value of things, free himself entirely by that means from the centrifugal fascination of the egotistical affirmation, realise the nullity of the egotistical notion of living and of the reality of the universal existing. Renouncing all false heavens he is given back to the Earth, he exists consciously, he 'is in the world' (Rimbaud: '*Nous ne sommes pas au monde*'), and his reconciliaton with the 'ex' allows him to be in possession of the 'sistere'. He *is* the original source when he agrees to be, by his organism, only a phenomenon, a passing emanation of this source, emanation without any special interest and whose individual destiny is without the slightest importance.

It is interesting to examine in its entirety the organism of the human being, his anatomy and his physiology, while asking oneself what is the use of all that one sees there. Digestion and respiration (and all the corresponding organs) serve to feed the blood with nutritive materials. The circulatory apparatus serves to deliver to all parts of the organism this nourishing blood. The delivery of this blood serves to maintain the bones, joints, and muscles; the bones are a framework without which the muscles could not carry out movements; the joints condition this use of the framework. The cerebro-spinal nervous-system releases and co-ordinates the muscular contractions; it regulates the execution of movements and the conception of movements to be made. The vegetative nervous-system controls the harmonious functioning of the viscera on which depend, as we have seen, the maintenance of the motor muscles. The endocrine system is connected with the vegetative nervous system and has the same harmonising function. All, in short, except the genital apparatus which we leave aside for the moment, converge towards the muscles and their movements; that is to say that all existing converges on living, on action; the human machine seems indeed to be made *for action*. But what purpose is served now by the action of this machine? We have seen that the ordinary man only attributes value, real usefulness, to action which affirms him egotistically. But this usefulness that is purely individual is illusory from the universal point of view; one cannot think that the human machine in general exists so that Mr. So-and-so may affirm himself in so far as he is Mr. So-and-so and not Mr. Somebody Else. This egotistical usefulness of action once eliminated, what purpose is served by the 'acting' of this machine-for-action which is the human organism?

Very numerous kinds of action evidently serve to maintain the acting-machine; man acts in order to get himself food, shelter, clothing, etc., or to get them for other acting-machines. There are other actions which have as much usefulness but of a less obvious kind; they are the actions which distinguish the man-animal from the non-human animals: scientific discoveries, artistic creation, intellectual research for the truth; that is to say search for the good, the beautiful, the true. But the good and the beautiful serve existence by tending to improve its conditions; truth also, since man expects of it the appeasement of his anxieties, and so the harmonious peace of his existing organism.

In short, if one looks at things objectively, the existing machine tends, through action, to maintain its existence, and one cannot perceive any object for existence other than existence itself. But is not that to say, at the same time, that existence has no object? (We are here leaving aside any thought of a cosmic utility for man's existence, utility of which the ordinary man cannot have any consciousness that is felt or experienced). The reproductive function, that we left on one side a moment ago, is not at variance with what we are saying now, since it seeks to maintain existence at the level of the existing human species.

Therefore, once the illusory utilisation of action for my egotistical affirmation as a distinct individual is eliminated, I see that my action, to which all the architecture of my organism tends, itself only tends towards the existence of this organism endowed with action; it only serves to prevent the cessation of existence, or death. The famous living, beside which existing seemed to me to be nothing, only tends to serve this existing. Action emanates from existence and serves it, therefore existence is the principle of action, and so infinitely superior to it (every principle being immeasurably superior to its manifestation).

Existence, seen thus as the first cause of the totality of my 'acting', first cause of all my phenomena, is no other than the First Cause of the microcosm which is my organism, that is to say also the First Cause of the universal macrocosm, which is the Absolute Principle. The apparent absurdity of this existence which wills itself and seems thus not to have any aim, is the apparent absurdity of the Absolute Principle from the point of view of the discursive intelligence which emanates from it and which, in emanating, could not be able to seize and comprehend it.

My existence, seen thus as first cause of my existing organism, and which transcends the totality of my phenomena, is entirely independent of the continuation or of the death of my organism. It is at once mine, personally mine, as long as I am not yet dead (immanence of the Principle), and at the same time not mine in so far as I am distinct but only in so far as I am universal, a link in a chain, and as such identical with every other link. Thus my existence is not touched by the death of my organism (transcendence of the Principle).

This allows us to understand that fear of death, a fear which dwells in the natural man and constitutes the centre of all his psychology, is related to the absurd contempt with which this man regards his existence. In one way which at first sight may appear paradoxical, the egotistical man trembles lest he lose his existence because, with regard to acting, to living, he looks upon existing as nothing. In existence resides, as we have seen, the Absolute Principle, this All that man does not know how to appreciate more or less, this All that can only be, for man, zero if he does not appreciate it, or the Infinite if he appreciates it. If man does not see any value in anonymous existence, he does not participate consciously in the nature of the Principle, he is consciously nothing, and in consequence incapable of supporting the subtraction which is death (which appears to him as a negative infinity). If, on the contrary, man sees an infinite value in anonymous existence, he participates fully in the nature of the Principle. He is then consciously infinite and in consequence the subtraction which is death appears to him as nothing.

One sees also the illusory character of the distressing questions which egotistical man puts to himself on the subject of an individual after-life. For these questions are founded on the illusory belief in the reality of the individual living and on the ignorance of the universal existing.

The error of certain philosophical conceptions called existentialist results, among other things, from the fact that the actions of existing and of living are there confounded. This confusion carries with it unfortunate consequences: existing assumes therein a purely phenominal character and, all idea of the First Cause having disappeared, the fact that existence wills itself results in an absurdity that is categorical and no longer merely apparent (it is like the idea of a material eye that itself sees itself). And this living, that is necessarily also absurd, is the capital thing; action, the 'doing and performing', become dogmatic necessities. The disappearance of the Principle entails logically this dualism torn asunder and heart-rending.

Let us return to the distinction that we have made between existing and living, and to the border-line that we have traced between the two. This border-line passes, as we have said, within the domain of actions, between the actions which serve my vegetative life and those which serve my egotistical affirmation. If I study all this in its bearing on my psychological consciousness it seems at first that existing comprises an unconscious part, my vegetative phenomena, and a conscious part, the actions of which serve my vegetative life. But, if I think about it more carefully, I perceive that these actions are as unconscious as my vegetative phenomena, since their object is null for my consciousness. I cannot pretend that I consciously maintain my existence since I am entirely unconscious of the reality of my existence. Let us quote here a dialogue taken from Zen literature:

A MONK: In order to work in the Tao is there a special way?

THE MASTER: Yes, there is one.

THE MONK: Which is it?

THE MASTER: When one is hungry, he eats; when one is tired he sleeps.

THE MONK: That is what everybody does; is their way then the same as yours?

THE MASTER: It is not the same.

THE MONK: Why not?

THE MASTER: When they eat they do not only eat, they weave all sorts of imaginings. When they sleep they do not only sleep they give free rein to a thousand idle thoughts. That is why their way is not my way.

The natural man is only conscious of images, so it is not astonishing that he should be unconscious of existing, which is real, which has three dimensions. In short I am unconscious of that in which I am real, and that of which I am conscious in myself is illusory.

The attainment of satori is nothing else than the becoming conscious of existing which actually is unconscious in me; becoming conscious of the Reality, unique and original, of this universal vegetative life which is the manifestation in my person of the Absolute Principle (that in which I am I and infinitely more than I; imminence and transcendence). It is that which Zen calls 'seeing into one's own nature'. One understands the insistence with which Zen keeps coming back to the maintenance of our vegetative life. To the disciple who asks for the way of Wisdom the master replies: 'When you are hungry you eat; when you are tired you lie down.' There is therein the wherewithal to scandalise the vain egotist who dreams of 'spiritual' prowess and of 'extatic' personal relations with a personal 'God' whose image he creates for himself.

It would be false to consider the revalorisation of the vegetative life, and of the actions which serve it, as a concrete inner effort on the plane of 'feeling'. The Zen master is too intelligent to advise the natural man to suggest to himself, when he satisfies his hunger, that he is at last in contact with Absolute Reality; that would be to replace the old imaginative reveries by a theoretical image of cosmic participation which would change nothing whatever. The natural man has not to revalorise his vegetative life, he has only to obtain one day the immediate perception of the infinite value of this life *by the integral devalorisation of his egotistical life*. The necessary inner task does not consist in 'doing' anything whatever, but in 'undoing' something, in undoing all the illusory egotistical beliefs which keep tightly closed the lid of the 'third eye'.

Indeed what we have just said on the unconscious character of our vegetative life was only an approximation. It would be more exact to speak of 'unconscious consciousness' or of 'indirect or mediate consciousness'; and to conceive of satori not as a consciousness being born *ex nihilo*, but as the metamorphosis of a mediate consciousness into an immediate consciousness. In speaking of indirect consciousness I mean to say that I am indirectly informed concerning the reality of my vegetative life in perceiving directly the fluctuations which menace the phenomena constituting this life. When I am hungry I perceive directly the menace with which inanition threatens my vegetative existence. If I had no kind of vegetative consciousness I would not be conscious that its phenomenal manifestation is menaced; by my hunger I am indirectly conscious of my vegetative existence. In the same way the joy and the sadness of my egotistical affirmations and negations denote diminutions and augmentations of the menace with which the outside world constantly threatens the whole of my vegetative existence; they constitute, then, the becoming-conscious indirectly of this existence.

In short all the positive and negative fluctuations of my affectivity spring from pure and perfect fundamental vegetative joy. This is not directly felt; it is so only indirectly, in the fluctuation of the security or insecurity of this vegetative life. And let us repeat that the direct perception of this perfect existential vegetative joy should not entail any fear of death but, on the contrary, should definitely neutralise this; indeed the fear of death presupposes the imaginative mental evocation of death; but the direct perception of existential reality in three dimensions, in the present moment, would cast into the void all the imaginative phantoms concerning a past or a future without present reality. Man, after satori, is perfectly joyous to exist as long as he exists, up to the last moment at which the disappearance of the mental functions entails the disappearance of all human joy or human pain.

I can say that I am not directly conscious of my existence, that is to say of myself existing, but only of the phenomenal variations of this existence; and that it is my actual belief in the absolute reality of these variations which separates me from the consciousness of that which is beneath them (and which does not vary: noumenal existence, principle of my phenomenal existence). I ought to understand the perfect equality of the varying phenomena (joy or sadness, life or death) in regard to that which *is* beneath these variations, and this understanding should penetrate right to the centre of me, in order that I may obtain at last the consciousness of that which *is* beneath the variations, that is to say of my existence-noumenon, my Reality.

Zen says that the slavery of man resides in his desire to exist. The intellectual apparatus of man develops in such a way that his first perceptions are not perceptions of his existence, but images both partial and biased which suggest the absence of all consciousness of existence and which implant in his mentality the seed of the desire of this consciousness. It is a part of the condition of man that he ought necessarily to pass through the desire to exist in order to reach the existential consciousness which will abolish this desire. And it is the checkmate, correctly interpreted, of all attempts to satisfy the desire to exist which alone can break through the obstacle constituted by this desire.

Among how many human beings can one observe the terror of 'ruining their lives'! Whereas there is in reality nothing to make a success of and nothing to spoil. But a certain temporal realisation is necessary for satori, of a kind that is in some sort negative. As long as man is in the impossibility of succeeding fully in his attempts to satisfy his desire to exist, he cannot go beyond this desire. It is in this sense that man ought to pass by the illusory

27

living in order to reach the real existing. In reality existing precedes living, in the sense that the Principle necessarily precedes its manifestation; but, in the unfolding of temporal duration, man ought to traverse the consciousness of living in order to reach that of existing, which is identical, as long as the human organism lives, with that of 'being'.

Chapter Five

THE MECHANISM OF ANXIETY

WHEN man studies himself with honest impartiality he observes that he is not the conscious and voluntary artisan either of his feelings or of his thoughts, and that his feelings and his thoughts are only phenomena which happen to him. It is easy to note this where feelings are concerned, it is less easy as regards thoughts; however, if I look into myself closely, I realise that my thoughts also just happen to me; I can deal with the subject with which my thought is concerned, but not with my thoughts themselves which I have to take as they come to me.

Since I am not the voluntary artisan of my feelings nor of my thoughts I ought to recognise that I cannot be the voluntary artisan of my actions either; that is to say I can do nothing of my free-will.

But these negative observations regarding a real consciousness and will, lead me to conceive the possible advent of these in man, in me, and I question myself concerning the means of realising these possibilities. I question myself with all the more curiosity in that I feel in myself, connected with this lack of mastery of myself, a fundamental distress which my 'moral' sufferings manifest directly and from which my joys only represent a momentary respite.

In the course of my researches for the means of liberating myself I note that the various teachings which admit the possibility of liberation or 'realisation' in the course of life can be divided into two groups.

The greater part of these teachings are founded on the following false theory: real consciousness and will are lacking to the ordinary man, he does not have them at birth; he must acquire them, build them up in himself, by means of a special inner labour. This labour is difficult and long; consequently the result of this work will be a progressive evolution, that is to say that the acquisition of consciousness and will is progressive. Man will surpass himself little by little, slowly climbing the steps of his development, obtaining higher and higher consciousness by means of which he will progressively approach the highest consciousness—'objective', 'cosmic' or 'absolute' consciousness.

This is a theoretical attitude radically opposed to that which Zen doctrine holds. According to this doctrine man does not lack this real consciousness and this real will, he lacks nothing whatever; he has in himself everything that he needs; he has, from all eternity, the 'nature of Buddha'. He needs absolutely nothing in order that his temporal machine may be controlled directly by the Absolute Principle, that is by his own Creative Principle, in order that he may be free. He can be compared with a machine which lacks not the smallest part in order that it should function absolutely perfectly. But the state of man at his birth comprises a certain modality of development which, as we shall see, entails a hiatus, a non-union which divides his mechanism into two separate parts, soma and psyche. In the absence of this union man does not enjoy the prerogatives of his absolute essence which is nevertheless entirely his own. One would be wrong in suggesting that this lack of union is a lack of some *thing*; the machine is complete, perfect in its smallest details, no part is missing which it should be necessary to manufacture and install in order to make it work properly; it is necessary only to establish a connexion between the two parts that are not joined. Leaving this mechanical comparison for a chemical analogy, let us say that no substance is lacking among the substances necessary for the desired reaction; everything is there; but a contact has to be established in order to set off the reaction. Or again, following another comparison of Zen, there is in man a block of ice to which absolutely nothing is lacking for it to take on the nature of water; but heat has to be generated so that this ice may melt and thus enjoy all the properties of water.

This conception necessarily entails the instantaneous, lightning-like character of man's 'realisation'. Either there is not union between the two parts of man, and then he does not enjoy his divine essence; or the direct contact is re-established, and there is no reason, since absolutely nothing is lacking, why man should not be instantaneously established in the enjoyment of his divine essence. *The inner work which results in the establishment of this direct contact, but not the deliverance itself, is long and difficult, and so, progressive.* In the course of this progressive preparation man brings himself nearer chronologically to his future liberty, but he does not enjoy an atom of this liberty until the moment at which he will have it in its entirety; all that he has in the course of his work is a diminution of his suffering in not being free. He is like a prisoner who laboriously files the bars of his window; his work is progressive and brings him nearer, in time, to his escape; but as long as this work is not completed this man remains entirely a prisoner; he is not free little by little; he is not free at all for some time, then he is completely free at the very moment the bars give way. The only progressive advantage that this man obtains from his work is an increasing alleviation of his suffering through being a prisoner; he is quite as much a prisoner one day as the day before, but he suffers less on that account because his instantaneous deliverance is getting nearer in time.

One can show the same thing again in another way, that which Jesus used in his interview with Nicodemus. Jesus said that man must die in order to be reborn. It is progressively that the 'old' man, by a process of special inner work, goes towards his death, but this death itself and rebirth in another state could only be the two aspects of an inner occurrence that is unique and instantaneous. The 'old' man can be more or less in a dying condition but not more or less dead; as for the 'new man' he is born or he is not yet, but he cannot be more or less born. *This unique and instantaneous inner event Zen calls 'satori' or 'opening of the third eye', and it affirms its sudden character.*

'At a single stroke I have completely crushed the cave of phantoms.'

'A light contact with a taut wire, and behold, an explosion which shakes the Earth to its foundations; everything that lies hidden in the spirit bursts forth like a volcanic eruption or explodes like a clap of thunder.'

Zen calls that 'to return home'. 'You have found yourself now; from the very beginning nothing has been hidden from you; it was yourself who shut your eyes to reality.'

This radical divergence of view between that which the Orient calls the 'progressive' method and the 'sudden' method has consequences that are capital to the conception and practice of the inner liberating task.

Let us see now in detail how one may, in accordance with the general doctrine of Zen, understand the ordinary state of man, this lack of inner union of which we have spoken, and all the functional consequences of this state.

We must first of all, in order to do that, sketch the state of the man who has attained realisation, who is perfect, enjoying his divine essence. This man is a psycho-somatic organism comprising a soma, or animal machine, and a psyche. The psyche of this man is a pure thought, or Independent Intelligence, functioning independently of all influence coming from the animal machine, not determined by this machine but determined by the superior influence of Absolute Truth; this psyche can be called also Divine Reason or Cosmic Intelligence. A force, emanating from this Intelligence and penetrating the animal machine, unites these two parts of the man in a ternary synthesis joined to the Absolute Principle and participating in its essence. The animal machine contains a certain substance which, combined with another substance contained in the Intelligence, constitutes the Absolute Substance of the total man who has 'realised' himself. The substance contained in the animal machine, substance deriving from Nature which makes this machine, we will call 'negative pro-divine substance'. The substance contained in the Independent Intelligence, substance deriving from 'supernatural' Truth, we will call 'positive pro-divine substance'. The force which emanates from the Intelligence and which penetrates the machine, a force which may be conceived as the true love of man for himself, is the hypostasis, the neutralising or conciliating force which permits the combination of the two pro-divine substances and the appearance of the Divine or Absolute Substance. The negative pro-divine substance can also be called feminine substance (as the ovum of the 'being'); the positive pro-divine substance may also be called male substance (as the sperm of the 'being'); the union of these two substances, thanks to the penetration of a force of Intelligence into the machine, is a sort of inner coitus, an act of love giving birth to the 'new man'.

Let us see now, by reference to this man who has attained realisation, how the natural development of the human-being takes place.

(A) STATE OF THE NATURAL HUMAN-BEING IN THE EARLIEST PART OF HIS EXISTENCE

The Independent Intelligence has not yet appeared; the positive pro-divine substance, then, has not appeared. The machine exists but incompletely developed; the brain, and the mentality which depends on it, are in process of construction but are not yet complete. Consequently the negative pro-divine substance is not yet present either, for it is connected with the synthesis of the animal machine fully completed. The mentality not being yet perfected, the child is not yet conscious of the distinction existing between the Self and the Not-Self; he is steeped in the outer world without consciousness of his own limits.

(B) COMPLETION OF THE MACHINE. APPARITION OF THE NEGATIVE PRO-DIVINE SUBSTANCE

The animal brain is now perfected (between one and two years of age). The machine is complete and the negative pro-divine substance is now present. The mentality is fully constructed as an animal mentality capable of concrete preceptions, that is to say such as it is in the non-human animal. But the Independent Intelligence that is to say the possibility for the mentality to function under the influence of Absolute Truth, is not yet present; the positive pro-divine substance, then, is not yet present; there is only the negative pro-divine substance, as in the case of the non-human animal. The development of the animal mentality allows of the becoming conscious of the distinction between Self and Not-Self. This access of consciousness necessarily constitutes a traumatism for the subject; he was living until then in the implicit unconscious conviction that the motor principle of his existence was the motor principle of the universe; nothing had autonomous existence in face of himself and so his existence had nothing to fear. Suddenly he becomes conscious that *his* principle is not the principle of the universe, that there are 'things' that exist independently of him, he

33

becomes conscious of it in suffering from contact with the world-obstacle. At this moment appears conscious fear of death, of the danger which the Not-Self represents for the Self. This entails in the psyche an effective state of war between Self and Not-Self; the subject desires to exist and he desires the destruction of that which exists outside himself and which is not favourable to his own existence. The infant expresses this when he says: 'Me only! Not you!' He affirms himself in saying No. The Self should be understood as everything that is favourable to the existence of the subject; the Not-Self is everything which menaces this existence or which, not showing that it favours it, conceals a possibility of menace. The affective situation so created is very simple: there are two opposing camps, two parties situated on either side of a barrier. The stake is life or death. When the mother of the baby is kind she is part of the Self, she constitutes a formidable defence against death, and the child is calm behind this ally; when she is unkind ('I don't love you any more, you are no longer my little boy'), she is part of the Not-Self, the formidable defence breaks down, and the child howls in the anguish of death (although evidently he has not yet any clear idea of what death is).

In the very simple situation constituted by this fight to the death against the Not-Self, the subject is entirely partial. Lacking Independent Intelligence he has not yet an atom of impartiality, he never puts himself 'in the other man's place'; his offensive and defensive manœuvres are only curbed in their manifestations by considerations of utility, of strategic opportunity. The attitude of the subject before the Not-Self only expresses itself by a No, pronounced effectively or not and with more or less violence according to the manner in which the combat takes place. The causes of the behaviour of the child are entirely affective and irrational.

(c) APPEARANCE OF THE INDEPENDENT INTELLIGENCE AND OF THE POSITIVE PRO-DIVINE SUBSTANCE

The Independent Intelligence appears, and only in the case of the human-being, at the period which is called the age of reason. The mentality then becomes capable of abstract, general, impartial perceptions. The subject can 'put himself in the other man's place', he can conceive of a Good that is distinct from the affirmation of the Self over the Not-Self, he can conceive as desirable an event that is unaffected by the issue of his fight against the Not-Self. Apart from the tendency to assure the building up of his own organism appears a tendency towards construction in general, towards participation in the cosmic construction. The subject can conceive the ideas of Good, Beautiful, True, in general, and can feel an urge towards them.

But, at the moment at which the Independent Intelligence appears, all the powerful affective mechanisms of the subject are already engaged in an entirely partial view of his situation in the universe. The abstract part of the human-being appears very late, at a moment at which his animal part is already solidly set up on the basis of a partial and personal mode of life. The thought of the 'Spirit' appears very much later than the animal thought which is radically contrary to it. The thought of the 'Spirit' affirms the Whole, one and multiple reconciled; the animal thought affirms, and can only affirm, the one by denying the multiple that is external to the one. The animal thought cannot rise towards pure thought; pure thought has to descend to animal thought; but, pregnant with impartiality, it turns from the partiality of the animal and reaches out towards the pure concepts which it fabricates (Eros, love of man for God). A chasm separates the two parties; they are going to live side by side without union. In default of this union the subject cannot enjoy an absolute consciousness. The abstract part, isolated from the animal part, only conceives forms without substance, images lacking a dimension. It conceives a universal ideal image or 'divine' image, beautiful-good-true, which in the absence of absolute consciousness projects itself on to the temporal image that the subject makes of himself, giving birth to an ideal, personal, narcissistic image or 'Ego'.

The two parts of man being unable to reunite naturally, man does not participate in the essence of the Absolute Principle, and he sets himself to adore an image that has no reality, the Ego. In default of a proper love of his abstract part for his animal part man only has an ersatz, self-respect, love of his abstract part for an ideal image of himself.

The unconciliated duality of his two parts results in man being possessed and actuated by two different energetic systems which interfere in various ways, supporting one another or counteracting one another.

IST CASE. THE INDEPENDENT INTELLIGENCE IS WEAK. THE TWO SYSTEMS MUTUALLY SUPPORT ONE ANOTHER. POLICY OF PRESTIGE

This dualistic man, without inner unity, but who has, by his absolute essence, need of unity, is going to cheat inwardly and to play within himself a lying comedy in order to give himself the impression of unity. To that end he is going to cheat either by playing upon his concepts to bring them into harmony with his animal part, or by doing the opposite.

The first case can be seen in the man whose Independent Intelligence is weak. In this man the perception of the abstract, of the general, is too feeble to prevent the concrete, the particular, from appearing to him more real. He lives in the concrete, that is to say, from the point of view of time, in duration and not in eternity. Accepting duration he wishes for *eventual* victory of his Self over the Not-Self, he accepts the momentary check without his 'divine' egotistical image being wounded thereby to an unbearable degree. This man desires to succeed in temporal duration, he seeks his egotistical affirmations in his effective temporal realisations. His abstract part tends towards the same thing as his animal part, it goes in the same direction and only accentuates the claims of the instincts. There is no inner laceration in this man; he rationalises his tendencies; he cheats in putting ideal 'principles' in harmony with his will-to-power, or more exactly in presenting to himself his practical problems in such a way that his reason approves his tendencies.

2ND CASE. THE INDEPENDENT INTELLIGENCE IS STRONG. THE TWO SYSTEMS OPPOSE ONE ANOTHER. 'FEAR' OF DEFEAT. DISTRESS

This man whose abstract part is strongly developed intellectually feels that the abstract, the general, is more real than the concrete, the particular. In the course of his search for success over the Not-Self the particular success is eclipsed by the general idea of success. He does not think in duration but from the angle of eternity; as in fact he lives in duration, and as the intersection of eternity and duration is the *instant*, he lives in the instant. He is the man of 'at this very moment'. He does not want his victory over the Not-Self finally, but at once; he desires to succeed in the temporal sphere instantly.

But this complete victory over an aspect of the Not-Self on the moment is manifestly impossible; nothing can be done on the temporal plane without duration. In order to avoid feeling rebuffed in the very centre of his being this man must do something; he must 'reason with himself', he must withdraw the pretention that he advanced to such a manifestation of his temporal omnipotence ('these grapes are too sour'). He adapts himself to the limiting conditions of his temporal existence, he pretends to accept them voluntarily, freely. In reality he does not and cannot accept them, he resigns himself to them merely, that is to say that, without accepting them, he acts as though he accepted them.

It is of capital importance to understand this distinction between acceptation and resignation. To accept, really to accept a situation, is to think and feel with the whole of one's being that, even if one had the faculty of modifying it, one would not do it, and would have no reason to do it. Man in his inner unconciliated dualistic state, with a separated reason and affectivity, is absolutely unable to adhere affectively to the existence of the Not-Self by which he feels himself repudiated. He can only pretend to accept, that is to say resign himself. Resignation contains a factual acceptation and a theoretical refusal. And these two elements are not conciliated, and are unconciliable in the inner state of this man; they are unconciliable because they are situated in two compartments separated by an unbridged gap. And this man preserves the necessary feeling of his inner unity by means of a mechanism of defence which blinds him to the theoretical refusal of his temporal state (mental scotomy). He makes himself believe that he accepts, that he is a 'philosopher', that he is 'reasonable'; he acts the part and succeeds in deceiving himself. The 'reasonable' discourse which he holds is indeed rational, is in accordance with the real order of things in the cosmos. But this man is wrong to be right, his rightness in that premature way is a pretence founded on two lies: he cheats in withdrawing an instinctive pretention which continues, in an underground manner, on its original course; and he cheats in declaring that he withdraws his pretention because it is reasonable while in reality he withdraws it in order to avoid seeing himself repudiated by the Not-Self. He is playing the angel, but he is not one.

If the word of the animal part were 'no', that of the abstract part is 'yes'. But this 'yes' is not the absolute 'Yes', it is only a relative 'yes'; it is not the 'Yes-noumenon', but only a 'yes-phenomenon', quite as illusory, from the absolute point of view, as the 'no' of the animal portion. The 'Absolute Yes' is to be attained ulteriorly by the union, in a ternary synthesis, of the relative 'no' and 'yes'.

Ignoring all that, the man congratulates himself on his 'yes', he sees it as proof that he is master of his animal portion, master of himself, whereas he is nothing of the kind. He thinks that he does right in saying this 'yes' more and more often, he believes that he is adapting himself to reality whereas he is only playing with himself the comedy of this adaptation. He splits himself into two personages: the 'yes' personage, the 'angel', has all his preference; he becomes as conscious of it as he can; he says that this is the personage *which is he*. During this time the 'no' personage, the 'beast', is despised and driven back; the man obscures, as much as he can, the consciousness of it which he is in danger of obtaining; and when he cannot avoid seeing it he says that *that is not he*. He says: 'I do not know what has come over me; that was stronger than I am.'

This 'no' personage, alone *in situ* at the very beginning, when the little child was becoming conscious of the opposition Self—Not-Self and rejected the Not-Self with the whole of his being, loses ground thereafter little by little in the measure that the mechanisms of adaptation are built up and consolidated. He is driven back more and more deeply, covered with layers of adaptive mechanisms ever more numerous and heavy, he is suffocated slowly and methodically. The voice which necessarily rebelled again the temporal state is gradually gagged and reduced to silence. Spontaneity is suffocated by shams, by 'reasonable' attitudes.

Sometimes, with beings of feeble instinctive vitality, this suffocation has a happy ending (if one may so call it). The 'beast' although not killed (for it could not be while the subject is not dead), is as though killed; and the man in which this happens is said to be 'civilised' and 'adapted'. One should ask oneself how this thing can be, how this man can come to believe that he accepts his temporal state, this limited and mortal state which is in reality affectively inacceptable, how he can live in this way. He arrives at it, essentially, through the play of his imagination, through the faculty which his mentality possesses of recreating a subjective world whose unique motor principle this time he is. The man could never resign himself to not being the unique motive-power of the real universe if he had not this consoling faculty of creating a universe for himself, a universe which he creates all alone.

The man who is going to interest us now, and who is truly interesting because his existence becomes little by little a drama, is the one whose instinctive vitality is too strong for the adaptive mechanisms to succeed in stifling the 'no', the 'beast'. For a certain time these mechanisms can attain their ends; the subject 'reasons with himself' vigorously; his imagination, a kind of balancing gyroscope, spins with speed and effect. A very handy adaptive mechanism will often be used; it is the projection of the 'divine image' on to the image of an aspect of the outer world, that is to say the adoration by the subject of some idol (adoration-love of another human-being, or of a 'just cause', or of a 'God' more or less personalised, etc. . . .). This mechanism, which seems to resolve the dualism between Self and Not-Self, arranges everything as long as it lasts.

But the situation becomes serious when all these adaptive mechanisms exhaust their effect, when the idol-making process breaks down or does not succeed in establishing itself, when the 'beast' can no longer continue to withdraw unceasingly its pretentions to overcome the Not-Self; and when the fox, as a result of declaring the grapes to be sour, begins to die of hunger and to hear his 'beast' growl with rage in the depths of his being.

At this moment appears *distress* and what one calls 'fear of defeat'. Let us examine what happens exactly, at this moment, in the human-being. We are going to show that the expression 'fear of defeat' is incorrect. It is in the abstract portion of the man that the phenomena that we are studying take their departure. But the abstract portion is intellectual, not affective; and so it could not be afraid strictly speaking. The man that we are studying claims, as we have seen, to succeed in the temporal sphere instantaneously, but he claims something that is impossible. In order to avoid

39

feeling repulsed by the concrete occurrence he has to withdraw the presentation of his claims; and so he withdraws it. The abstract portion has no fear of the concrete repulse; let us say rather that a powerful mechanical determinism forbids him to envisage it, to conceive of the eventuality, and that as a result he refuses it. In order to refuse it, in order to repell it, he refuses and denies the conflict with the Not-Self—a combat whose issue could only be defeat, given the total and instantaneous character of this man's pretention. Unable to be sure that the Not-Self will be totally and instantaneously defeated the abstract portion pretends to be ignorant of the existence of this concrete Not-Self and takes refuge in the world re-created by his imagination. The animal portion for a certain time has accepted that his superior friend shall act thus; in effect this desertion in face of the dual between Self and Not-Self has brought certain advantages from which the animal portion has benefitted—the friendship of others, the approval of others, and so a guarantee of certain allies against the Not-Self. But little by little life has disappointed these hopes of reward for having been kind and good; misfortunes, felt as unjust, have supervened; the animal portion no longer believes in these chimeras, it decides that it has been duped and that it has had enough, it no longer wishes to avoid the combat, no longer feels in agreement with a pacific attitude which brings no benefit; it is deaf now to promises of ulterior benefits which never seem to come to hand and it now only wishes to take up arms. Being in this new frame of mind it can no longer feel the defection of the abstract portion otherwise than as an act of cowardice in face of danger, as a frightful collaboration with the enemy. This man is comparable with a besieged citadel, in which the soldiers, who can only feel and act, want to save their skins, and in which the leader, who only thinks, does not wish to hear a word about fighting and orders the laying down of arms. The army of soldiers cannot understand this absurd order, and at the same time it cannot, in the absence of an order or at least of an authorisation from above, fight as it wants to. It feels itself abandoned, dismayed by the abandonment; it feels anguish. And this anguish is not at all the fear of a particular repulse implied in the present circumstances; it is the fear of death, this ancient fear that has been in the depths of the being ever since its first meeting with the Not-Self, the selfsame fear that the baby experienced when his mother seemed to withdraw from him her alliance.

Anguish is then a phenomenon in two periods, and it is of capital importance to examine these two periods into which it can be resolved. It is 'the head', 'the reason', 'the angel' which leads the way; the head pretends to be ignorant of the existence of the dangerous Not-Self and escapes into its dreams; acting thus it implicitly affirms the Not-Self in matter-of-fact reality, it goes over in fact to the enemy's camp. Then the animal portion, 'the beast', is distracted with fear, not with a relative fear of the relative defeat which is impending, but a total fear of the total danger of death which the Not-Self represents for a Self that the desertion of the head leaves powerless. In what one calls, incorrectly, 'fear of defeat' there are then two distinct elements: an intellectual refusal of defeat, and an affective anguish not of defeat but of death.

The erroneous belief implied in the fear of defeat explains how the vicious circle of anguish is closed. Our subject does not realise that he trembles in the face of death and that he does so because his head abandons his organism in face of the menacing general Not-Self. He believes that he trembles before such and such a concrete negative aspect of the outside world (which may be in fact a very little thing, the low opinion of Mr. X, for example). Seeing this concrete aspect of the world as the spectre of death, of total destruction (since in reality it is death which is feared) he sees this aspect of the world as a total negative Reality, as an absolute negative, and consequently as indestructible. And this vision of the obstacle of the world, as indestructible and absolute, evidently reinforces in the abstract portion his refusal to undertake the struggle. The vicious circle is thus closed.

One understands why anguish is fatally the lot of those beings who are, in a sense, the best, the richest, in whom the impartial and abstract portion is very strong and the partial and animal portion very strong also. On the contrary anguish will not be the lot of beings, on the one hand, whose abstract portion is weak and who live in a comfortable egoism ('materialists'); or, on the other hand, of beings whose animal portion is weak and who live in a comfortable altruistic renunciation ('idealists'). Among the former the 'no' triumphs in fact, among the latter the 'yes' triumphs in fact; in both cases the scales have tipped to one side or the other and have come to a standstill. But the unhappy man whose two portions are strong is torn inwardly by the tugging of a 'yes' and of a 'no' which are unconciliated. This man is unhappy but, at the same time, he is invited to the total realisation that is represented by the conciliation of the 'yes' and the 'no'; the others are comfortable but are not invited to this realisation.

It is interesting to study attentively the relations that exist between anguish and imagination, for this study will inform us of the exact nature of 'moral suffering'.

Let us recall the two psychological phenomena which are at work in anguish; the abstract portion capitulates in face of reality because, claiming instantaneous omnipotence, it sees the normal resistance of the outside world as insurmountable, unshakable, absolutely forbidding. It escapes by flight into the world of the imagination. The concrete rebuff is thus avoided by the mentality, but, if the concrete rebuff is indefinitely postponed, in suspense, the image of the rebuff remains present to the abstract portion which turns away from the practical struggle for existence. The animal portion suffers then from the fear of death, since the defection of the 'head' leaves it paralysed in face of the aggressiveness of the Not-Self.

One sees clearly the double rôle played by the imagination in anguish. It plays the rôle of protector towards the egotistical and revendicative illusions of the abstract portion, and the rôle of destroyer towards the animal machine by abandoning it to the fear of death. It protects the Ego, which is illusory, and crushes the machine, which is real.

If one looks into it closely one perceives that the anguish is illusory since its causes are illusory (and that the effect of an illusory cause could not be real). Its immediate cause is illusory since that is the imaginative film, an artificial creation of the mind. Its efficient cause is equally illusory. In fact, if the mind turns away from the obstacle of the world and takes refuge in the imagination, it is because it presents to the world an absolute claim; and if it presents this absolute claim it is on account of its illusory ignorance of its divine filiation. Man only seeks to deify himself in the temporal sphere because he is ignorant of his real divine essence. Man is born the son of God, participating totally in the nature of the Supreme Principle of the Universe; but he is born with a bad memory, forgetful of his origin, illusorily convinced that he is only this limited and mortal body which his senses perceive. Amnesic, he suffers from illusorily feeling himself abandoned by God (while he is in reality God himself), and he fusses about in the temporal sphere in search of affirmations to support his divinity which he cannot find there, without realising that he would not be searching for Reality if he did not participate in it by his own nature (for one cannot lack something without any knowledge of that thing).

Anguish is then an illusion since its causes are illusory. Besides this theoretical demonstration we can obtain a practical demonstration of it; we can prove directly, intuitively, the illusory character of anguish. If in fact at a moment at which I suffer morally, resting in a quiet spot, I shift my attention from my thinking to my feeling, if, leaving aside all my mental images, I apply myself to perceiving in myself the famous moral suffering in order to savour it and to find out at last what it is—I do not succeed. All that I succeed in feeling is a certain general fatigue which represents, in my body, the trace of the anxiety-phenomenon and of the wastage of vital energy which has taken place through the fear of death. But of suffering itself I do not find a scrap. The more I pay attention to the act of feeling, withdrawing thereby my attention from my imaginative film, the less I feel. And I prove then the unreality of anguish.

One will understand this still better by comparison with physical pain. If I have a painful gumboil, the more I imagine the less I suffer physically; the less I imagine, on the contrary, shifting my attention from thinking to feeling, the more keenly I am aware of my pain. This is because the pain is real, not imaginary.

We do not mean to say that there is no perception in the course of moral suffering; we say that it has an illusory suffering, which is not the same thing. If a man sees a mirage in the desert one cannot say that he does not see it; he sees, indeed, but that which he sees does not exist. In the same way, when I suffer morally I perceive, but I perceive nothing that really exists.

What then happens in me when I suffer morally? There is, as we have seen, in my feeling, the fear of death; this fear uses up my vitality and so impoverishes my reserve of organic energy; there is in that then an injury inflicted on my organism, on my body. This injury is not the same as that of physical pain; the injury of physical pain affects a part of the body, it affects the body-as-an-aggregate-of-parts. The injury of the moral suffering, loss of energy at its source, affects the body-as-a-whole; which is not indicated in the sensibility of the organism by any precise pain, but by a general discomfort, by fatigue, depression, a lowering of vitality. In the course of the moral suffering there is therefore at the body level, a general depressive discomfort. During this time, at the psychic level, there are unpleasant, menacing images. The moral suffering results from the association of menacing mental images with a depressive somatic condition. The loss of organic energy without counterpart (for there is then no exchange with the outside world) tends evidently in the direction of death; and so the unpleasing images have an inner taste of death and are perceived as external aggressors tending to kill me. Therein dwells the mirage of which I am the victim. I perceive assassins coming in my direction, and I am persuaded of their real existence; yet they do not exist at all, any more than the lake on the horizon of the desert. That is what Zen calls the 'cave of the phantoms'.

Let us remember that, where anguish is concerned, it is the 'head' which leads the way, and takes the initiative in the process. Doubtless an organic depression of physiological origin favours the appearance of anguish (our humour can be gloomy all day as a result of having slept badly); but, even in this case the anguish depends on the mind, for if I shift my attention on to 'feeling' I only feel tired and not distressed.

The man suffering from anguish has his attention turned towards the screen of his imaginative film by which he tries to escape from the dangerous and real Not-Self; and the anguish assails him from behind, coming from the direction towards which he is not looking, on which he turns his back. The inner gesture of which we have spoken above, and by which I shifted my attention from my 'thinking' on to my 'feeling', is a radical *volte-face*, of one hundred and eighty degrees, by which I turn my back on the imaginative screen and look in the direction from which came the anguish a moment ago; I say 'came a moment ago' because, during the moment at which this *volte-face* is accomplished, when the image-making mind which holds the initiative of the process is annihilated, the anguish ceases and there only remains from it a certain

44

mental fatigue. The spectre only exists illusorily as long as I turn away my eyes from the place where I suppose it to exist; as soon as I dare to look at this place I see that there is nothing there.

All this does not lead to an immediate remedy for anguish. One of man's errors is to search for an immediate remedy for his anguish, for this symptom, without bothering about the cause of the symptom. Nevertheless the theoretical understanding of the mechanism of anguish is useful for the intemporal realisation which alone can save man from his illusory sufferings. I am not able to consecrate myself to the task of realisation if I have not first perfectly understood the character, equally illusory, of the two affective poles 'pleasure-pain'.

Chapter Six

THE FIVE MODES OF THOUGHT OF THE NATURAL MAN—PSYCHOLOGICAL CONDITIONS OF SATORI

THE psychological consciousness of the natural man functions in five different ways which form a single series.

1st mode: Deep sleep, without dreams. The mentality contains no images. A mode of functioning which is non-functioning.

2nd mode: Sleep with dreams.

3rd mode: Waking with reveries.

4th mode: Waking with definite thought that takes account of the real external present.

5th mode: Waking with pure intellectual thought.

Except in the first mode the mentality contains an imaginative film but of a kind which differs from the second to the fifth. An imaginative film, of whatever kind it may be, is characterised in one respect by the nature of its images; these may be concrete, particular, based on the concrete reality of the present or not present; or they may be abstract, general (based on general reality, to which the words 'present' and 'not present' no longer apply). An imaginative film is characterised in another respect, by the manner in which the images are arranged in it, the style of their association. Three styles can be distinguished: symbolical, realistic, pure intellectual.

The imaginative film, or, to put it in a simpler way, the thought of sleep-with-dreams, is characterised before all else by its symbolical style of association. In this symbolical style the meaning of the film does not lie in its form, in its expression; it lies behind the form, and this merely serves to indicate it. There is a difference between form, which is only a means, and informal substance, which is its aim (and at the same time evidently its principle).

The thought of waking-with-reveries is intermediary between the dream thought and the thought of man adapted to the real external present. It can be very near the dream thought, with the same apparent absurdity. It can also be constructed no longer in the symbolical style but in the realistic style such as we shall see in the fourth mode.

The realistic thought of man adapted to the real external present is composed of images which are no longer content to suggest meaning without containing it within themselves. These are concrete images which claim to have a real immediate meaning that is adequate for the concrete reality. The meaning of this thought lies less behind its expression than within it. We do not say, however, that the meaning of the thought does not lie at all behind its expression; indeed the meaning, which is the relative truth of the thought, is a manifestation of inexpressible primordial Truth; and this thought would be meaningless, would not even exist, if it had no meaning behind its form; it is by virtue of this latent meaning that the form contains a certain manifest and relative meaning.

Pure intellectual thought, in the man who reflects, who meditates, is no longer constructed in the realistic style but in the pure intellectual style. Its images are abstract and, in contrast to what applied to realistic thought, correspond with nothing that the sense-organs can perceive. The Hindus regard the mind as the sixth organ of sense; this view is very defensible, in the sense that the mind, like the sense-organs, transmits nothing that is not relative; but the mind differs in another respect from the sense-organs in that it alone transmits perceptions that are abstract and general. In this mode of thought the images pretend to much more than in realistic thought. Rejecting, categorically this time, the modest rôle of indirectly suggesting the truth, they claim to contain in themselves a meaning of general import. Formal expression is at its apogee, the substance behind the form is at its minimum.

Considering these five modes of thought spread out serially, we necessarily ask ourselves what hierarchy there is among them. Current opinion sees in the succession from the first mode to the fifth a *progression*; it rates the state of the man who deals with external reality above the state of the man who sleeps, and it rates the state of the man who meditates on general laws above the state of the man who deals with concrete reality.

This opinion is partially correct. But we will see first wherein it is wrong, wherein the Vedanta is right in regarding the state of deep sleep as superior to the state of sleep-with-dreams, and this as superior to the waking state. From the absence of thought (sleep-without-dreams) to pure intellectual thought (meditation), the perception of inexpressible truth claims more and more to take upon itself a mental form; but the mental form, or imaginative form, is comparable with the plane section of a volume. This section certainly gives information concerning the volume, but it differs from it radically; the more the section is made with ability and precision the more precise the information which it gives; but at the same time the pretention of the section to be the volume increases, and so the more precise the information given by the section, the more it deceives the person who considers it, and the less it tells him in reality. With the man who meditates (fifth mode) the error is at its greatest since he takes his images as adequate for objective reality of general import. With the man who deals with concrete reality the error is less since he takes his images as adequate for a lesser reality. The man who day-dreams deceives himself less in his turn; he is less pretentious; he does not confuse his 'reverie' with 'reality'. The error is less again with the man who dreams while sleeping; his images are more modest, they no longer claim to do more than indicate indirectly a truth which they do not possess in themselves.[1] Finally, the man who sleeps without dreaming no longer deceives himself at all since the pretentions of his formal thought have vanished with the thoughts themselves.

From the first mode of thought to the fifth there is, then, in a sense, degradation. The form seizes more and more firmly the sense of the thought, until informal and original substance becomes ever poorer behind the curtain of images. The images, less and less

[1] Note that the highest 'esoteric' teachings always and necessarily use symbols and myths.

backed up, may be compared with bank-notes against which the gold-reserve disappears.

This way of looking at the series of modes of thought, as a hierarchy successively graded down from the first mode to the fifth, would be the only and indisputable way if man had only to be regarded from the point of view of the moment. It is no longer so as soon as one regards man as being capable of evolution in duration. At the moment the man who sleeps profoundly deceives himself less than the one who meditates; but, if one considers duration, the man who meditates is superior to the one who sleeps profoundly because, in meditating, in playing to the utmost the illusory game of his state as a natural man (egotistical state shut up in the subject-object dualism), this man comes near to the instant of satori when the 'old' man, deluded, will disappear and will give place to the 'new man', in possession of the informal original thought (immanent and transcendent thought as compared with the five modes of ordinary thought).

As we will see later, the thought of the fifth mode, or meditative thought, cannot by itself release satori, but without this thought man could never find out how to obtain this release, and in consequence he could never obtain it. It is by using this thought, the most abstract, the most pretentious, and in a sense the most completely erroneous, that man can arrive at an understanding of the vanity of all his functions of perception and of research for intemporal realisation, and can understand how he ought finally to proceed in order to relax inwardly and to present himself thus, ready for the explosion of satori.

In short, in this series of the five modes of thought of the natural man, there are at the same time two inverse hierarchies. If one looks at the question from the point of view of the moment one sees the thought decline in value from the first mode to the fifth; if one looks at the question in duration, from the point of view of the man's possible metamorphosis, one sees the thought increase in value from the first to the fifth.

Let us point out, in a short digression, the analogy which exists between the evolution of the individual man and that of humanity. Some people maintain that, with the passing centuries, humanity progresses; others maintain that this scientific or intellectual progress is a sign of progressive decomposition. The truth, as always, conciliates the opposing points of view; in a sense there is degradation in proportion as the knowledge of humanity emerges from its informal state in order to crystallise itself in forms that are more and more expert and precise; in another sense there is progress by means of cyclic advance towards a collective explosion, analogous to individual satori (although at the same time very different) when an old humanity, learned and without wisdom, will die, and a new humanity, unlearned and wise, will be born.

Let us return to the modes of our individual thought and consider them from the angle of satori that we hope some day to obtain. In order that satori may be released, man should organise in his psyche certain favourable conditions that we shall see further on. But, to begin with, at the first stage, he ought by patient intellectual work to understand what are these favourable conditions and how to organise them. It is only with regard to this first stage that the five modes of thought differ in effective value, and that the fifth mode is the highest. The non-human animal is incapable of satori because he only possesses the first four modes of thought, and not the fifth. Abstract meditative thought is necessary in order to understand the vanity of all the direct efforts that man can make in order to satisfy fully and definitely the aspirations of his nature. This thought alone is capable of conceiving other new methods in view of this satisfaction, then to realise that these methods also are vain, and to succeed at last, after a long process of elimination, in reaching the heart of the problem.

But the primacy of meditative thought only applies to this preparatory phase of the acquisition of theoretical understanding. If we suppose now that the man has discovered the inner conditions which, by establishing themselves and growing within him, are ultimately going to lay him open to the explosion of satori, this man has at the same time discovered that none of his five modes of thought constitutes by itself these necessary inner conditions. He has understood that for this final phase of the inner labour the five modes of thought are equally ineffective; dreamless sleep is inefficacious because the Not-Self is absent from it; and the four following modes of thought are ineffective because, as soon as the mind works in order to take hold of reality, this formative instrument separates man from any immediate union with Informal Reality.

The condition necessary for the release of satori consists in a perception that we are going to try to demonstrate, and which is not natural or spontaneous in the ordinary man as are his five modes of thought.

In order to succeed in our attempt we shall have to make a few digressions. Let us study, to begin with, the circumstances of a certain psychological phenomenon which no doubt a good many men have experienced. One day, comfortably installed, I am in process of reading a book which takes up my attention without in any way reminding me of the preoccupations of this period of my life; I do not identify myself with any of the heroes of my book and I follow their adventures as a completely detached spectator. With regard to my personal life I am enjoying an absolute truce, my fears and my hopes have been expelled from my mind; the discourse represented by my book is, in my mind, purely a monologue, without any other voice intervening either to comment upon it or to interrupt it with reflections concerning my cares or my personal hopes. My body, very comfortable, does not send to my mind any message to trouble it and everything runs smoothly in me. Then the attention, already so slight and relaxed, that I was paying to my book, is removed from it altogether; at this moment the calm in me is so pure that it amounts to a veritable suspense (we will see in a moment suspense of what). Suddenly a sense-perception (an object which enters my field of vision, or a sound which reaches me) breaks this suspense; I see the object, or I hear the sound, as I never see or hear habitually; as if, habitually, forms and sounds only came to me through a screen which deformed them, whereas in this special moment, they come to me direct, in their pure reality. Still more interesting, my sense perception communicates to me simultaneously a knowledge of the outside world and of myself; in this moment I feel no longer any separation between the world and myself although they remain distinct; Not-Self and Self, while remaining two, are joined together to form a unity. Then, at the end of a few seconds, in the course of which I have mentally realised what I have just described, my new vision of things fades away and I return to my usual condition.

If one compares this experience with the accounts that certain Zen masters have left us of their satori, many points in common become obvious; great calm at first with a sensation of suspense in which the subject is as though awake and asleep at the same time, cessation of all mental agitation (the Zen monk says that he is then 'like an idiot, like an imbecile'), the rôle of a sense-perception in the release of a new perspective of everything, the suddenness of this release, and the impression of clarity and of unity in this new perspective. But there is otherwise a great difference; the experience of which we are speaking leaves nothing but a memory, whereas satori inaugurates a new life definitely freed from the dualistic-egotistical illusion.

How should we interpret these resemblances and these differences? First of all for what reason did this little transitory satori come to me? Because an exceptional tranquility is realised in my mind; my mind is functioning in the course of my reading, but in a uniform rhythm, regular, without jerks, weaving a film made of light images, without relief. These images even fade away in the end, and my mind turns in then on its centre without projecting anything on to the surface. At this moment the habitual spasm of the mind has disappeared although the mind continues to function (I am not in a state of deep sleep); thus relaxed without being asleep, my mind is able to receive, motionless, this non-dualist perception of existence to which it is habitually opposed on account of its agitation. It is like a prisoner living in a prison the door of which is made to open inwards, and who habitually pushes this door in order to open it. The more he pushes the less the door can open, but if he stops pushing for a moment the door opens by itself. Why, then, did not my little satori last? Because the conditions which allowed the releasing of it were based on an artifice; it is thanks to a momentary forgetfulness of my personal preoccupations that this perfect tranquility was realised in me; I had withdrawn outside the range of any circumstance that could concern my Ego. When, later, I became conscious of my little satori in saying to myself that it is to me that it has happened, all my egotistical life, which had been momentarily cast out of my mind, burst in again with all the usual consequences of its illusory agitation.

True, definitive, satori supposes that a perfect tranquility has been realised in the mind of a man who has not withdrawn from the circumstances that concern his Ego, but who, on the contrary, lives them fully.

How is that possible? And first in what exactly consists this tranquility of the mind? Something is in suspense, we have said, but what? It is not a suspending of all mental functioning, since the subject remains awake, since he does not sleep. The mind functions, it works. Only it works smoothly, without jerks. Something is stopped, but not the mind, only its jerks, the irregularities of its rhythm. With what then do these jerks correspond? They correspond with the emotions. The little satori of the experience described above happened to me because I had been for an hour or two without emotions; I had left outside my mind all images concerning my personal life, my book held my attention without moving me the least in the world, my body, being comfortable, kept quiet; I felt neither joy nor grief. It was this absence of emotion which conditioned the functioning, without jerks, of my mind, and it was this functioning which conditioned the sudden release in me of the non-dualistic consciousness of existence.

What then is emotion? We must know this in order to discover the means of eliminating emotion from our psyche. (We will speak later on of the reason that leads the natural man to rebel so violently, as a rule, when one speaks to him of eliminating the emotions of his psychic life.)

Emotion represents a short-circuit of man's vital energy flowing between his instinctive, negative centre and his intellectual, positive, centre. This short-circuit consists in a disintegration of the energy at a point which one regards as a third centre and which one calls the emotional centre. (After satori this point is no longer a centre similar to the others, situated on the same plane, but the apex of the triangle of his ternary synthesis.) The short-circuit that produces emotion occurs when the intellectual terminal is not insulated. To what does this lack of insulation of the intellectual terminal correspond? To the passivity of the mind in face of the ultimate problem of man's state as this problem is manifested in the present moment. All man's movements, interior and exterior, have a unique prime motor, his natural need to-be-as-a-distinct-entity, that is to say his natural need to 'exist', which resides in his instinctive centre; but man is not conscious of this need at the moment when this need comes into play in so far as it comes into play at the given moment. Man can be conscious of it theoretically, but not concretely, in so far as this need is experienced in the instant. Everything works in the man on the basis of a 'given-that-I-must-exist' which remains implicit; his mind can become actively conscious of all the manifestations of this primary need, but this consciousness of manifestation excludes consciousness of that which it manifests.

Let us try to say that again in another way. Behind everything that man experiences there is debated within him the illusory question of his being or his nullity. Man's attention is fascinated by the fluctuations of this dispute, and these appear to him unceasingly important and new; and he is unconscious of the dispute itself and of its constant monotony. Man is attentive to the forms of his psycho-somatic states, to their qualitative variations which are always new; he does not see, behind the formal manifestations of his momentary state, the quantitative variations of what we will call the in-formal sensation of his existence. If, at any moment, I wish to perceive, by means of an intuitive inward movement of perfect simplicity, the in-formal impression that I have of existing more or less, I can do so; but as soon as I cease to wish it I cease to do so and my attention is seized once again by formal perceptions. When I voluntarily perceive my in-formal sensation of existing (quantitatively variable), my mind is active concerning the ultimate reality of my condition at the concrete moment that I am living, and then my intellectual centre is insulated, and I experience no emotion. As soon as I cease this voluntary perception, which is unnatural, my intellectual centre ceases to be active, ceases to be insulated, and my emotions begin again.

My in-formal sensation of existing varies quantitatively, from annihilation to exaltation, but without a special effort I do not pay attention to that, though it is nevertheless that which is in question for me in my actual egotistical-dualistic condition. I am attentive to the mental forms which reveal my state, annihilated or exalted.

My mental passivity, seduced and held captive by the forms of my humour, constitutes a non-insulation of this centre which exposes it to emotional short-circuits, to jumps, to agitation (what the Hindus call 'the mad monkey').

The man who desires some day to obtain satori should train himself progressively to insulate his intellectual centre in order to protect it against emotional agitation. And he should do so, without eliminating or modifying artificially the circumstances which concern his Ego and which try to move him, fully in the course of his natural life as it comes to him. In order to do that he must unceasingly reawaken the possibility that he has (and which tends unceasingly to fall asleep again) of perceiving, beneath the forms pertaining to his states-of-mind, his in-formal sensation, more or less positive or negative, of existing. This attention does not lead to turning his back on concrete egotistical-dualistic life, but, on the contrary, to keeping himself in the very centre of his being, accomplishing it by living it in the motionless inner point at which appears the very first dualism, that of existence—non-existence. When man's attention is fixed exactly on this source of all his agitation, then and then only, tranquility begins for him. When this tranquility is firmly established the inner conditions are at last favourable for the opening of satori in which dualism is conciliated by integrating itself in a ternary synthesis.

It is clearly impossible to describe this presence within oneself which is the immediate and in-formal perception of the degree of existence at the moment, precisely on account of the in-formal character of this perception. Let us suppose that I ask you: 'How are you feeling at this moment?' You will ask in reply: 'From what point of view? Physically or morally?' I answer: 'From all points of view together, how do you feel?' You are silent for a couple of seconds, then you say, for example: 'Not so bad', or 'So-so', or 'Very well', or something else. . . . Of the two seconds during which you were silent the latter does not interest us for you were using it in order to put into a form of expression your perception of your total state-of-mind; you had then already slipped away from the inner presence which interests us. It is during the first second that you perceived what is really in question for you all the time, and of which you are habitually unconscious, being conscious only of forms which derive from this unconscious perception or of forms in connexion with which this unconscious perception exists. If someone, after having read this, tries to obtain the in-formal perception of which we are speaking, let him beware; there are a thousand ways of believing that one has it, whereas one has it not; in any case the mistake is the same and consists in one complication or another which comprises forms; one is not simple-minded enough. *In-formal and immediate perception of existence is the simplest kind of perception there can be.* Correctly carried out it can be obtained in the middle of the most intense external activity and without disturbing that; I do not have to turn away from what I am doing, but rather to feel myself existing in the very centre of the formal world of my activity and of the attention that I pay to it.

The natural man, as we have said above, is loath to envisage a diminution of his emotions. He resembles a caterpillar that can become a butterfly if it passes through the stage of a chrysalis. The caterpillar only moves along the ground. It cannot fly, or profit by the height dimension; but at least it moves; compared with this movement the immobility of the chrysalis might seem to it to be horrible. Nevertheless the temporary renouncement of an imperfect movement procures him ultimately a superior movement. Emotions are like the movement of the caterpillar; it is not flying but it resembles it and, with imagination, one succeeds in mistaking it for that. Man holds on to the bright sparks of his inner short-circuitings, and he has to reflect long and honestly in order to understand that these simple fireworks could never lead to anything. There is no real renunciation as long as one continues to attach value to that which one renounces.

We will take up again now, in another way, the whole problem studied in this essay.

That which popular language calls 'physical' and 'moral' corresponds with two domains which co-exist in us and which appear to us to be clearly different. The impressions by means of which I feel myself to be living, I range in my somatic or in my psychic life; for instance when I feel my life negatively, when I feel it is menaced, attacked, that may be through physical pain or through moral suffering. It is as though my 'being' presented two faces to make contact with the outside world, one somatic, the other psychic, and penetrated by the constructive or destructive influences of the outside world.

My impressions are released by the outside world, but I feel them well-up in myself; my physical pain may be due to a blow, but I feel that it springs from my body; my moral suffering may be due to any external event, but I feel that it takes its rise in what I call my 'soul'. If I try to see from where, in myself, these impressions come to me, I do not succeed; my painful somatic sensation reaches my consciousness from a source in which it is unconscious. It is the same with the moral suffering; I see clearly

56

that this suffering is connected in me with such and such a mental image, but from where has this image risen up in my consciousness? Here also I have to reply, from an unconscious source. This source I conceive necessarily as the source of my life, and I conceive it as unique, for I have the intuitive impression of being one, a single synthesis beneath the duality of my reactive manifestations.

If I study thus, working up-stream, the flux of my somatic life and that of my psychic life, I see these two currents join together at the central point of a unique source. I understand then why the physical seems to react unceasingly on the moral, and the moral on the physical; and the notion of a third term, the notion of the synthetic 'being', unites the two parts which appeared to be separate. I realise that I did not properly understand the reactions of my two lives upon each other; in reality the outside world never directly touches my 'body' or my 'soul' in so far as I am aware of it; it always touches directly this central cross-roads from which my two conscious lives branch off; and it makes contact either through the somatic face which I present to it, or through the psychic face. Once the centre has been touched I shall experience impressions from it which can be situated above all in the domain (psychic or somatic) through which my profound centre has been touched, or even above all in the domain opposed to that by which the contact has taken place. This distribution of the impressions which are going to predominate, either in the physical domain or in the psychical domain, depends to some extent on the nature of the contact which comes from the outside world, but also to a great extent on the structure of the subject. To this corresponds the distinction that psychiatrists make between the obsessional neurotic type and the hysterical type; the obsessional neurotic has above all psychic impressions, the hysterical predominantly somatic impressions. A bad digestion will sometimes to the 'psychic' man no abdominal impression, but only black thoughts; bad news is often expressed, where the hysterical subject is concerned, principally, or even uniquely, by physical discomfort.

The two domains, physical and psychic, are not really separated, and the problem of their apparent reciprocal reactions is not worth bothering about. It is useless to enquire what bridge links them together; no bridge joins them, but they are in direct contact at the point at which they are born, at the central unconscious cross-roads of my 'being'. These two kinds of manifestation reveal the same principle and they are not obliged to react one against the other; when I drink alcohol and it gives me cheerful thoughts, why speak of the reaction of my physical side on my moral? My centre has received a certain influence from the outside world, which has reached it via my somatic facet; then, crossing this central cross-roads, this influence expresses itself reactively at the same time in my somatic domain (gaiety). Good news, or the joyous animation of a meeting with friends, can, without the absorption of alcohol, produce in me exactly the same phenomena; it is because the influence which has reached my centre, although it has arrived this time via my psychic facet, has acted in the same manner and has so produced the same double reaction.

This central cross-roads of my 'being' is, as we have seen, unconscious. It is the original Unconscious from which flows all my consciousness. It should not be conceived as a mere absence of consciousness, but as the Absolute Thought which is up-stream of all conscious manifestation and from which this latter springs. It is the No-Mind of Zen, from which issue all our manifestations, mental and physical. We find again here the Creative Triad: above the psychic (positive force) and the physical (negative force) lies a superior conciliatory pole to which, by virtue of the apparent primacy of the inferior positive force over the negative, we ought to give the name of Absolute Mind (and not Absolute Matter), or, as in Zen, of No-Mind (and not No-Body).

With regard to these essential ideas we necessarily ask ourselves what difference there is between the natural man and the man who has attained 'realisation'. These two men exist by virtue of this central cross-roads at which sits their creative principle; basically there is no difference between them; and it is that moreover which Zen affirms. Zen affirms that these two men are identical in constitution and that the natural man lacks nothing; the man who has attained realisation has not acquired something which the natural man lacked. However, if these two men are identical, their manifestations differ. Why? Does it mean that the unconscious central cross-roads has become conscious at the moment of satori? This would have no sense, the principle of consciousness being necessarily always above consciousness itself, outside it, unconscious. No, the true answer is otherwise: Let us say that everything happens in the natural man as though his central cross-roads were asleep, passive; and that everything happens in the man who has attained realisation as if his cross-roads were awake, active. It is relatively easy to imagine the sleeping cross-roads of the natural man; it is indeed only a cross-roads, that is to say a place at which pass by all the influences coming from the outside world. Crossing this simple 'place', the influxes from without reach the secondary centres of the somatic and psychical domains, centres which respond to them by automatic reactions. The natural man, whose cross-roads is asleep, is an automaton. With the man who has attained realisation the central cross-roads is not asleep, the Absolute Original Thought is functioning there (although, once again, always unconsciously). This Thought interprets the influx that has come from without; conceiving things in their totality it sees this particular influx in the totality of the universal context; it sees it, then, in its relativity, that is to say that it sees it as it is really. It is to this vision, interpreted, 'enlightened' (the 'third eye' opened in the centre of the unconscious), and no longer to a vision deformed by lack of context, that the secondary centres are going to react now, and their reaction will be adequate to the reality. The natural man was a machine whose reflexes were conditioned by such and such a particular aspect of the outside world; the man who has attained realisation is a machine whose reflexes are conditioned by the totality of the cosmos as represented by such a particular aspect; he is identical with the Cosmic Principle (in so far as this manifests itself), and he manifests himself, like this Principle, in a pure independent invention.

This Absolute Thought, Universal, Unconscious, when it functions in the centre of man, constitutes Absolute Wisdom, incommensurable evidently with any formal intelligence; in fact this Wisdom is in-formal, preceding all form, and is the first cause of all form.

We have said that the Unconscious Universal Thought sleeps at the centre of the natural man, and that it is awakened at the centre of the man who has attained realisation. Let us see now that the sleep of this Absolute Thought knows degrees, and that these degrees are disposed in inverse order to the five modes of thought of the natural man. When the natural man sleeps without dreams, the Absolute Thought is as though awakened in him (more precisely, is not asleep), and this man is altogether like the man who has attained realisation; but this does not manifest at all in his consciousness because he has not at that time any consciousness; it is manifested only in the harmonious and re-creative operation of his vegetative life. As soon as this man begins to dream, that is to say as soon as his formal mind begins to function, that corresponds with a certain weakening of the Absolute Unconscious Thought, and the man is already less 'wise'. When this man awakens (in the ordinary meaning of the term), the Absolute Thought weakens more markedly and it is all the more enfeebled in that the formal mind is about to function in a manner that is pure, abstract, and generalised. It is nevertheless thanks to these moments of maximum enfeeblement that a certain evolution will take place in the man whose abstract intellect is at work, and in his life as a whole the Absolute Thought will sleep gradually less profoundly. This man will be able to live according to a relative and increasing wisdom. It is as if the sleep of the Absolute Thought at the moment [1] suscitated its awakening in duration; at the utmost one has the right to conceive of the positive and definitive awakening of the Absolute Thought (satori) as being released by an instant in which there will have been apprehended the total sleep of this Thought, an instant at which the mind will have reached the extreme limits of its dualistic functioning.

Let us say that again in a different way. The man who sleeps without dreams has withdrawn to the centre of himself; he who dreams has already moved out of his centre; the awakened man who day-dreams is still more 'ex-centric'; the man who adapts himself to external reality, and he who meditates, are ever further from themselves, more remote from their centre. The man who sleeps without dreams is in possession of his Reality but without being aware of it; the more he climbs thereafter the graded modes of formal thought the more this Reality disappears in proportion as the means wishing to seize it increase; as if the man were withdrawing from a centre of warmth in proportion as his sensibility to heat increased. In the instants which precede satori man is as

[1] *Duration*, composed of past-present-future, as opposed to *the moment*, i.e. the present that has no duration.

far from his centre as is possible. Then the inverse relation which has operated up till then is broken at the moment of satori, and the man finds himself definitively installed at his centre in his capacity as universal man, although able to withdraw himself at the same time into the various modes of formal thought in his capacity as personal man.

Man attains satori, then, as a result of turning his back, as thoroughly as possible, on his centre, as a result of going right to the ultimate limits in this centrifugal direction, as a result of pushing to its ultimate degree of purity the functioning of the discursive intelligence which keeps him away from Wisdom. He ought to *accomplish* formal thought to the point of breaking up the form. In order to do that he ought to make his formal mind function in a persevering attempt to perceive, beyond its limits, the in-formal; an attempt that is absurd in itself but which brings about the release one day of the miracle of satori, not as crowning the success of the ridiculous efforts accomplished, but as the defeat, definite at last, and triumphant, of those efforts. It is like a man separated from the light by a wall and who cannot touch this wall without making it higher and higher; but a day comes when all these absurd efforts have built up the wall to such a height that it becomes unsteady and collapses suddenly, a catastrophe that is final and triumphant, and which leaves the man bathed in the light.

It is this absurd but necessary effort that we accomplish when we oblige ourselves to perceive our in-formal sensation of existing-more-or-less in the course of all the episodes of our daily life. This effort towards an in-formal perception of existence is not similar to the reflex mental efforts that we make habitually and which are mental contractions that form images. It is even quite the contrary; it is an effort of de-contraction made in order to escape from the habitual contractive reflexes, an effort towards perfect simplicity in order to escape from the complexities that we habitually introduce, by way of reflex, into the question of our existence. We learn, by this effort, not to do something new, but no longer to do the inward actions, useless and agitating, which are usual with us. We learn to obtain from our mind not the most ingeniously clever gestures, but the pure gesture which is the essence of all the others and which rejoins immobility. This simple mental functioning

61

represents the highest accomplishment of our thought as natural man; it breaks through the ceiling of the fifth mode of our thought. Starting from the in-formality of sleep without dreams it finds again the in-formal by closing a complete circle—or more exactly, since the final point of the circle dominates its point of departure, a complete spiral turn.

Chapter Seven

LIBERTY AS 'TOTAL DETERMINISM'

IN order to tackle profitably the problem of liberty it is necessary to come back to the basic idea that the whole cosmic architecture consists of the exact, rigorous equilibrium of two inferior principles, positive and negative, brought about by a conciliatory principle which is above them. Seen in the perspective of our actual state, in which we have not yet attained 'realisation', the conciliatory principle takes on two aspects:

1 When we consider particular phenomena we see the conciliatory principle under a partial aspect, and we can call it the 'temporal conciliatory principle'. It is the Demiurge who presides at the creation of the Ten Thousand Things, at constructive and destructive phenomena, anabolism and catabolism, all of which manifest the cosmic metabolism;

2 When we consider the spatial and temporal totality of the cosmos we arrive at the conception of the Intemporal or Supreme, or Absolute Conciliatory Principle, which presides at the Unity of phenomenal multiplicity, the Intemporal Principle in which there does not yet exist any dualistic manifestation and for which the temporal conciliatory principle represents a sort of inferior delegate.

This Supreme Conciliatory Principle is the First Cause, anterior to all manifestation, and it is to it that our abstract thought tends when it reascends the universal chain of effects and causes.

The existence of the Demiurge between the First Cause and phenomena leads us necessarily to distinguish two determinisms:

1 A partial determinism according to which the temporal conciliatory principle determines the phenomena;

2 A total determinism according to which the Supreme Conciliatory Principle determines the temporal conciliatory principle and, through it, the phenomena.

63

Each of these two determinisms is manifested by laws. But it is interesting to see the differences which exist between the laws of partial determinism and the law of total determinism.

The laws of partial determinism operate only on the concrete plane, temporal and spatial. Each particular manifestation of these laws operating in the partial is apparently disordered. This man, for example, has an unhappy destiny during the whole of his existence, while that other man has a happy destiny. The partial determinism, operating in appearance, appears to be un-balanced, unjust, disordered.

The law of total determinism operates not only on the plane of particular phenomena, but in the universal. We can only conceive this determinism as perfectly ordered. The totality of positive phenomena is exactly balanced by the totality of negative phenomena. Each phenomenon is integrated in a totality in which it is counter-balanced by a phenomenon that is exactly complementary.

The partial determinism, phenomenal, apparent, visible, dis-ordered, is not 'real' since it is partial (and there can only be Reality which includes totality). But the ignorant man takes the visible for the real; also he believes in the unique reality of this partial determinism; and this is revealed by the fact that he calls it 'determinism'. Besides, this man has a certain innate intuition of Reality, that is to say of the Supreme Principle, which he conceives as endowed, among other attributes, with liberty. Since, for him, determinism only exists at the partial level, and since he does not conceive total determinism as operating at the level of the Supreme Principle, he opposes the only determinism that he knows to the liberty of the Supreme Principle. Thus he finishes up with the opposition between 'determinism and liberty'. In reality this opposition is illusory. What is not illusory is the distinction between 'partial determinism and total determinism', a distinc-tion which is not at all an opposition, but which expresses two different views, one at the individual level, the other at the universal level, of one and the same Causal Reality.

The natural egotistical man desires to be free, unconditioned, while thinking of himself as a distinct individual. I can envisage myself thus as a distinct individual, as a psycho-somatic organism, but I ought then to understand my liberation from partial determinism as a passing-beyond, an accomplishment of this partial determinism in the total determinism of the Supreme Principle. When I have attained Realisation my psycho-somatic organism will no longer be governed only by the apparently disordered laws of partial determinism but by the total law of universal and cosmic equilibrium, a law rigorously ordered which is the principle of all the apparently disordered laws of partial determinism. If I suppose myself to be liberated by Realisation I ought not to imagine my organism escaping all determinism, but as being conditioned at last by the total determinism of the Supreme Principle which is my 'own nature'; I ought not to imagine my organism no longer obeying any cause, but as obeying at last the First Cause which is its own Reality. In short my liberty does not reside in the absence of all causation geared on to my organism, but in the perfect equivalence in me between that which is caused and that which causes it, between that which is conditioned and the Principle which conditions it. If, at the moment at which I attain Realisation, I cease to be constrained, it is not because that which was constraining me has been wiped out, but because that which was constraining me has expanded infinitely and has coincided with the totality in which Self and Not-Self are one, in such a way that the word 'constraint' has lost all sense.

Failing the understanding of that, the natural egotistical man fatally envisages an act of free-will as an act of fantasy, gratuitous, arbitrary, connected with nothing, and he ends up thus at absurdity, at that which no longer has any meaning. This illusory liberty, which is on this side of partial determinism, and not on the other side, chimerically excludes our organism from the rest of the cosmos and thus contains an internal contradiction which wipes it out. In a book on Zen that appeared recently a Western author affirms that the man liberated by satori can do anything in any circumstances; but this is radically contrary to a true understanding, for the man liberated by satori can only perform one single action in a given circumstance. He can no longer do anything but the action that is totally adequate to that circumstance; and it is in the immediate, spontaneous elaboration of this unique adequate action that the enjoyment of the perfect liberty of this man lies. The natural egotistical man, activated by partial determinism, elaborates in a mediate manner one of the innumerable

65

inadequate reactions to the given circumstance; the man who has attained Realisation, activated by total determinism, elaborates with absolute rigour the unique action that is adequate.

On this side of the adequate act of free-will there exists a whole hierarchy of actions more or less inadequate according to the narrowness or the amplitude of the partial determinism which rules it. Right at the bottom of this hierarchy it is purely reflex action, without any *reflection*, in which we see come into play a spontaneity on this side of reflection. Then, reflection intervening more and more, we see this inferior spontaneity disappear little by little; the action becomes adquate to an ever-wider aspect of surrounding circumstances. After satori reflection is left behind and the action finds quite a new spontaneity at the same time that it becomes perfectly adequate, adequate to the spatial and temporal totality of the phenomenal universe.

In the range of this intermediate hierarchy there is a direct proportion between the discipline of the act and the inner impression of liberty which accompanies it. The more the rigour of the determinism increases, the more the action is felt inwardly as free. If, for example, someone asks me to name any substantive, I feel uncomfortable, a confusion of which I am prisoner; I do not know what to say. If someone asks me to name a musical instrument of any kind I like, I feel a lesser degree of discomfort and I reply more readily. If someone asks me to name the smallest instrument of a quartet, the confusion of which I was prisoner disappears entirely; by naming the violin I experience within an impression of liberty which is bound up with my certainty of being able to reply adequately. According to the degree in which my possibilities of reply are restricted, in which my exterior liberty of reply decreases, in the same degree my impression of interior liberty increases; in other words, my mind is freer in the degree in which that which I have to elaborate is more rigorously defined.

The modern evolution of art is a striking illustration of the disorder which seizes the human spirit when it rejects all discipline. In refusing to accept limitations man deprives himself of the impression of liberty which he feels when he is within accepted constraints; with this impression of liberty he loses a tranquillity of which he has need in order to receive the message of his deeper inspiration. And so the artist who refuses all discipline, and who

66

even makes a virtue of outraging it, cuts himself off from his deeper source and no longer succeeds in expressing himself; he mumbles and even ends up by feeling himself impotent, restricted by his exterior liberty.

A discipline which we accept spontaneously is necessary in order that our life may not be a suicidal chaos. But let us admit, on the other hand, that if it is dangerous for our temporal life not to have discipline, this discipline constitutes at the same time an obstacle to Realisation. Indeed it procures us an impression of interior liberty; but, before satori, we are not really free at all. This impression of liberty is illusory and it constitutes a palliative, a compensation for our dualistic condition that is not yet conciliated. The counterfeit joys which flow from it consume vital energy which we are not able to save from them.

Therefore discipline is, as regards intemporal realisation, at once favourable and unfavourable; it is favourable indirectly since it favours temporal realisation without which there could not be intemporal realisation; and it is unfavourable directly to intemporal realisation in giving to man the illusion that all is going well in him henceforward.

The Zen adept resolves this contradiction by opposing to it a method that is also contradictory: he refuses all particular discipline (no 'morality', no asceticism, no 'spiritual' exercises) and he adheres, as his understanding advances, to the total discipline which consists in depriving himself pitilessly of all particular discipline. 'Cease to cherish opinions', 'The perfect way is closed to all preference', 'Awaken the mind without fixing it on anything', etc. . . . This man gradually faces up to the distress inherent in complete external liberty. By rejecting all opinion he tastes to the full the inner servitude of our egotistical state; he maintains himself in the middle of our illusory prison right up to the moment of this culmination of impotent immobility in which satori entirely overthrows appearances and rebuilds them in the new light of a liberty that is real, that transcends its own inner and outer aspects.

Chapter Eight

THE EGOTISTICAL STATES

A T the centre of myself, in this centre which is still uncon-
cious to-day, resides the primordial man, united with the
Principle of the Universe and through it with the whole of
the Universe, totally sufficient unto himself, One from the beginning, neither alone nor not-alone, neither affirmed nor denied,
up-stream of all duality. It is the primordial Being, underlying all
the egotistical 'states' which cover it in my actual consciousness.

Because I am ignorant to-day concerning what are in reality
my egotistical states these states constitute a sort of screen which
separates me from my centre, from my real Self. I am unconscious
of my essential identity with the All and I only consider myself as
distinct from the rest of the Universe. The Ego is myself in so far
as I consider myself as distinct. The Ego is illusory, since I am
not in reality distinct; and all the egotistical states are equally
illusory.

In the fundamental egotistical state I feel myself as Self opposed
to the Not-Self, an organism in which the 'being' is opposed to
the 'being' of other organisms. In this fundamental state everything that is not my organism is Not-Self. I love my Self, that is to
say that I desire my existence, and I hate the Not-Self, which
means that I desire the disappearance of its existence. I am greedy
for the affirmation of my Self, as distinct, and for the negation of
the Not-Self, in so far as it pretends to exist beside my distinct Self.
In this fundamental egotist state 'to live' is to affirm my Self by
defeating the Not-Self. It is material victory by the acquisition of
material goods, subtle victory by the acquisition of renown—
recognition by the Not-Self of the existence of the Self; the acquisition of glory which 'immortalises' the Self that is distinct.

The fundamental affective state of the natural man is therefore

68

simple; this man loves his Self in opposition to the Not-Self, and he hates the Not-Self in opposition to his Self.

On this fundamental state there can be built five altruist states comporting the appearance of the love of others.

I. APPARENT LOVE OF OTHERS BY PROJECTION OF THE EGO [1]

This is idolatrous love, in which the ego is projected on to another being. The pretention to divinity as 'distinct' has left my organism and is now fixed on to the organism of the other. The affective situation resembles that above, with the difference that the other has taken my place in my scale of values. I desire the existence of the other-idol, against everything that is opposed to him. I no longer love my own organism except in so far as it is the faithful servant of the idol; apart from that I have no further sentiments towards my organism, I am indifferent to it, and, if necessary, I can give my life for the safety of my idol (I can sacrifice my organism to my Ego fixed on the idol; like Empedocles throwing himself down the crater of Etna in order to immortalise his Ego). As for the rest of the world, I hate it if it is hostile to my idol; if it is not hostile and if my contemplation of the idol fills me with joy (that is to say, with egotistical affirmation), I love indescriminately all the rest of the world (we will see further the reason, in the fifth variety of apparent love). If the idolised being rejects me to the point of forbidding me all possession of my Ego in him, the apparent love can be turned to hate.

2. APPARENT LOVE OF OTHERS BY LOCALISED EXTENSION OF THE EGO

For example: the binding love of a mother for her child, the binding love of a man for his country, etc. This is possessive love. In idolatrous love there was first of all projection of the Ego, and

---

[1] This simplified exposition of the doctrine of projection, known to all classical psychologists, may appear to ignore the detailed analysis of this process expounded by some. Terms such as 'Ego' have not, however, a standardised meaning, and the reader may be well-advised to understand the word here as including any aspect of the psyche whose image might be projected.— *Translator's note.*

afterwards need of possession of the projected Ego in a material or subtle possession of the idol. Here there is first of all possession of the other (it happens by chance that this child is my child, this country is my country). The affective situation which results much resembles that of idolatrous love; however the joys are less conscious, and one often sees the fear of losing the loved object predominate. Idolatrous love gives what man calls a meaning to his life; possessive love also does this, but it is often a meaning that is less positive, less satiating.

3. APPARENT LOVE OF ANOTHER BECAUSE THIS OTHER LOVES US WITH ONE OF THE TWO PRECEDING KINDS OF LOVE

The other loves his Ego in me, but he gives me the impression that he loves my Ego. And so I desire his existence as I desire the existence of everyone who desires my existence.

4. APPARENT LOVE OF OTHERS BECAUSE MY IDEAL IMAGE OF MYSELF REQUIRES IT OR BECAUSE MY IDOLATROUS LOVE COMPORTS IT

I love others because I need to see myself as aesthetic in order to love myself and because to love others is aesthetic.

Or again I love others because I love mystically a divine image on to which my Ego is projected, because I consider that this divine image wishes that I may love others, and because I desire that which is desired by this divine image (identified with my Ego).

5. APPARENT LOVE OF THE NOT-ME BECAUSE MY EGO IS MOMENTARILY SATIATED

The man who is momentarily filled with an intense egotistical affirmation loves the whole universe. This love without particularity does not correspond with a momentary apparition of primordial universal love, but with a momentary inversion of the fundamental egotistical hatred of the Not-Self coinciding with a relaxation of egotistical revendication. Besides, this state only lasts a little time. It is comparable with the voluptuous sensation of ceasing to suffer; this voluptuousness is only comparative, however, and it ceases as soon as the period of comparison comes to an end.

These five kinds of apparent love-of-others represent so many indulgences of my Ego experienced in situations which affirm me as distinct. With every diminution of one of these situations corresponds the appearance of distress and of aggressiveness.

The more a given man is called upon to attain intemporal realisation the greater his need to experience these kinds of love; these states resemble indeed, more or less, the affective state of the man who has attained realisation (who loves everything) by seeming to join him to something other than himself.

Nevertheless the more this man advances in the knowledge of himself the more these kinds of love lose value in his eyes and lose their compensatory effectiveness. This man loses little by little his 'positive', 'altruistic' sentiments. His understanding sees through these clever counterfeits and leads him back willy-nilly towards the fundamental egotistical state in which he has always hated that which is not his Self; the state of 'night' and of solitude. He suffers distress on account of his refusal to combat the Not-Self (cf. Notes on the Mechanism of Anxiety).

This man, robbed little by little of all possibility of cheating inwardly, sees himself hounded towards the task of realisation. He will address himself more and more often to his impartial thought in order to query the legitimacy of his egotistical claim, of that pretention to be distinct which engenders solitude and fear. The Ego becomes ever more contracted, more and more hemmed-in in its last stronghold. There is a limit to this compression, a limit beyond which the Ego explodes in satori. Then the Ego is diffused throughout, accomplishing itself and annihilating itself at one and the same time.

Chapter Nine

THE ZEN UNCONSCIOUS

THE psychological consciousness of the natural man contains perpetually two different layers of perception; it pays attention to two different orders of things. The natural man's attention is continually held on two planes of perception; it is divided between these two planes. It is a mistake to suppose that one can only pay attention to one thing at a time; one continually pays attention to two things at a time; but, as we are about to see, in two different ways.

On the first plane of perception the attention is held by particular aspects of the outside world, effectively present or rendered present by the imaginative film. On this plane I live, in duration, my particular dispute, qualitatively changing all the time, with the Not-Self.

On the other plane of perception my attention is held by the situation, at the moment, of the hearing of my profound general lawsuit between 'to be' and 'not to be'. This action is always the same, so this plane of perception is qualitatively entirely monotonous. If, on this plane, things change unceasingly also, it is quantitatively. My state therein is more or less 'white' (impression of 'being') or 'black' (impression of 'not being'). Apart from these fluctuations between the white and the black there occur quantitative fluctuations between calm and agitation; we will return later to these two kinds of fluctuation.

It is interesting to study the relations which exist between these two planes. The plane of my particular perceptions, or surface plane, depends (in so far as my imagination influences thereon my perception of the outside world or re-creates on it aspects of the outside world) on the plane of my profound general perception, that is to say, on my state. A white state peoples my imaginative film with positive forms, a black state peoples it with negative forms. An agitated state accelerates my imaginative film, a calm state slows it down. Apart from that this surface plane evidently depends also on outside circumstances.

The profound plane, that is to say, my state, depends in part on the forms present on the surface plane. The affirming or negating events that I perceive there influence my state; and the forms imagined under the influence of my state react on this state in a positive and negative vicious circle. But my state depends also on my physiological coenaesthesis;[1] insomnia, indigestion, blacken it; alcohol, opium, whiten it.

In short I am unceasingly occupied by two things at the same time; I am occupied at once by my existence in the outside world and in calculating inwardly the chances of a favourable or unfavourable verdict in the general action concerning my being and my nullity. My attention is divided between these two occupations; this explains why the neurotic patient often presents disturbance of superficial mental concentration and disturbance of perception of the outside world. So great a part of his attention is taken up in calculating the verdict of his action, so little is left to him for his contacts with the outside world, real or imagined, that he receives an impression of the unreality of the outside world and of the impossibility of managing his surface mentality.

My state, white or black, agitated or calm is non-formal. Light shows up forms but it is itself without form. Agitation is likewise without form; forms are more or less in a state of agitation, but agitation itself is without form. Therefore all perception of the profound plane is without form. On the contrary perception on the surface plane is formal. Therefore perception on the surface plane is evident to me, while my perception of my state is latent. I can only become conscious of it as of a coenaesthesis more or less agreeable or disagreeable, the agreeable corresponding with the white and the disagreeable with the black.

It is important that I distinguish between these two consciousnesses which correspond with the two planes which divide my

[1] The word 'coenaesthesis' indicates the total inner perception that we have of our organism. Beside the five senses by means of which we perceive the outside world our coenaesthesis is a kind of sixth sense by means of which our organism perceives itself in its ensemble.

attention, and that I indicate them by different names. I will call my surface consciousness '*objectal* consciousness' and my profound consciousness '*subjectal* consciousness'. These two consciousnesses are the two unconciliated parts between which is torn in pieces my psychological consciousness in my dualistic egotistical condition in which I perceive everything from the angle of the opposition subject-object. I say 'subjectal' and 'objectal' and not 'subjective' and 'objective' because these two latter words should correspond with the two conciliated aspects of the consciousness of the man who has attained Realisation.

My objectal consciousness is evident, or manifest, my subjectal consciousness latent. I debate my outward problems knowing that I am debating them; I debate my profound inward problem without being aware of it. The fact is that in these two consciousnesses the manner in which my attention is held differs. I am in agreement with the capture of my attention by outward forms, I lend myself to it, I am in favour of it; on the contrary I am against the capture of my attention by my inner state; I can say that I cause my attention to be captured in my objectal consciousness and that it is captured in spite of me in my subjectal consciousness. I am oriented in a centrifugal manner, towards the outside; it is outwards that I look; and I turn my back, on the contrary, on my state. The part of my attention which is captured by my subjectal consciousness is stolen from me from behind; the part of my attention which is captured in my objectal consciousness I myself offer, in front of me, to the outside world of form. I am to be compared with a man sitting in a cinema, with a screen in front of him and the projector behind; I look at the forms on the screen and I turn my back on the projector, on my state which projects on to the screen form and colour.

My subjectal consciousness, this consciousness unknown to classical psychology, is the latent face of my psychological consciousness that is torn apart in duality. This thought which works unceasingly, monotonously, on the dispute between my being and my nullity, is, in a sense, unconscious. But the unconscious in question here is not the fundamental Unconscious of Zen; it represents the very first apparition of dualism, immediately after the fundamental Unconscious has become conscious of itself; it is the very first dualistic manifestation of the fundamental Unconscious. One does not know whether one ought to call it unconscious or conscious since it is exactly at the border-line between the fundamental Unconscious and consciousness. One sees it to be unconscious if one looks at it from the point of view of consciousness (the Freudian point of view); one sees it to be subjectal consciousness if one looks at it from the point of view of the fundamental Unconscious. It is from this point of view of the fundamental Unconscious that the Zen master looks at it when he deplores, in the natural man, the misdeeds of the dualistic psychological consciousness. The Zen master says to us: 'You are unhappy because you are established, in fact, in consciousness and not in the Unconscious'; and he sees the Freudian unconscious not indeed as a real unconscious but as the deepest and most obscure source of the discoursive consciousness, that is to say as the first mode of dualistic consciousness.

Sharing this Zen point of view we ought to regard this subjectal consciousness as our latent consciousness and not as the Unconscious. Although latent it is no less active for that, and for our misfortune. The more active it is, that is to say the more we debate our illusory problem being-nullity, and the more we are distressed by doubt concerning our being, the more we are deprived of the joyous original light, and the more our attention is captured by the obscure depths. When a very great amount of our attention is thus captured there only remains a little for our adaptation to the outside world; it is what has been called 'lowering of the psychological tension', with impossibility of concentration and all the symptoms of psychasthenia.

Since my subjectal consciousness is latent, since it is a kind of unconscious consciousness, one can ask oneself by what means we have knowledge of it and how we can speak of it. It is the observation of my surface consciousness, and the need that I experience of understanding why it functions as it functions, which lead me little by little to understand, by mediate reasoning, the existence and the nature of this profound subjectal consciousness in which is debated the action between my being and my nullity. The immediate inner intuition of my profound state does not reveal to me forms within it but gives me information concerning its luminosity (from white to black, from light to dark) and concerning its dynamism (from calm to agitation).

This intuitive perception is interesting, for it allows me to observe the relations which exist between my inner state and my comportment, sentiments and actions. Just as the meaning of a dream is found in its latent content and not in its manifest content, so the meaning of my life, this other dream, is to be found in my latent consciousness, subjectal, and not in my manifest consciousness, objectal. It is the thought of my latent consciousness which determines my comportment and my manifest consciousness.

In my latent consciousness in which is tried the action concerning my being and my nullity, I desire to be acquitted, I desire to feel myself as being, and I am terrified of my nullity. Let us see how the two phenomenal dualisms of my being—'light-darkness' and 'agitation-immobility'—are connected with this fundamental dualism being-nullity. Everything happens in me as though light were identified with being and darkness with nullity, and as though agitation were identified with being and immobility with nullity. That is to say my innate partiality for being is expressed by a partiality for a 'luminous state, in motion'. But it is possible to specify still further my partiality; the particular modalities of life and of my personal inner structure are not always such that I can have at the same time light and agitation; I am obliged sometimes to choose between the two; I then perceive, by my comportment, that I still prefer agitation to light. I can say, still more accurately and speaking now in the negative mode, that, if my deep fear is fear of darkness and of immobility, my fear of immobility is greater than my fear of darkness; I encounter more strongly the terrifying impression of not 'being' in the absence of movement of my subjectal consciousness than in its character as black. (Thus a child will prefer to see his mother scold him than not pay attention to him at all; he would prefer that she paid attention to him by kissing him; but if he fails to obtain that he will prefer her scolding to her neglect. So also, the masochist, if his greatest preference tends, as that of every man, towards vibrant joy, likes better, since he has not succeeded in obtaining this vibrant joy, to vibrate by suffering rather than not to vibrate at all.) Everything happens, then, as though I feared more than anything the immobility of my deep state, and secondarily the darkness of this state; as if I feared more than anything not to feel myself living (and so, vibrating, movement being the essential criterion of life), and secondarily not to feel myself joyous. Man generally pretends to desire happiness; this pretention corresponds with the sound intuition that the deep state of the man who has attained Realisation will be luminous and motionless. But in fact this pretention does not accord with the natural man's comportment; the natural man does not live for happiness, he does not tend to obtain for himself a luminous and motionless state; he tends to obtain for himself a state that is, above all, vibrant and, secondarily, luminous.

It is not surprising that the natural man does not attain happiness, since he does not tend towards it. And the fact that his preference for agitation is stronger than his preference for light explains why his joys are so precarious; when he is joyous he attaches more value to the agitation by means of which he strives for still more joy than he attaches to his joy itself. This is expressed by an unlimited demand for joy which always ends by his stumbling on the limits of the temporal plane and by bringing about the collapse of the joy. (Consider a man who has a great piece of luck; at once he wishes to celebrate it and to add as much gratification as possible to his original gratification.)

Of the two distinct preferences experienced by the natural man in connexion with his states, the secondary preference for the light is sound; but his primordial preference for agitation is erroneous, and it is the cause of all his miseries. It is because he desires unceasingly to feel his life vibrating in him, that is to say, in the egotistical situation in which he still is, to feel himself affirmed as distinct, that he remains plunged in the miseries of dualism and its lacerating contradictions.

Only comprehension can deliver man from this absurd preference; comprehension reveals to him that this inner immobility of which he is terrified not only is not to be feared but represents salvation. Indeed, in the egotistical situation in which he is at present, he cannot have at the same time light and immobility; if he brings himself, being initiated, to prefer in fact, that is to say to seek, immobility, he will have darkness at the same time; the 'Night' of Saint John of the Cross, if it is motionless is at the same time dark. But this night is very bearable when I am established in this immobility of which I am no longer afraid, in which on the contrary I put my hopes.

This inner task does not consist in 'doing' anything new whatsoever; it consists only, because one has understood, in spontaneously remembering the absurdity of the hopes that we place mechanically, naturally, in our inner agitation, and of the harmful absurdity of this agitation. Each time that I conceive this revealing non-natural thought my agitation ceases more or less completely. Abandoning my pretension of settling my action between being and nullity I confide myself to my Principle so that it may scatter the phantoms of this absurd action. I *do* nothing further, I leave everything to my invisible Principle, in which I believe without seeing it. I have only, for my part, to maintain and to increase my understanding by honest intellectual work, so that the spontaneous effects of this understanding may grow richer as well.

Chapter Ten

METAPHYSICAL DISTRESS

W HEN I am distressed in connexion with any circumstance of my life, what is happening in me? My distress is the result of meeting the Not-Self, it expresses my fear of being defeated in this encounter. Since I unceasingly try the action between my being and my nullity in connexion with the particular circumstances of my life, my distress expresses my fear of being condemned in this action. I have tried to conquer the Not-Self, and here I am, afraid that I may not succeed, and of being brought face to face, in this failure, with the negation of my being.

But I would not have tried to conquer the Not-Self and to win the case of my being if this case had not first of all existed in the depths of me, if a doubt had not dwelt in me regarding my being. As a result, behind the distress that I have felt in the momentary failure of my case, there is another distress, a permanent distress which supports my case itself. Behind the phenomenal, or physical distress, felt on the plane of phenomena, there is a noumenal, or metaphysical distress, which dwells up-stream of my phenomena.

This metaphysical distress is the original, or primary distress which conditions my ordinary, secondary distress. We will try to specify its nature.

First of all it is unconscious. The man who has not attained Realisation is conscious of phenomena only; he could not, therefore, be conscious of a distress which is up-stream of phenomena. Besides let us see what happens in us when we are joyous; I am joyous because I feel myself to be affirmed in the antagonism Self-Not-Self, because my inner lawsuit is momentarily going well, in process of being won. But, behind this joy which depends upon the turn for the better of my lawsuit, this lawsuit still goes on, and so a doubt concerning my being, and so metaphysical distress; metaphysical distress lies at the origin of my joys as well as of my conscious distress; and it is the unconscious element therein.

Unconscious metaphysical distress, then, is also characterised by permanence. It is always there, always the same, behind all our affective phenomena and their dualism Joy-Suffering.

We will demonstrate besides that it is illusory, unreal, that it 'is' not (although it has seemed to us to 'be' just now, noumenally), but simply that all our affective phenomena occur as though it existed.

Let us note that it constitutes, with the joy and the suffering that it conditions, the triangle that we know already, whose apex represents the conciliatory principle and whose inferior angles represent the inferior positive and negative principles:

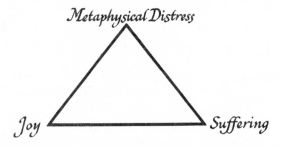

But this triangle may surprise us; as opposed to what we have seen in all the other cases the superior principle here carries a negative appellation. Why? This corresponds with the fact that Faith is asleep in the man who has not attained realisation, with the fact that this man whose Faith is asleep does not see his Buddha-nature. Because this man does not see his Buddha-nature everything happens in him as though this nature, which however is his, were lacking in him. Because the Being is not awakened in the man's centre everything happens in him as though, in this centre, there reigned a Nullity which it then becomes necessary to refute. Because the perfect existential Felicity is not awakened in the centre of this man everything happens as if this centre were occupied by a primordial distress. But this primordial distress 'is'

not. We understand thus that our recent triangle was badly drawn; it would be more accurate to draw it thus:

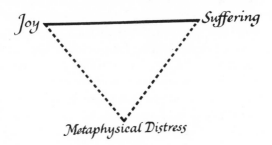

It is a triangle illusorily inversed by ignorance. In the case of the man enlightened by satori this inversion disappears and the triangle becomes:

Metaphysical distress cannot be conscious since it is entirely illusory. Man cannot become conscious of it without it annihilating itself. One cannot even say that satori results from the fact of becoming conscious of metaphysical distress; it is better to say that satori occurs when the man's centre awakens, this centre in which the metaphysical distress is supposed to reside as long as the centre is asleep.

All the forms of distress that man can feel consciously are secondary distress; none deserves the name of primary or metaphysical distress. Sometimes man is distressed concerning the great philosophical problems that touch on his condition, that is to say he is distressed concerning metaphysical questions; but this man is tormented by mental images, by phenomena, by forms; he suffers on the phenomenal plane—physical not metaphysical. Another man can be distressed at the thought of renouncing certain illusory compensations; he can then believe that this distress at the idea of losing his personality and merging in the universal deserves the name of metaphysical distress. But this man has a false conception of renunciation; he does not know that true renunciation is a passing beyond that which has been depreciated by the understanding interpreting experience; this man is not, as he believes, distressed by the universal but by the particular values to which he is still attached and which are menaced by a false conception of Realisation. No distress that is consciously felt could be called metaphysical; there could not be distress at the level of the Principle, at the level of our creative source.

On the other hand, we repeat there cannot exist any distress, consciously felt, which has not at its origin unconscious metaphysical distress, the reversed unconscious image of dormant existential Felicity. This fallacious unconscious image is the efficient cause of all our 'moral' suffering; the circumstances of our life, in connexion with which we suffer, are only, despite what we habitually believe, immediate causes. A mother who has lost her child does not suffer, as she believes, because her child is dead; she suffers, in connexion with this death, because she believes herself to have been abandoned by her Principle, she suffers because the occurrence has realeased in her the profound impression of not 'being'.

If no distress that is consciously felt can be the primary metaphysical distress it is important to see that our secondary distress is more or less removed from the fallacious primordial distress. Our distress is graded in a qualitative hierarchy according to the degree of depth of our understanding. My distress is at its furthest from my source if my understanding of the inner life is null, if I am fully persuaded that my concrete and particular grief is the real cause of my suffering. In proportion as I advance in the correct understanding of the inner life I escape from this trap; my belief in the causal rôle of the particular accidental circumstance decreases; I relate my suffering less and less to that which happens to me personally, and more and more to my universal human state, this state which I share with all human beings. In the degree in which this understanding works effectively in me the lawsuit between my personal being and my personal nullity ceases to be pleaded; that is to say in the degree in which the causes of my distress become universal in my understanding I cease to suffer. The more my mental images lose their fascinating density, the more my distress becomes subtle and draws near its source, and the more this distress at the same time is attenuated. Thus one can perceive how understanding frees man little by little from his distress; the more profoundly I understand that my distress depends on a state that is in no way particular to me, the more there fades in me the famous and absurd lawsuit 'to be or not to be' from which comes all my misery. Understanding does not bring the lawsuit to a settlement, it scatters the phantoms of the illusory suit, and reduces progressively all the emotions which come from this 'cave of phantoms'. Thus we make our way towards satori. According to the descriptions of the Zen masters the inner states which precede and announce the release of satori are states of serenity, of affective neutrality. The consciousness of this man has gradually approached his centre, this centre at which it was supposed that metaphysical distress, mother of all distress, resides; the nearer he approaches it the lighter is his distress, so tenuous that it disappears altogether in the last moments which precede satori. The more he approaches the point at which metaphysical distress was supposed to reside, the more he recognises that he does not see it, the more he assures himself in this way that it has never been there. The painful belief disappears then in serenity; together with it there is abolished the spasm which was closing the 'third eye' and which forbade him until then the vision of perfect existential joy.

Chapter Eleven

SEEING INTO ONE'S OWN NATURE
THE SPECTATOR OF THE SPECTACLE

WE would like to revert to the psychological conditions of satori and to the necessity of training ourselves to perceive inwardly, up-stream of all form, our impression of existing-more-or-less. There indeed lies the heart of the concrete inner work aiming at our transformation.

Zen says to us: 'Look straight into your own nature.' Certainly, but I, as a natural man, realise that I do not succeed in doing so. This way of looking depends on the 'opening of the third eye', and everything takes place in me as though this third eye was always closed. I have understood that the third eye exists in me and that no film covers it; there is nothing wrong with it, it does not have to be cured; but it is used to remaining shut and I have to do something in order to get rid of this habit. I ask myself, therefore, how I am to lose this habit from which spring all my sufferings. I have understood that there ought to be a certain way of using my two ordinary eyes, that is to say with my ordinary attention, which should gradually do away with the spasm of the eyelid of the third eye and enable me one day to see suddenly and definitively into my own nature. I ask myself then what this way may be. What is this way of looking which, possible in my present state yet incapable by itself of giving me the 'vision into my own nature', will nevertheless modify my state in such a way that it will cease to oppose the 'opening of the third eye'? I know that the effective effort will not be an effort of contraction but an effort of relaxation; but I ask myself: 'What exactly is this effort of relaxation that I must make and which although fruitless in itself— since an inferior manifestation could not be the cause of a superior manifestation—will make me subject, ultimately, to the direct action of Intemporal Reality?'

This effort of relaxation consists in a certain glance within. This inward glance, as we have said, is that which I make towards the centre of my whole being when I reply to the question: 'How are you feeling at this moment from every point of view at the same time?' If someone asks me: 'How are you feeling at this moment from a physical point of view?' I look into myself so as to perceive what is called my coenaesthesis, what I shall call here my physical coenaesthesis. If someone asks me: 'How are you feeling at this moment from the "moral" point of view?' I look into myself so as to perceive that which I will call my psychic coenaesthesis (that which is called also my state of mind or my mood). And when someone asks me: 'How are you feeling at this moment from every point of view at once?' I look into myself so as to perceive what I shall call my *total coenaesthesis*. It is this last way of looking which constitutes the essential effort in order to obtain one day the 'sudden' release of 'vision into my own nature'.

In order to study this special inner perception which is total coenaesthesis we will use the similarities which relate it to physical coenaesthesis. Two points are interesting. First of all coenaesthesis is a perception obtained by a de-contraction; the coenaesthetic sensation of my right arm, for example, which consists in feeling the existence of my arm, or in feeling my arm from within, cannot be felt if my arm is contracted; in this state of contraction the sensibility of my arm is projected to the surface; I must decontract my arm in order to feel it in its central axis, as though its sensibility flowed back then into the marrow of its bones. Again, coenaesthetic perception is in-formal. When my arm is contracted I feel its form; when on the contrary it has lain as relaxed as possible for some minutes and its sensibility has flowed back entirely into its central axis, I feel this arm certainly, I feel it as existing (this corresponds with the painless sensation of the missing limb that a man has, whose limb has been amputated), but I no longer feel its form. If I think of it from the spatial point of view I feel it to be as big as the whole universe, as though its form had burst and was dissolved in the totality of space; I have therefore certainly an in-formal perception of it.

These two points, de-contracted perception and in-formal

perception, are common to the three coenaestheses. But the physical coenaesthesis differs from the two others from a point of view that is capital, the point of view of time. The perception of my physical existence is capable of continuity in duration; I can feel my arm, or the whole of my physical body, 'from within' during a certain continuous period. On the contrary, when I perceive my total coenaesthesis, that is to say when I feel myself from within in my psycho-somatic totality, it is only in an instantaneous flash, and I cannot hold it with the least temporal continuity; this perception escapes me at the same moment that it reaches me. It escapes me in its in-formal purity and drifts at once towards formal perceptions. For a moment, for example, I feel 'not very well' without this discomfort having any form; then, at once, I feel the manner of my discomfort, how I am not very well; then why, in my opinion, I am thus; then what I envisage in order to feel better, and so on. . . .

Thus, then, my effort to perceive purely my total existence has only resulted in perceiving my actual and instantaneous *state of existence*. And so the view which this perception gives me is at once a view which sees and which does not see; it sees something of that which it is looking at, since it sees an instantaneous aspect of it which is not without reality, but it does not see what it is looking at in the moving reality which sustains all its instantaneous aspects. One dimension is lacking, that of time. It is this dimension which must be conquered in order that my perception of existing may be a real subjective consciousness, a consciousness of self.

This difference which separates my total coenaesthesis from my somatic coenaesthesis is the cause of another difference between these two perceptions. If my global perception of existing has all the same a certain reality it is in the measure in which this instantaneous perception is opposed to a previous perception, that is to say in the measure in which I feel myself to exist more, or less, than a moment ago. If I withdraw myself from the stimulations of the outside world in order to consecrate myself to repeated efforts of perception of my state of existence, these efforts soon cease to have any result. Since my state of existence does not vary in its impermeability to outside influences, my instantaneous states are identical, they are not in opposition. The time element which was represented by these oppositions from one moment to the next, in the *memory* that I had in that moment of the moment before, has disappeared, and with it all in-formal perception of existing. If, as we have said, the time dimension is lacking in the consciousness of the natural man, it is still necessary that time should be represented there by memory, and that it manifest thus in connexion with modifications of my state of existence—in order that there may be a certain perception of existing. In any case this perception is relative; in my state of natural man I am not able 'merely' to feel myself existing, I can only have, as in-formal perception, that of existing-more-or-less-than-a-moment-ago. (It is different where my physical coenaesthesis is concerned; and it is because the perception of the physical existence of my arm participates in the absolute, in the intemporal, that a man who has suffered amputation still feels the existence of the arm which he no longer has.)

The perception of existing, of which alone I am capable to-day, is then a perception limited to the moment, and it is relative; it is only an instantaneous perception of existing-more-or-less-than-a-moment-ago. My impression of existing varies unceasingly according to the ups-and-downs of my relations with the outside world. It is comparable with a bottle-imp, the kind that bobs up and down inside a vase. According to whether I see myself affirmed or denied by the outside world my bottle-imp rises or falls. And my perception of existing-more-or-less consists in perceiving instantaneously the position of this bottle-imp in relation to that which it occupied a moment before.

I perceive the positions of the bottle-imp in their reciprocal relations, I see the bottle-imp higher or lower than it was a moment ago. But I cannot, actually, see it move; I can only indirectly see its displacements by perceiving the difference between my successive instantaneous observations of it; I do not perceive them directly. These displacements of the bottle-imp, these modifications of my states, express my profoundest vital movement. They represent the first phenomenal manifestation of my noumenal existence, of my Principle, of the Universal Supreme Principle, of that which the Vedânta calls the Self. I perceive instantaneous states, different and contrasted, of the manifestation of my Principle, not that manifestation itself in its continuity. The Principle alone sees its manifestation in its continuity; and my consciousness will only benefit by its identity with its Principle when it sees, in its continuity, this manifestation which is the spectacle of my creation, or as the Vedânta also says, when I shall be the Spectator of my Spectacle.

Often this notion of a Spectator of the Spectacle is imperfectly understood; some believe that the spectacle in question is at the level of our formal inner phenomena, that it is the imaginative film of our ideas and sentiments. This is a serious mistake; it pushes us towards ordinary introspection which subjects us more and more to our imaginative world. The problem, attacked on this lower level, is insoluble; we cannot be the active spectators of our imaginative film; we only see it when we are not actively looking at it; every active look stops it. The spectacle of which we have to become Spectator is situated at a level above the imaginative film; it is at the level of our first, profound, in-formal movement, from which derive thereafter all our formal inner movements. And this first movement is that which we have called the movement of the bottle-imp, displacements upwards or downwards of our total inner state, synthesis and source of our states both somatic and psychic.

In short, to obtain satori, it is a question of obtaining the transformation of these instantaneous perceptions of existing-more-or-less-than-a-moment-ago into a continuous perception which will then be just perception of existing. Man can arrive at that by training himself to have more and more of these instantaneous perceptions. A comparison will help us to understand what happens in the course of this work. Let us suppose that someone projects a cinematograph-film at the speed of one image every 10 seconds, and we see each image clearly; let us suppose next that the projection is accelerated progressively, and for a certain length of time we still see clearly the images in their discontinuity; but a moment will soon come when we will no longer see them clearly in their discontinuity and when we will not yet see the film clearly in its continuity. Finally, the speed of projection becomes sufficient for us to see clearly the film in its continuity. Zen well describes the intermediate stage which separates the clear and dead vision (ordinary consciousness) from the clear and living vision (consciousness after satori); at its height this intermediary stage is called by Zen 'Tai-i' ('Great Doubt'), and it is described to us as a mental state of complete confusion without form (confusion so complete and so lacking in form that it is in no respect a state of chaos and resembles the transparent purety of an immense crystal behind which there would still be nothing). The idea of the three successive stages of which we are speaking is found also in this passage of Zen: 'Before a man studies Zen, for him the mountains are mountains and the waters are waters; when, thanks to the teaching of a good master, he has achieved a certain inner vision of the truth of Zen, for him the mountains are no longer mountains and the waters are no longer waters; but later, when he has really arrived at the asylum of rest, once more the mountains are mountains and the waters are waters.'

Let us come now to the practice of the inner work such as we envisage it at this moment. As regards the manner of this work we can say nothing more than what we have already said; let us merely repeat that the difficulty of this looking inwards comes from its simplicity. When one fails in looking as one should it is always because one is looking for difficulties where none exist; the question is simply to see if one feels better altogether or less well altogether, if the bottle-imp has bobbed up or dropped down.

This way of looking, let it be said, is only useful if the man who is training himself has profoundly understood, with true intellectual evidence, that, the attainment of satori being the only possible solution of his present state of distress, it is absolutely without importance whether the bottle-imp be high up or low down; the only thing that matters is to obtain the continuous perception of his movement, and not to be happy or unhappy, to tremble or to be self-assured, etc. Above affective preferences, which evidently persist, the impartiality of intellectual comprehension should be firmly established. In the same order of ideas it is evident that the way of looking of which we are speaking assumes the understanding of the equal nullity of the forms of all our mechanisms. At the beginning the man should analyse his mechanisms in order to understand in what the inner mechanics consist; but the concrete inner work assumes that all this has been done and that one has ceased to attach importance to his complexes. The work of theoretical understanding should have been done, and well done, before the concrete inner work can be undertaken.

But an important question remains which we must study. Since, like every natural man, I have five different manners of thinking, which of these manners will constitute the most favourable psychological climate for my efforts to 'see into my own nature'? The reply is simple: there is only one manner of thinking which is compatible with this perception, that is the fourth manner, that of the man who adapts himself to the real outer world. When the variation of my states of existence depend on the non-real and non-present outer world that my imagination creates, that is to say on an imaginative film that I fabricate outside present reality with the materials of my reserve of images, at that moment my mental apparatus is entirely occupied by this fabrication, and it is not available for active perception. I can only actively perceive my varied states of existence when these variations depend not on my activity but on another activity than mine, on the activity of the Not-Self, of the present real outside world. And this activity of the present real outside world only concerns my psychic mechanism during the periods when I join myself to this world, when I adapt myself to reality. One could object that, even at that moment, the variations of my states depend on a certain activity of my mind; which is true, but re-active activity; re-activity, not activity. When I adapt myself to the real outside world the initiative of the mechanisms which will result in my states is outside me, not in me, and it is that which matters. From the moment that this initiative is outside me my initiative is available to me for an active perception.

Experience proves to us, better than any reasoning, what I have just said. If I wish to perceive my state of existence at a moment when I am day-dreaming, or at a moment when I am meditating, I must suspend my activity in order to achieve it; I must suspend that which is my life of that moment, and stop living. If, on the contrary, I want to perceive my state of existence at a moment when I have real concrete occupation I realise that I can do so without interrupting my action, that I can feel myself even in the middle of my action. The imaginative film that I have in my mind when I am paying attention to the present outside world is an accurate reflection of this world; it is reactive; it is the outside world which determines it. This reactive imaginative film does not hinder my perception of my state of existence; it is like a wheel which turns with the regular rhythm of the cosmos and at the centre of which my attention can direct itself to the perception of my state of existence at this moment. Every active imaginative film, on the contrary, fabricated by my mind without contact with the present outer world, forbids me the perception of my state of existence. The inner work is, then, incompatible with sleep, with day-dreaming, and with meditative reflection; it is only compatible with life that is adapted to the present concrete world.

Thus are we able to understand why Zen masters have so often repeated that 'the Tao is our daily life'. A monk one day asked his master to instruct him in Zen; the master said to him: 'Have you had your breakfast, or not?' 'I have had it,' replied the monk. 'Very well then, go and wash your dishes.' Zen says also: 'When we are hungry, we eat: when we are sleepy, we lie down; where in all that does the finite or the infinite come in? It is only when the intellect, fertile in restlessness, comes on the scene and takes command that we cease to live and that we imagine that we lack something.'

The inner task consists in an effort of decontraction, in a non-action opposed to our reflex inner agitation; it is a simplicity opposed to our natural complexity; and Zen insists often on this simplicity, this relaxation. Sometimes then we come to think that the inner task should be easy, that we do not have to take trouble; on account of our ignorance of the non-action we believe that it is only in order to 'do' something that we have to take trouble. Let us try, however, to decontract our whole body and to maintain it in a state of complete decontraction for five minutes; we will see then what trouble we must take to remain vigilant, without which one group of muscles or another will quickly slip back into a state of tension. That is why Zen, if it often recalls the simplicity of the inner task, says also: 'Inner peace is only to be had after a bitter fight with our personality . . . the fight should rage with extreme force and virility; otherwise the peace which follows will only be a sham.' This battle with the personality is not on the plane of form, it is not, for example, a battle with shortcomings; it is a fight against the mental inertia which engenders all our formal inner agitation, a struggle against that current in order to remount it little by little right up to the reintegration of our consciousness with the in-formal source of our being.

We must now complete what we have said concerning the relations of compatibility or of incompatibility which exist between the effort to 'see into our own nature' and our five manners of thinking. We ought further to enlarge the distinction that we have made between the reactive imaginative film, based on the present outer world, and the active imaginative film, fabricated by our mind with the material of our reserve of images. This distinction is parallel with a distinction that the observation of our concrete psychological life imposes on us: we live at the same time on two distinct planes, the plane of sensation and the plane of imagery. Most men, for example, crave for riches, luxury; they expect from that affirmation of themselves; in fact the rich man obtains from his wealth affirmation of himself. But these affirmations are of two kinds. My wealth affirms me on the plane of sensation by favouring my organic life (good food, good sleep, refreshing sensory impressions, etc.), and on the plane of imagery 'I feel that I am "someone" because I have all that.' The plane of sensation corresponds with physical coenaesthesia, the plane of imagery with psychical coenaesthesia. Notice at the same time that the plane of sensation is real while the plane of imagery is illusory; in fact the plane of sensation corresponds with the man in so far as he is as all other men, that is to say universal man; while the plane of imagery corresponds with the man in so far as he sees himself and wishes himself unique, distinct, that is with the egotistical personal man, who has the illusory image of an Ego. It is illusory because, if each man differs from every other, it is only in formal factors and not at all in his specific condition.

The natural man, except when he sleeps deeply, never lives on just one of these two planes; he lives always on both planes at once. His mind never limits itself to building up a reactive film (plane of sensation) or even an active film (plane of imagery); he builds up unceasingly two films at the same time, one reactive, the other active; his attention shifts from one to the other of these films and it is only on one at each moment, but the two films are unceasingly built up together. It is easy enough at first to see that I do not live on the plane of sensation without living at the same time on the plane of imagery: the lawsuit between my being and my nullity is pleaded unceasingly within me and it is influenced by everything that happens to me on the plane of sensation; according to whether I experience physical discomfort or well-being I mistrust myself or I have faith in myself, etc. On the other hand it may seem that I live sometimes only on the plane of imagery; we will see, however, that it is not so, and we will even realise that the plane of imagery is based on the plane of sensation, that it depends upon it, that it results from it. Let us study to that end a case in which the play of the plane of imagery is nevertheless carried to extremes. A rich financier goes bankrupt and he kills himself in order to escape from a life curtailed, in which he would no longer be important. This man destroys his body in order to save his image of himself; it would certainly appear that such an act is performed entirely on the plane of imagery and that there is here priority of this plane over the plane of sensation. But let us look more closely: this man kills himself in order to avoid a loss of consideration; but this loss of consideration is only unbearable to him because it is the loss of a consideration on which he placed an extremely high price. And he only envisaged this price of the consideration of himself by others because this consideration, this affirmation of himself by others, represented an alliance of the others with him in his combat against the Not-Self, a protection of his organism against death. However paradoxical the thing may seem, this man kills himself in order to preserve that which virtually protects him against death. In the light of this example I understand that the plane of imagery is a sort of illusory construction which my active imaginative mind builds on the plane of sensation; everything that I like on the plane of imagery, everything which affirms me on this plane, I see as affirming me because I see it as favourable ultimately to my organism. I say 'ultimately' because there is no immediate coincidence between my imaginative affirmation and the organic affirmation from which it derives. Here, for example, is a powerful business-man who works unceasingly and becomes very rich; this daily agitation is a negation of the plane of sensation; he leads, according to the popular expression, a dog's life, nevertheless if he clings to his position it is because the power that it confers upon him represents a virtual protection of his organism against death. This man also kills himself by degrees, in order to maintain and to increase that which protects him against death. There is no immediate coincidence between the affirmation that he obtains on the plane of imagery and that which his wealth procures him eventually on the plane of sensation; it is nevertheless this last affirmation, however virtual it may be, which determines and supports the first.

The natural man lives, then, unceasingly on these two planes at once. These two planes correspond with the two domains, somatic and psychic, that we studied in another chapter. Let us recall that every episode of our lives results ultimately in concomitant re-actions in us in these two domains, but that the contacts with the outside world which will release these reactions in the two domains together come to us via the one or via the other. I am touched by the outer world either on the plane of sensation (the outside world effectively present), or on the plane of imagery (the outside world recollected), but I experience each of these two contacts at the same time on the two planes.

If the natural man lives unceasingly on the two planes at once we have said that he only pays attention to one of them at each moment. When a man dreams, when he day-dreams, and when he meditates, his attention is fixed on the plane of imagery only, on the active imaginative film only; the reactive imaginative film is developed alongside it, but the attention is not on it. It is only when he adapts himself to the present outside world that a man experiences his life at the same time (thanks to the rapid alter-nations of his attention) on the plane of sensation and on that of imagery. If I observe myself well I realise that I day-dream always a little, and very often enormously, at the same time that I adapt myself to the real present in order to join myself with the outer world and use it. Knowing that, we can now reconsider more exactly the compatibility which exists between the fourth manner of thinking and the inner task. Theoretically this compatibility is absolute; concretely everything happens as though it was not absolute because I am never unreservedly in the fourth manner of thinking. My attention alternates incessantly between the fourth manner and the third, I am astride these two manners of thinking. The aim of the inner task is precisely to install myself some day, by means of satori, entirely in the fourth manner of thinking, to adapt myself at last really to the outside world, to reach Reality by the elimination of the dream.

Experience demonstrates it to me. As soon as I begin to make the right kind of efforts in order to perceive my instantaneous state of existence I realise that these efforts curb the active imaginative film which is in me and which is incompatible with these efforts. More exactly these efforts have a solvent effect on my illusory film, by taking my attention from it and placing it on the real reactive imaginative film. In short my efforts dissolve my life-on-the-plane-of-imagery and purge of it my life-on-the-plane-of-sensation. The inner work eliminates my psychic coenaesthesis, which is illusory, from my physical coenaesthesis, which is real; it eliminates my egotistical life, which is illusory, from my organic life, which is real. I realise that there is in me a real 'Earth', my organic life with my perceptions, reactive to the real present, and an illusory 'Heaven', my active imaginative life. On account of this illusory Heaven I really have to-day neither my Earth nor Heaven. The inner work, by abolishing the illusory Heaven will give me back to my Earth; and this restitution of my Earth will be at the same time the enjoyment of the true Heaven. Such is the sense of that phrase of Zen: 'The Earth, that is Paradise.'

This understanding, which re-valorises our organic life and de-valorises our imaginative life, exposes us to the temptation to devote ourselves directly to our organic perceptions, to our organic coenaesthesis. Such an inner proceeding would be sterile and dangerous. It is impossible artificially to wipe out our imaginative life; we would thus make merely an absurd pretence. It is not on the dualistic plane where the real and the illusory manifest that there can be effected the subtle distillation which will eliminate illusion; our formal inner manipulations are powerless there. Only our Principle can effect this alchemical distillation, this purification. We have only to stop opposing this action of our Principle; and it is by means of the instantaneous total inner relaxation of which we have spoken that we can learn to stop our habitual opposition.

The progressive dissolution of our life-on-the-plane-of-imagery brings us nearer to delivery, to our birth in Reality. But, looked at before satori, this dissolution represents the laborious agony of the 'old' man. Consequently the inner work carried out in order to 'see into one's own nature' constitutes the veritable asceticism (of which exterior kinds of asceticism are only imitations), the veritable purification, the veritable mortification. (Let us make it clear that the veritable asceticism evidently requires no modification of the outward manner of living.)

It is important clearly to understand the immensity of what we have to abandon, in our actual way of looking at things, and at the same time the perfectly painless character of this abandonment. This plane of imagery that I am going to lose is more than immense for me to-day, it is everything; it is the salt of my life, it gives it all its meaning. It may be the scene of my terrors, but it is also the scene of my delights, fervours, compassion, and of my hopes. The natural man can only imagine the disappearance of sentiment from his life, the disappearance of the dualistic sensibility of his 'soul', as the death of his being; this illusory Heaven, with its tempests as with its sunshine, seems to him to be more precious than anything, in particular more precious than his Earth, than his body. But the dissolution of life-on-the-plane-of-imagery represents the definite renunciation of this illusory Heaven, of all that we see as 'sacred', 'super-natural', in our actual condition.

However, this renunciation is perfectly painless; the agony of the old' man is laborious (that is the bitter fight with our personality), but it is not painful. This renunciation indeed only takes place according to the degree in which, without snatching from me anything regarded as precious on the plane on which I see it as such, I obtain, in procuring a displacement of my attention which encourages in me the plane of sensation, the dissipation of the mirages which caused me to see value where there is none. The plane of imagery is not taken away from me—which would be horrible—it is I who leave it; no regret is possible to me for what I thus leave, since the plane of imagery only exists illusorily for me when I am on it. An inner task that is painful is badly done; it directly attacks the emotions; the correct inner task, the effort 'to see into my own nature', acts in us at the point from which the emotions spring. How could I be painfully moved in escaping from emotion? We have nothing to fear from forms in the course of efforts correctly carried out towards the in-formal; in dissipating this shadow the light dissipates all the shadows.

Chapter Twelve

HOW TO CONCEIVE THE INNER TASK ACCORDING TO ZEN

IT is difficult to understand wherein consists practically the inner task according to Zen, this work which should one day bring us to satori. In fact the Zen masters, when they speak of it in a positive manner, utter generalities which are liable to seem to us somewhat ironical: 'It is enough for you to see into your own nature'; or again: 'Be entirely detached from everything'; or again: 'You are Buddhas and, in consequence, it is not a question of becoming, but of acting as Buddha. . . . Man, then, has only to fulfil his active rôle of Buddha', etc. Very good, the disciple thinks, but that hardly helps me forward in the practice of my inner life. Then he imagines, as best he may, such and such a practice which may effectively bring him nearer to satori; and he goes to the master in order to submit his idea to him. There he receives nothing but snubs. If he were proposing to perform some good deeds the master assures him that that would not help him at all. If he were proposing to meditate on some sacred texts, the master says to him: 'Don't let yourself be upset by the Sutra, rather upset the Sutra yourself.' If he were proposing to exercise himself in the mental void the master shows him that therein lies only gradual suicide. If he were proposing an intellectual task, patient and profound, the master says to him: 'Reflection and discursive thought lead to nothing; they are like a lamp in full daylight; no light comes out of them.' When the unfortunate disciple asks at last, with humility, to be given a ray of light on the mystery of Zen, the master replies to him: 'To imagine that Zen is mysterious is the gravest error, into which many fall. . . . We have not to avoid contradiction, but to live it.'

97

Doubtless the Zen masters are right not to try to express the inexpressible, while declaring at the same time that this inexpressible is in no wise mysterious; doubtless they are right only to reply to the suggestions of their pupils by negations, to hound them thus from error to error right on to a kind of despair, accepted and so without sadness, in which the whole being decontracts and opens itself to Reality. Nevertheless we will try to do that which the Zen masters do not, that is to say speak positively of the inner task, conceived in the spirit of Zen, without remaining on that account in abstract generalities.

Zen instructs us that the real inner task does not consist in any 'doing', but in a 'not-doing'. But this would only lead us into discouragement if we did not understand that that which is not-doing on a certain plane corresponds to doing on another plane, and that we have, in that way, the possibility of looking for and finding this other plane on which the inner task will appear to us under a positive aspect. In order to understand what we have just said we will make use of a comparison taken from the working of our body. In the course of our movements the contraction of each of our muscular fibres is controlled by the activity of a nerve-cell situated in the spinal marrow or medullary cell. The function of this cell is to cause the muscles to contract, and, if nothing intervened to interfere with its action, the muscle would be in a constant state of contraction. But the medullary cell is not free to act all the time. Another nerve-cell, seated in the brain, sends out a long fibre which joins the medullary cell, and, by means of this fibre, the cerebral cell, when it is active, inhibits the activity of the medullary cell. Thus, therefore, when my muscle is relaxed, at rest, this rest corresponds, at the level of the medullary cell, to not-doing (for as soon as this cell acts the muscle contracts); but this not-doing of the medullary cell corresponds to doing of the cerebral cell, since the activity of this superior cell consists in suspending the activity of the inferior cell. The muscular decontraction which is not-doing on an inferior plane is at the same time doing on a superior plane.

Let us see now how the vital energy operates in us, in the totality of our being, and how we can find here again two planes of such a kind that non-activity on the inferior corresponds with activity on the superior. Only thus can we understand why Zen assures us that we have nothing to 'do', and proclaims elsewhere that the inner task requires an activity, faultlessly attentive, 'as if we had our head in the fire'.

Our organism conceals energy; that is evident, since we see unceasingly well-up in us forces which move us, which make us think and act. We have no direct perception of the source of these forces, but observation of our phenomena leads us to infer, by induction, the existence in us of a source of energy. We can only conceive of this source as a sort of reservoir, without defined limits, where lies, latent, immobile, invisible, untouchable, potential vital energy. This source, whose activity is going to manifest in my individual person, should not, however, be regarded as individual. This reservoir of energy which is still potential, un-manifested, ought to be regarded as universal since the particular individuality only begins with the manifestation. This source is then the Principle of the Universe at the same time that it is my Principle; it corresponds with that which Zen calls Cosmic Mind or Unconscious.

From this source forces will surge-up in me under the influence of impulses from the outer world. These impulses can come to me by way of the psyche or by way of the physique. In any event the impulse consists in a bi-polar tension existing between the outside world and me. For example, if I drink some alcohol, or eat some bread there is, between what I absorb and my own substance, bi-polar tension. Or again, if I see myself in danger of death, there is between this outer image and an imagination of immortality, claimed by me and existing in me, bi-polar tension, etc. . . .

The gushing-up in me of vital force in response to the excitation of the outside world represents, with regard to the potential energy of my source, a first disintegration (we will see that there will be a second), comparable with atomic disintegration. Bergson has clearly shown the existence in us of these 'explosive' phenomena; his mistake was only in localising this explosion in the psychic domain, whereas it takes place up-stream of the two domains, psychic and physical, at the exit of the common central source.

At the moment at which this force wells-up from its source it is constituted by a certain quantity of raw vital energy, pure, not yet differentiated, in-formal. More exactly, it is intermediary between the in-formal and form. It is between the source and my phenomena, as the positive and negative principles of creation are between

99

the Supreme Principle and the world of phenomena; the micro-cosm is constructed like the macrocosm. In consequence this vital force springing from the source can present two aspects, one positive and the other negative. If the excitation of the outer world is felt by me as an affirmation of myself, the force springing up is positive; I feel it as a surplus of life to expend, as a pressure, with an urge towards the Not-Self (desire and benevolence). If the excitation of the outer world is felt by me as a negation of myself, the vital force springing up is negative; I feel it as a waste of life, a void, a deficit, a de-pression, which aversion from the Not-Self (flight, disgust, or aggressivity).

Although this vital energy, welling-up, primitive, has thus two aspects according to which it takes the sign + or the sign − ; although it may be thus coloured by the confines of the formal world, it is nevertheless still up-stream of this formal world, and we should call it in-formal. Thus the two principles, positive and negative, of creation, although at the confines of the temporal world, ought to be called in-temporal.

This vital force at its birth, in-formal force, we should perceive by a direct inner intuition. We cannot describe it, since it is in-formal, but we can perceive it. If I have just heard some good news I can chase from my mind all ideas concerning the fortunate circumstance, and can feel directly in myself a kind of bubbling of life in excess; when a misfortune happens to me I can chase away every idea on the subject, and can feel directly in myself a sort of void, a suction which draws me towards annihilation. Conse-quently it is possible for me to fix my attention on my central source, at the very point whence issues its manifestation. It is possible for me to lift my attention up to the in-formal plane, con-cerning which we shall see that its activity, its 'doing', corresponds to a non-activity, to a 'not-doing', on the formal plane of my psycho-somatic phenomena.

What I have just said is absolutely concrete. If, for example, I have just lost some money and I leave my attention where it is habitually (on the formal, phenomenal plane), I experience a lively imaginative activity in which I chew over my worries present and future. If at this moment I fix my attention, as I have just said, on this intuitive perception of vital wastage (which I am obliged to name in my text but which is in reality without form), then I find that my imaginative agitation ceases. That is a fact of experience that anyone can test. So my activity on the in-formal plane controls my inaction on the formal plane. The in-formal plane, when my attention is on it, is the break, the inhibitor, of the formal plane.

The manner in which the attention is fixed, either naturally on the formal or voluntarily on the in-formal, controls the destiny of the vital energy welling-up. Naturally, in his ordinary ignorant condition man always leaves, in practice, his attention fixed on the inferior formal plane; he is fascinated by the phenomena which occur outside himself and within. When attention is there the vital energy, emerging from its source, will necessarily complete its disintegration by setting in motion the human machine, that is to say by taking upon itself *form* as energy-phenomena, somatic and psychic. At the moment at which the in-formal welling-up of energy begins to take form and to flow, dissipating itself as it does so, on the slope of phenomena, it becomes emotion. Emotion is thus a primary inner phenomenon, which is not yet either somatic or psychic, but which will engender physico-chemical movements and imaginations.

When attention is thus fixed a vicious circle is necessarily established; the imaginations which result from the process at once act as stimulants which cause new forces to spring up whose fate is identical with that of the preceding force etc. . . . .

On the contrary, if my attention, at first fixed on the exciting outer world, turns back thereafter internally towards the in-formal force at the point of its initial springing-forth, and remains there for a moment, during that moment the vital energy escapes from the disintegrating mechanism of form, and it does not produce any movement of my machine, either actions or thoughts. On the other hand it does not return to its source, for the first disintegration which has given it birth is irreversible. What becomes of it? Certain doctrines, insufficiently freed from the fascination of form, teach that this force accumulates in the total form of the organism, but different from that which we know, more subtle, and that it constitutes thus little by little a second body, which is subtle, within the first body, which is gross (illusory theory of an 'astral body'). Zen, which anyhow does not 'believe' in anything, does not believe in that. How can we then conceive the destiny of this pure vital energy, saved from phenomenal disintegration, in the light of Zen thought? We can suppose that this energy accumulates in us indeed, but not within a form, however subtle one may wish to imagine it; it accumulates without form on the plane of the two inferior creative principles, positive and negative, principles which although giving birth to all forms are themselves in-formal. It accumulates there and could be qualified as potential, actualised energy; as potential energy, it no more acts, phenomenally, than potential energy acts when at its source; but, actualised, it accumulates for ulterior action. This ulterior action is satori. Vital energy is comparable with an explosive powder which, without co-ordinating action from within, burns packet by packet in simple fireworks, powerless to change the structure of the being (these fireworks are our emotions and their psycho-somatic effects). The inner work from time to time saves a certain quantity of this powder and stores up these little packets, manufacturing thus a kind of delayed-action bomb. This bomb will only burst when a sufficient quantity of the powder has thus been accumulated. But this delayed explosion will have nothing in common with the emotional fireworks; while the emotions used the human organism because these little explosions occurred within the form of this organism, the formidable explosion of satori will not touch a single cell of the human organism. It will occur in the in-formal, and its action on the formal plane, on phenomena, will be comparable with a catalysis which allows the conciliated combination of temporal duality, in consequence suppressing definitively all inner tension of anxiety.

During the period of accumulation of the in-formal energy, without satori yet being possible, this accumulation is revealed by the appearance in the man of a relative wisdom, or, more exactly, of a relative diminution of his habitual folly. If certain men, as they grow older, become wiser, that is in the measure in which, losing their illusory beliefs by contact with experience, they accord less of their attention to forms, outer or inner, and thus bring about to some extent, without knowing it, this displacement of the attention of which we are speaking from the formal on to the in-formal. These men work inwardly without knowing it. But, because they do not know it, they do it too little for the production within them of the great accumulation of in-formal energy which satori requires.

Let us come back now to this displacement of the attention. In order to render it understandable we have shown on what intuitive perception our attention must come to be fixed; and we ought to proceed thus in fact, for it is impossible to withdraw our attention from a point without having another point towards which to direct it. But it would be entirely wrong to believe that this in-formal intuitive perception towards which we voluntarily direct our attention positively presents the least interest (illusory conception of spiritual as opposed to temporal 'possessions'). It is only a point of orientation, a simple means of which we avail ourselves to preserve our energy from the meshes of the formal machinery which would seize upon it but for that. Thus to displace attention, that is to work inwardly, is not then to 'do' anything but what one would do ordinarily, it is to 'do nothing', or more exactly actively to inhibit every 'deed' that can be described.

This conception of the two planes, formal and in-formal, of such a kind that 'to do' in the second corresponds with 'to do nothing' in the first, enables us to understand the real positivity of the negative terms which Zen uses so readily, 'no-mind', 'no-form', 'no-birth', 'emptiness', 'void', 'Unconscious', etc. . . . .

The practice of the 'koan' is understandable also. The cryptic formula on to which the Zen monk incessantly brings back his attention, has, certainly, a form; but this form is such that it quickly ceases to be perceptible on account of its apparent absurdity. When the Zen monk fixes his attention on his koan it is not this last which possesses the slightest interest; what is interesting and efficacious is by that means to tear the attention from the plane of form.

The displacement of attention which constitutes the inner task should really be a displacement, and so a coming-and-going of the attention between the formal and the in-formal. It would be impossible to fix the attention on the in-formal (as also on any kind of form) with stability. To begin with that would amount to suicide. But, above all, the excitation of the outer world is absolutely necessary for the surging-up of the in-formal energy from its central source. The inner task is then necessarily discontinuous; in that it conforms to the law of alternation which dominates all creation (day-night, summer-winter, systole and diastole of the heart, etc.).

It is not a question, either, of wishing to save from phenomenal disintegration all our vital energy. To think incessantly of the energy which wastes itself in us would be to fall back into the distressing error of 'salvation' regarded as a 'duty'. There would then be contraction, not relaxation. It is only when I no longer trouble myself to contract that I can relax.

The Zen masters say to us: 'You should not in any event hinder or disturb the course of life.' The inner task is performed in the course of our life, but it does not disturb it because it is done in parallel with it and not in it. That is to say that it is not concerned with forms, with the manner of life, and does not try to modify them; the attention, in leaving the plane of form, is content to ignore form. The man who works according to Zen becomes ever more indifferent to his actions, to his imaginations, to his sentiments; for all that is precisely the formal machinery with which he is obliged to share his energy. This man can work inwardly all day, in the alternating manner of which we have spoken, without this work comprising the slightest spiritual 'exercise', the least intentional discriminative reflection, the slightest rule of moral conduct, the least trouble to do 'good'. Turning his back on the visible and its phantoms, fair or ugly, he accumulates in the invisible the charge of energy which will one day blow up in him all the 'cave of phantoms', and will open to him thus the real plenitude of his daily life.

Chapter Thirteen

OBEDIENCE TO THE NATURE OF THINGS

ACCORDING to Zen man is of the nature of Buddha; he is perfect, nothing is lacking in him. But he does not realise this because he is caught in the entanglements of his mental representations. Everything happens as though a screen were woven between himself and Reality by his imaginative activity functioning in the dualistic mode.

Imaginative mental activity is useful at the beginning of man's life, as long as the human machine is not completed, as long as the abstract intellect is not fully developed; it constitutes, during this first period, a compensation without which man could not tolerate his limited condition. Once the human machine is entirely developed the imagination, while still retaining the utility of which we have just spoken, becomes more and more harmful; it brings about in fact a wastage of energy which otherwise would accumulate in the interior of the being until the crystallisation of intuitive non-dualistic knowledge (satori).

The misfortune is that man takes the relief which imagination obtains for him for a real amelioration of his state; he takes the momentary relief of his distress for progress towards its abolition. In reality his momentary relief merely results in a progressive aggravation of the condition from which he wishes to be relieved. But he does not know this, and he cherishes an implicit belief in the utility of his imaginative activity and of his mental ruminations.

Experience should, one would think, contradict sooner or later a belief so mistaken. More often than not, however, it is not so. Why then does man believe so strongly in the utility of his agitation in spite of the experience which proves it to be harmful?

Man believes in the utility of his agitation because he does not think that he is anything but that personal 'me' which he perceives in the dualistic manner. He does not know that there is in him something quite different from this visible personal 'me', something invisible which works in his favour in the dark. Identifying himself with his perceptible phenomena, in particular with his imaginative mind, he does not think that he is anything more. Everything happens as though he said to himself: 'Who would work for me except myself?' And not seeing in himself any other self than his imaginative mind and the sentiments and actions which depend on it, he turns to this mind to rid himself of distress. When one only sees a single means of salvation, one believes in it because necessarily one wishes to believe in it.

However, if I look at the life of my body I observe that all kinds of marvellous operations are performed spontaneously in it without the concourse of that which I call 'me'. My body is maintained by processes whose ingenious complexity surpasses all imagination. After being wounded, it heals itself. By what? By whom? The idea is forced upon me of a Principle, tireless and friendly, which unceasingly creates me on its own initiative.

My organs appeared and developed spontaneously. My mediate dualistic understanding appeared and developed spontaneously. Could not my immediate understanding, non-dualistic, appear spontaneously? Zen replies affirmatively to this question. For Zen the normal spontaneous evolution of man results in satori. The Principle works unceasingly in me in the direction of the opening of satori (as this same Principle works in the bulb of the tulip towards the opening of its flower). But my imaginative activity counteracts this profound genesis; it wastes by degrees the energy generated by the Principle, which otherwise would accumulate until the explosion of satori. As an old Zen master said: 'What conceals Realisation? Nothing but myself.' I do not know that my essential wish—to escape from the dualistic illusion, generator of anguish—is in process of being realised in me by something other than my personal 'me'; I do not believe that I can count on anyone but on myself: I believe myself therefore obliged to do something. I take fright in believing myself alone, abandoned by all; necessarily then I am uneasy and my agitation neutralises by degrees the beneficial work of my deeper self. Zen expresses that in saying: 'Not knowing how near the Truth is, people look for it far away . . . what a pity!'

This manner of thwarting the profound spontaneous process of construction is the work of mechanical reflexes. It operates automatically when I am not disposed to have faith in my invisible Principle and in its liberating task. In other words, the profound spontaneous process of construction only makes progress in me in the degree in which I am disposed to have faith in my Principle and in the spontaneity, always actual, of its liberating activity. Faith does not move mountains, but it procures that mountains shall be moved by the Universal Principle.

My participation in the elaboration of my satori consists, then, in the activity of my faith; it consists in the conception of the idea, present and actual, that my supreme good is in process of being elaborated spontaneously.

One sees in what respects Zen is quietist and in what respects it is not. It is, when it says to us: 'You do not have to liberate yourselves.' But it is not in this sense that, if we do not have to work directly for our liberation, we have to collaborate in thinking effectively of the profound process which liberates us. For this thought is not by any means given to us automatically by nature. The outer world unceasingly conspires to make us believe that our true good resides in such and such a formal success which justifies all our agitations. The outer world distracts us, it steals our attention. An intense and patient labour of thought is necessary in order that we may collaborate without liberating Principle.

Arrived at this degree of understanding, a snare awaits us. We run the risk of believing that we must refuse to give our attention to life. We run the risk, thinking we are doing the right thing, of going through life like a somnambulist, incessantly bringing back, into our surface mind, the fixed idea of the Principle operating in us. And this could only lead to mental derangement.

We must proceed otherwise. At moments when outer and inner circumstances lend themselves to it we reflect upon the understanding of our spontaneous liberation, we think with force, and in the most concrete manner possible, of the unlimited prodigy which is in process of elaboration for us and which will some day resolve all our fears, all our covetousness. In such moments we seed and re-seed the field of our faith; we awaken little by little in ourselves this faith which was sleeping, and the hope and the love which accompany it. Then when we turn back to life we go on living as usual. Because we have thought correctly for a moment a portion of our attention remains attached to this plane of thought, although this plane penetrates the depths of our being and is lost to sight; a portion of our attention remains there while the remainder goes where it always goes. The man who has adored a woman or a piece of work which he is in process of conceiving will understand what we are trying to say. While he goes about his usual business it will happen that he no longer thinks consciously of the woman he loves, as though he were forgetting her; nevertheless when his thought comes back to this beloved image he realises that he had never entirely left her, that he had remained all the time beside her as though in a secondary state, on a subterranean plane of consciousness.

When it is a question of our participation in our liberation this secondary state is not granted to us gratuitously; we have to obtain it by means of special moments of reflection on the borderline of our practical daily life. Nevertheless these necessary moments are not what really matters; what will be really efficacious will take place when we are once more in our daily life and when our faith, now more or less awakened and vigilant on a subterranean plane of consciousness, will dispute victoriously with the outside world a part of our attention and, in consequence, a part of our energy.

In the measure in which this second subterranean attention develops we will perceive a less compelling interest in the world of phenomena; our fears and our covetousness will lose their keeness. We will be able to learn how to be discreet, non-active, towards our inner world, and we will thus become able to realise this counsel of Zen: 'Let go, leave things as they may be. . . . Be obedient to the nature of things and you are in accord with the Way.'

Let us note that the natural man sometimes has an attitude that is correct, discreet, non-active; he has it during deep sleep. There he stops being restless with the idea of doing himself good; he effaces himself, he 'lets go', he 'leaves things as they may be', he abandons himself to his Principle and lets it operate without interference. It is because man is then non-active that sleep has such a wonderful recuperative effect.

But the man who sleeps only behaves wisely through a kind of syncope of his mind; the pernicious egotistical imaginative film is only stopped because the imaginative film based on the real exterior present is stopped also. The harmful part of the mind only stops because its healthy part (that which perceives directly things that are present) stops too. And on that account sleep could not bring Realisation.

We can achieve wisdom without the whole of our mind coming to a full-stop. Each progression of our faith in our liberating Principle weakens our egotistical imaginative film without weakening our imaginative film based on the real present; the appearance and the growth of our faith establish by themselves a discrimination between our two imaginative films. Thus we go little by little towards a state in which deep sleep and the waking state are reconciled. There again let us affirm that this astonishing conciliation is established by itself; our inner manipulations are powerless to establish the slightest real harmony in us. For our Principle, which is the only artisan qualified for this Great Work, to operate in us it is enough that we think correctly, or more exactly that we cease to think wrongly.

In order to understand more clearly what has been said above we can use a symbolical illustration. Man, in his development, may be compared with a balloon-figure progressively inflated. At his birth he is like a little balloon very slightly inflated, without many indications of form, a little spherical mass. Then, the Principle inflating the balloon, it increases in volume; at the same time its form departs more and more from the simple form of the sphere; reliefs and hollows appear; a figure develops whose structure is unique in its particularities. It is the development of what one calls the character, the personality, of that by which I am 'I' and nobody else. That corresponds to the development of the human machine, soma and psyche.

If man's ignorance did not intervene to counteract his normal evolution, this is what would happen. The balloon, at the moment at which the human machine is fully developed (towards puberty, when the somatic machine is complete with the appearance of the sexual function and when the psychic machine is complete with the appearance of the impartial intelligence, abstract and generalising), the balloon then is fully inflated and it attains in surface an extension which it can no longer exceed. But the

Principle continues to inflate it; and this brings about a state of hypertension. Under the influence of this hypertension the inextensible surface will be deformed so that its content may increase, that is to say that it will flatten out its folds, reduce its reliefs and its hollows, progressively become spherical, since the simple form of a sphere corresponds to the greatest possible capacity for a given surface. Little by little the irregularities of the balloon-figure disappear. Finally the perfectly spherical form is attained; no increase of contenance is any longer possible. The Principle still inflating, the balloon bursts.

In the course of this normal evolution one sees three phases succeed one another. The little sphere at the beginning, little spherical bundle of the balloon as yet uninflated, that is the phase which is up-stream of man's temporal realisation, up-stream of the development of his personality, of his Ego. One might say that the small child is still spherical. The second phase, that of the developed personality, corresponds to the figure endowed with particular contours, complex and personal. In the third phase, which precedes the final explosion, the irregularities are smoothed out, the personality is blurred according to the degree in which the thought attains a universal point of view, or, more exactly, frees itself from the narrowness, from the rigidity of personal points of view. Man comes back to his initial spherical form, but this time down-stream of his temporal realisation. This phase then resembles the first although it is in a sense its opposite (one recalls the words of Jesus: 'In truth I say unto you, whoever will not receive the Kingdom of God like a little child shall not enter therein').

Let us note that this third phase appears to us necessarily at the same time as progress and as regression. It is progress from the point of view of the universal, since the balloon increases its capacity and approaches an explosion which will make it coincide with the immense sphere of the cosmos; but it is at the same time regression from the point of view of the particularities of shape, from the point of view of the personality. That which distinguishes this man from all others grows less, he becomes more and more ordinary, his reliefs disappear; the 'old' man wastes away and approaches death in the measure that the birth of the 'new man', with the bursting of the balloon, comes nearer. (One can thus understand the words of St. John the Baptist: 'Prepare ye the way of the Lord; make smooth his paths. Every hollow shall be filled up, every mountain and every hill shall be made flat.')

The outcome of the third phase, the bursting of the balloon, is the explosion of satori, the instant at which every limitation disappears, and at which the one is united with the all.

We have said that man's ignorance thwarts this normal evolution. In fact man, before any initiation, does not recognise any reality in what his balloon-figure contains, but he sees reality that is indisputable and unique on its surface and in the particular shape of this surface. In this ignorance his will to 'be' expresses itself only by the will to 'be as one distinct'. This ignorant balloon, built up into a figure, refuses to accept the smoothing-out of its distinctive reliefs: it stiffens itself in its particular form, it is opposed to any stretching of its folds which would increase its capacity by tending towards the spherical. The hypertension being unable to resolve itself in this normal manner must resolve itself otherwise; and there comes into play the man's imaginative-emotive activity, a kind of safety-valve by which is released the pressure caused by the continuous inflation of the Principle. This corresponds to the wastage, of which we have spoken, of energy which ought to have been accumulated with a view to an explosion.

Every man who observes himself realises that he is unceasingly more or less overstrained inwardly. He feels it through the agitation of his emotive states, positive or negative, exalted or depressed, states which correspond with the unconscious resistence which he opposes to the opening-out of the folds of his personal form. But, if it is easy to see to what the hypertension in our concrete psychology corresponds, it is less easy to see in what consists the normal inner release of this tension. This release occurs at the moment at which I become conscious of my tension while neglecting the contingent circumstances in connexion with which this tension appeared, and at which I accept it in myself.

In the extent to which I have overcome ignorance, in the extent to which I have understood that reality is not at all to be found in the external forms which are the object of my fears and of my covetousness, but that it resides in the vital hypertensive pressure itself; to this extent my attention abandons forms and directs itself towards my centre, towards my source, the place from which wells-up my vital pressure. I can do this if I have understood that my Principle is engaged in leading me to my true fulfilment and that I need not trouble myself about anything in this matter. Then my imaginative-emotive activity stops for a moment, and I feel my hypertension yield. That is all that I feel, but I know furthermore that the capacity of my balloon has just increased a little as a result of the simplification of its form. Evidently this docility to the opening-out of folds, which helps my realisation, is passing, instantaneous, and this 'letting go' has to be done afresh with perseverence as often as may be necessary.

The comparison we have just used may be criticised, like all comparisons. But it can help us to understand the modalities of our normal growth, and above all the essential notion that this growth will take place by itself right up to its perfect accomplishment if, having faith in it, we cease to oppose it by our restlessness and our inner manipulations.

Let us return to this idea that man, in the measure in which he is still ignorant, is lacking in faith, and consequently also in hope and in charity. We will show that, faith being absent, everything happens in man in a sense radically opposed to the normal. The normal direction is from above downwards: when man abandons ignorance his understanding (which pre-existed through all eternity but which was sleeping in unconsciousness) awakens in his intellectual centre. Of the three theological virtues it is Faith which leads the way, intellectual intuition of the absolute Principle and certainty that it is 'my' Principle. The awakening of Faith carries with it the awakening of Hope: there is no longer anything to fear, I can hope for everything, from the moment that the absolute Principle is 'my' Principle. Thus that which began in the intellectual centre continues in the emotional centre. Finally the awakening of Faith and of Hope brings the awakening of Charity. It is in error that Charity is often thought of as an emotion, as adoration-love; it is in reality desire-love, an appetite felt by the whole of our organism for a kind of existence that the spectres of duality have ceased to conceal from us. It is a constant appetite for all aspects of existence. Thus that which began in the intellectual centre, and which continued in the emotional centre, ends up in the animal or instinctive centre;

that which began in the head has passed by the heart in order to finish up in the entrails.

In so far as man is still in ignorance the succession is reversed. That which begins in him is the appetite to exist, the desire to affirm himself as distinct, the desire for the positive aspects of existence only. This natural awakening of the desire to exist carries with it the awakening of all sorts of 'hopes' (which are the opposite of Hope), hopes of this or that success on the plane of phenomena; that which began in the animal centre continues in the emotional centre. Finally the awakening of the desire to exist, and of hopes, entails the awakening of 'beliefs' (the opposite of Faith) which build up false values, the aims which the hopes need, the image-idols necessary to polarise the impulses coming from below. That which began in the animal centre and has continued in the emotional centre has risen to the heart, and then to the head.

One observes the radical opposition which exists between these two directions that man's life takes. The natural direction is from below upwards: appetite for the positive aspects of existence, then hopes, then beliefs. The normal direction is from above downwards: Faith, then Hope, finally Charity or appetite for all aspects of existence.

The natural direction exists only at the outset of life. Realisation consists in the appearance of the normal direction and in its final triumph. This final triumph is satori. Before satori the normal direction should appear in concurrence with the present natural direction and should play an ever bigger part at the expense of this natural direction. ('He must increase and I must decrease.')

When we study the problem of Realisation we incessantly come across all sorts of paradoxes. 'He who loses his life shall save it,' says the Gospel for example. These paradoxes cease to embarrass us when we thoroughly understand that there are in us two life-currents; one is natural, given to us and starting from below to move upward; the other is normal, possible to us and starting from above in order to descend. The natural life can thus be called the 'life of the "old" man', the normal life the 'life of the "new" man'. ('It is necessary to die in order to be reborn.')

The new current should appear while the old natural current is still flowing. The new current begins, let us repeat, at the place at which the natural current stops, in the intellectual centre.

The life of the new man takes its departure in the Independent Intelligence, pure thought, intellectual intuition removed from affective influences. The work of the Independent Intelligence destroys little by little the 'beliefs' which polarise the natural current, ascending, and without which this current could not flow. In the extent to which man 'ceases to harbour opinions', as Zen says, he abolishes absolutely the natural current within him. Faith increases in him in the extent to which beliefs decrease.

But it is on the emotional plane that we shall find in its most interesting aspect this inverse evolution. It is there that we shall best be able to understand the 'letting go' of Zen. Just as Faith pre-existing from all eternity but asleep, awakens in the measure that beliefs are abolished, so Hope, pre-existent from all eternity but asleep, awakens in the measure that 'hopes' in general are wiped out. That which is sunrise in the new life is sunset in the old; that which is triumph in the new life is disaster in the old. Satori can only be foreseen by the 'old' man as the most radical of all imaginable disasters.

If I observe myself I see that I struggle incessantly and instinctively in order to succeed; whether my enterprises are egotistical (to win, to enjoy, to be admired, etc.) or altruistic (to affirm others, to become 'better', to uproot my 'faults', etc.) I struggle incessantly, instinctively, to succeed in these enterprises; I struggle unceasingly 'upwards'. Incessantly I am agitated by upward-tending contractions, like a bird which continually makes use of its wings in order to rise, or to fight against a downward motion which a down-blowing wind imposes on it. I conduct myself as though my hopes were legitimate, as if the real good which I need (Realisation, satori) were to be found in the satisfaction of these hopes. Nevertheless just the contrary is true; my hopes lie to me, they are part of a vicious circle in which I wear myself out in useless efforts. All my upward-tending exertions are only gestures of ignorant resistance opposed to the happy spontaneous transformation that my Principle is always ready to bring about. Perfect Felicity does not await me above, but below; it does not await me in that which I see actually as a triumph, but in that which appears to me actually as a disaster. My perfect joy awaits me in the total anihilation of my hopes.

One must thoroughly understand that the total disaster in the middle of which satori awaits us does not necessarily coincide with a practical exterior disaster. The realising disaster, the satori-disaster, consists in an understanding, an intellectual intuition of the radical absurdity of our natural ascending current, in the clear vision of the nullity which is at the end of all our hopes. The realising despair does not consist in the practical ruin of hopes which would continue to exist in us (this would lead to suicide, not to satori), but in the annihilation of the hopes themselves. The man that one habitually calls 'desperate' is definitely not desperate; he is filled with hopes to which the world opposes a flat refusal; therefore he is very unhappy. The man who has become really desperate, who no longer expects anything from the world of phenomena, is flooded by the perfect joy which at last he ceases to oppose.

Here is the way in which I can, in practice, make progress in the annihilation of my absurd and deplorable 'hopes'. I am not going to set myself to organise the failure of my enterprises; to hope to succeed in ruining myself instead of hoping to succeed in enriching myself would not change anything in any way. No, I let my instinctive and emotive life go on as usual. But my under-standing, initiated into the reality of things, works in parallel. At the moment when I suffer because my hopes come up against the resistance of the world I remind myself that my old successes have never brought me that absolute accomplishment in which I had placed my hopes; all my surface satisfactions, sometimes so intense, were in the last instance deceptions in depth, that is to say in truth. Profiting by this experience, correctly interpreted, of my fallacious successes I think now of the new successes which I am in process of coveting; I imagine their concrete realisation, and feel afresh their vanity. The bad moments, the moments of anguish, are the best for this work; the suffering felt by the organism-as-a-totality curbs the illusions which show us satori in the opposite direction from that in which it awaits us. On the condition that all our essential hopes have been more or less fulfilled in the past our actual hope, recidivist, is the more readily annihilated as it is thwarted by the world. It is easier for me to let go when my muscles are very tired. Zen affirms: 'Satori comes to us unexpectedly when we have exhausted all the resources of our being.'

What we have just been saying should not be understood as a masochistic appetite for torment. The man who works according to Zen has no love of suffering; but he likes suffering to come to him, which is not at all the same thing, because, in helping him to 'let go', these moments will make easier for him that inner immobility, that discretion and silence, thanks to which the Principle works actively in him for Realisation.

One perceives how much the 'progressive' doctrines which invite man to climb up an ascending hierarchy of states of consciousness, and which more or less explicitly conceive the perfect man as a Superman, turn their back on truth and limit themselves to modifying the form of our hopes. Zen invites us on the contrary to a task which, up to satori exclusively, can only appear to us as a descent. In a sense everything becomes worse little by little up to the moment when the bottom is reached, when nothing can any longer become worse, and in which everything is found because all is lost.

We can imagine nothing of the transformation of satori; therefore we risk a new idolatry if we try to imagine anything of it whatsoever. At the point at which we are to-day we are not able to see the true evolution except as a progressive annihilation of all that we call 'success'; we are not able to see the man who has attained realisation otherwise than as a man who has become absolutely ordinary. Only he who has obtained satori can say: 'A wandering cur who begs food and pity, pitilessly chased away by the street urchins, is transformed into a lion with a golden mane, whose roar strikes terror in the hearts of all feeble spirits.'

Chapter Fourteen

EMOTION AND THE EMOTIVE STATE

CLASSICAL psychology, in studying emotivity, misunderstands an extremely important distinction from the point of view of the inner evolution of man. It certainly describes this 'movement of the soul' which wells-up as a result of an impulse from the outside world, in response to an image consciously perceived, a movement of anger, of love, of remorse, etc. . . . . But the play of emotion, in us, is not confined to that. I often feel the existence in me of a durable emotive 'state' concerning which I see clearly that it is not released in me by images that I have in my head at that moment; I am more or less gloomy, for example, while thinking of a thousand harmless matters. If then I demand what images have brought me this state, sometimes I do not find any, but often also I find the worry which lies underneath my surface associations and which releases my sombre state of mind. When I was not thinking about it my worry was motionless in my mind (fixed idea) and released a durable emotive 'state' that seemed motionless. Now that I think of my worry, when I evoke an imaginative film about it, emotive movements are produced in me, like those of which we spoke at the beginning; but I feel that there persists beneath these movements the motionless emotive state, and I feel that this state was certainly in relation with the worry that I have just brought up to my surface mind.

Inner experience shows me then that, under *dynamic* emotions, there exists a *static* emotion. But how is one to understand this last? Its name even seems paradoxical; emotion implies movement; can one speak of static movement? In order to resolve this contradiction and show how the emotive state can be at once a movement and an immobility it will suffice to compare those 'movements of the soul' which are emotions with the movements of the body which are our muscular contractions. If a muscle can contract dynamically in a *contraction* it can also contract statically in a *spasm,* or cramp. Emotions connected with conscious images are psychic *contractions,* the emotional state connected with subconscious images is a psychic *spasm.*

In order to be clear we have, to begin with, thus established our distinction by means of words of approximate exactitude. We can now be more precise. The phenomenon 'emotion' represents a short-circuit between the psychic pole and the somatic pole of our organism. One should not speak in connexion with emotivity, of psychic contraction or of psychic spasm, but of contraction or spasm of our psycho-somatic organism; the emotional centre is half-way between the intellectual (or psychic or subtle) centre and the instinctive (or somatic or gross) centre. Similarly if we spoke at the beginning of emotions and the emotive state released by images, that is by psychic, subtle, excitations, we must not forget that our emotivity can equally be released by somatic, gross, excitations. A somatic indisposition can be the releasing cause of my gloom, which is an emotive spasm of my psycho-somatic organism. In any case, whether the releasing cause has been psychic or somatic, the spasm that results always affects both the psyche and the soma; a certain muscular spasm (of my muscles striated or non-striated) always accompanies my psychic spasm based on a subconscious image and vice versa.

Coming back to the idea that emotivity in general represents a short-circuit of energy between the intellectual and the instinctive poles, let us see how, from this point of view, dynamic emotion (we will call it simply 'emotion' in future) is distinguished from the static emotional state (or emotional state for short). Making use of an electrical comparison one can say that emotion corresponds with a spark uniting the two poles. This spark can last for a certain time, but it is not static, for the reason that the contact which it establishes between the separated poles is a contact in continual repetition, a contact which shifts; the spark does not simply fly from one pole to the other, it also flies in a lateral direction. The emotive state, on the contrary, can be compared with a passage of energy which occurs between the two poles when they touch one another directly along a surface that is more or less considerable.

This comparison already shows us one of the factors which renders the emotive state more dangerous than emotion. Emotion, because it shifts, is visible, conscious; the subject is made aware of it by his inner sensibility; on account of that divers defensive mechanisms come into play at once, which succeed in reducing, then in interrupting, the short-circuit that eats up energy. On the contrary the emotive state does not give the alarm quickly enough to the defensive mechanisms; it only gives the alarm tardily, when its regrettable consequences have become visible; and the defensive processes which are necessary at this moment carry a very tiresome aspect; they are neurotic (giving this word its widest meaning), and reduce the contact between the two poles through a certain deterioration of the poles themselves. Emotion is comparable also with a visible hæmorrhage which disturbs the sufferer and endangers the treatment; the emotive state is comparable with an invisible and continuous hæmorrhage which undermines the sufferer. He will have himself treated nevertheless some day, but at a time when the curative value of the treatment will be much less effective.

But these somewhat rough comparisons leave aside the most important considerations. In fact in these comparisons we assumed that the combustion of energy in the spark was similar to the destruction of energy in the contact of the poles. In reality it is not so; there is a fundamental difference between the two phenomena. In the case of emotion the two poles are separated; the spark which unites them is not, properly speaking, a short-circuit; in this spark the energy burns and frees itself, something is produced. In the emotive state, on the contrary, the two poles touch, there is a real short-circuit; the energy passes from one pole to the other; the total energy of the subject—energy which depends on the difference of tension between the two poles—is destroyed since this difference of tension is reduced, and it is destroyed without producing anything. The emotion is part of the manifestation, of the life which manifests the 'being'; therefore it can be called normal. The emotive state on the contrary is not 'alive'; it is destructive without a counterpart. The energy which it consumes cannot be used for liberation, and since it cannot lead us to our norm we must call it 'abnormal'.

Another comparison may help us to understand all this better.

Let us imagine a horizontal wheel, which turns but whose centre of rotation does not coincide with its geometrical centre; its rotation is eccentric. This wheel is set in motion by two kinds of forces; first a rotative or 'dynamic' force; but the wheel as a whole is affected by a centrifugal force which tends to move it from its centre of rotation; and this force, which has no effect, can be called 'static'. The movement of rotation, which in this illustration represents the emotion, can be used; if I fix a belt to my wheel it will be able to work machines. On the contrary the static force which tends in vain to project the whole wheel far from its centre of rotation, cannot be used; it symbolises the motionless spasm, a cramp of the emotive state.

The man who has attained realisation, man after satori, may be compared with a wheel whose centre of rotation coincides with the geometrical centre; he will have emotions, but he will not have an emotive state. The natural man, before satori, may be compared with our eccentric wheel. And this image of the eccentric wheel allows us to demonstrate certain important aspects of our affective life. Everything happens in me as if there exists, between the centre of rotation of my wheel and its geometrical centre, an elastic band which tends to make them coincide. When my wheel turns slowly, when I have little emotion, the centrifugal force is weak and the elastic suffices to maintain the centre of rotation not far from the geometric centre. But now violent emotions arise in me; my wheel begins to turn rapidly, the centrifugal force increases; despite the elastic my centre of rotation moves away from my geometric centre. This shows us how the emotions determine the appearance of the emotive state; when I have just experienced violent emotions, I feel myself thereafter quite 'ex-centric', as though out of my axis, internally displaced, and a certain time has to elapse before my elastic exercises its action and brings together my two centres, of rotation and geometric. Never before satori can the two centres of my wheel coincide absolutely; indeed where the natural man is concerned, who does no correct inner work, if the emotions may sometimes be of slight intensity they are never inexistant. The wheel turns sometimes slowly, but it turns all the same; there is always a certain centrifugal force which prevents the elastic from making the two centres coincide.

Satori corresponds, in our image, with a moment in which the wheel entirely stops turning; it is an instant without duration, but this instant suffices for the two centres to coincide. When they have coincided, if only for a single instant, they will never again be separated from one another; however fast the wheel turns now, its rotation can no longer bring about the appearance of any centrifugal force. After the moment of satori, in which there is neither emotion nor the emotive state, there will again be as many emotions as one may care to suppose, but never again an emotive state. The elastic of our image corresponds to the profound nostalgia which man carries within himself for satori. This nostalgia is not, indeed, felt as nostalgia for satori since the natural man cannot have any conception of this event (it is felt as a nostalgia for such and such temporal things or for an inadequate image that we make of satori), but it is none the less nostalgia for satori. The further a man is, in his emotive states, from satori, the further his elastic will be stretched, the more intensely will he experience the nostalgia of its attainment in whatever way he may envisage it; the nearer a man approaches satori, the more his elastic slackens, the less strongly does he feel his nostalgia for its attainment. On the verge of satori, in the moments which precede it, all nostalgia of its attainment disappears; then, for lack of any nostalgia, he who attains to satori does not feel it at all as an attainment; he can say, with Hui-neng, 'There is no attainment, there is no liberation', liberation only existing in the eyes of him who is not liberated. In our image liberation is the complete slackening of the elastic; but, in satori, the elastic is destroyed and there could no longer be any question of its slackening.

Man before satori can imagine nothing positive concerning man after satori. In a negative manner only can he conceive that the emotions experienced after satori will be profoundly different from those experienced before satori, since they will no longer release that emotive state, that inner spasm, which was responsible for our distress. This leads us to a fresh understanding of the distinction between 'emotion' and 'emotive state' which we are studying at this moment. Emotions can be positive or negative, joys or sorrows; but the emotive state is always negative. Following our image, the wheel can turn in one direction or in the other;

but in both cases the centrifugal force remains centrifugal. A concrete examination of our affective life shows us this; when something very pleasing happens to me, releasing in me violent emotions of joy, the central displacement, or shifting of the axis, of which we spoke a moment ago, takes place in me just as it takes place as a result of violent negative emotions; distress appears under my joyous images, distress connected psychologically either with the fear of losing the affirmation which has come to me, or to the unsatisfied demand which my affirmation endlessly increases right up to that absolute accomplishment of myself that I am always waiting for in the depths of my being.

The emotive state, or profound emotivity (opposed to the surface emotivity which the emotions create), corresponds with that profound psychic, or subconscious, plane on which is tried the 'case' of my Ego in connexion with the situations in which I am involved with the outer world. The emotive state is always in relation with a doubt concerning my 'being'; this doubt, this dilemma between 'being or nullity', menaces me unceasingly, and my 'case' goes on in the unrealisable hope of a definitive temporal absolution.

Some euphoric people appear to be constantly possessed by a positive emotive state, and this fact seems to contradict what we have just explained. The study of the apparent happiness of the natural man is very interesting because it can help us better to understand what the emotive state is. If I observe myself continuously I perceive that I am occasionally euphoric and that this state corresponds with a moment at which my doubt of myself is transitorily asleep. An external situation that is moderately affirming and which appears sufficiently stable, added to a good physical condition, puts my inner 'trial' to sleep; for lack of incidents in court judge and witnesses have gone to sleep. My subconscious psychological plane is drowsy. At the same time I am in an agreeable 'state'. But this agreeable state does not correspond with a positivity of the emotive state in activity, it corresponds with a non-activity of the emotive state; it does not correspond with a decision, favourable at last, of the trial, but with a temporary suspension of this trial; it does not correspond with a destruction of my illusory belief that I lack something, but with a temporary quiescence of this illusion. How is this possible? Since the Ego continues to exist how can its trial thus be suspended?

An examination of the man who is habitually euphoric will give us the answer. Where this man is concerned the need of the Absolute is weak, often practically non-existant. When his desire for egotistical affirmation is assured of a certain degree of satisfaction this desire is calmed and asks no more; this man can rest satisfied with what he has. Soothing mechanisms have developed in him: he knows how to present to himself the situations which face him in the outer world in such a way as to look at their affirming aspects and to avoid seeing their negating aspects. For the profound inner trial there is substituted on the surface a monotonous apology for oneself; the trial is almost always asleep. It is interesting to observe that this man is particularly unsusceptible; one can criticise him fairly severely without wounding his self-respect, and this anaesthesia of self-respect corresponds with the putting-to-sleep of the trial. This man appears more or less devoid of an Ego. The Ego exists nevertheless but, on account of the weakness of the need for the Absolute, the compensations that have been established keep all their efficacy in the use that is made of them. Doubt of oneself is put on one side beneath a shelter that time does not weaken; such a man does not tire of the attitudes (compensations) which he assumes before the external world. But the apparent positivity of his emotive states only corresponds with the neutralisation, with the inhibition of the emotive state which is, by its very nature, negative. This man experiences plenty of joys, but these joys file across in front of a background of sleep, of absence; the background which conditions them is not a real, profound, flexibility (or relaxation of the emotive state), it is unconsciousness, by inhibition, of the deep spasm. (It is analogous to the courage of the man who does not perceive danger.) And this is possible on account of the congenital weakness of the need of the Absolute, a weakness which renders the compensations sufficient and everlasting.

In the case, on the contrary, of the man in whom the need of the Absolute is intense, the compensations are effectively established with difficulty (this man is too exacting, his appetite for egotistical affirmation is too revendicative in quantity and in quality) and these compensations, if nevertheless they are established, are little used. Also the trial is rarely very drowsy, perhaps never. The further this man's life proceeds the more his possible compensations deteriorate beyond repair; his trial knows no more suspensions; this man more and more clearly envisages everything that happens to him, all his situations in face of the Not-Self, from the angle of self-doubt; in his subconsciousness, never asleep, he lives unceasingly in the expectation of an illusory verdict on which he feels that his absolution or his final condemnation depend. His self-respect is incessantly in question in one direction or in the other; he is touchy, and this constant excitation corresponds with the permanent activity of his subconscious emotive state and of his irritability. Whereas the man who has little craving for the Absolute is calm, the man who has a great need of the Absolute is hyperexcitable, overstrained. Everything concerns his Ego, he envisages everything that he perceives from the unique angle of his self-respect.

Let us finish this passage by affirming that the emotive state can only be negative, a spasm of distress, and that the activity of the subconscious in which this emotive state operates is in relation to the need of the Absolute and consequently to the need of intemporal realisation. The presence of distress and the need of satori are intimately connected in any given individual.

After satori if a man still experiences emotions he no longer experiences them against a background of constant distress; and this modification of the background is a modification so immense, so fundamental, of our whole affective life, that we cannot correctly imagine anything about the emotions of a man after satori.

The inner work to attain satori should aim at this moment, perfectly non-emotive, the necessity for which we have seen. This work of restraint of our emotivity cannot be correctly understood as long as the distinction between emotions and the emotive state is not understood. The emotive state by itself is abnormal and contrary to satori; emotion itself is normal and not contrary to satori. But it is a thousand times easier to perceive the emotions than the existence of the emotive state. And so man often believes that it is good to curb the emotions; and all his work is vain because it is misdirected.

Correctly directed, the work will aim at curbing the emotive state; it will aim at obtaining not a disappearance of the contractions of the psycho-somatic organism which are the emotions, but the disappearance of the spasms of this organism. It is for the organism as a whole as for the aspect of it that is merely gross: the virtuoso pianist has not suppressed his muscular contractions: he has suppressed the spasm which, at the beginning of his apprenticeship, was the troublesome background against which his muscular contractions took place.

But how can one obtain the annulment of the emotive state, of the distress-spasm which constitutes the basis of all our affective life? It would be vain to attempt it directly. One might think it would be useful to make an effort of voluntary muscular decontraction, in the hope that this partial decontraction might automatically bring about a general decontraction. Such efforts, directed against a particular object, are in reality powerless to touch the generality of the being; a central spasm necessarily accompanies the effort by which I relax one aspect of myself; I cannot envisage anything particular without spasm. One could also try to fight against the emotions, since the emotions release the emotive state; but that would be to injure our very life; the problem is to relax the emotive state without touching the emotions, without touching anything particular.

We cannot obtain any modification of our total organism except by using the law of Three. That is why any direct effort that tends to reduce something within us is inoperative as regards our totality. On the contrary we ought to respect, directly, what we deplore in ourselves and bring up face to face with it the antagonistic and complementary element; this brings into play the conciliatory principle and, as a result, the resolution of the regrettable element. This element is reintegrated in the whole and disappears by losing its illusory autonomy.

Let us see how this law applies here. The profound spasm of my total organism, although affecting my organism as a totality, is not itself total, it is not absolute. It is more or less intense, but always partial; at each moment only one part of my possible spasm is found to be effective, while all the rest is ineffective, unmanifested. My deep attention (the attention which functions on the profound plane) is, in a natural manner, always focussed on the manifested part of my spasm. The disequilibrium resides precisely in this natural partiality by which I am only attentive to the manifested part of my spasm. The desirable equilibrium consequently requires that I be attentive to the non-manifested part of my spasm at the same time that I am attentive to its manifested part; in other words, at the same time that I am attentive to my interest in such and such a particular thing I ought to be attentive to my indifference towards all the rest of the manifestation.

This time again there arises the temptation, to which we are so well used, to act directly; I am tempted to make a voluntary effort by which I may perceive my indifference to everything with which I am not concerned at the moment. But this is impossible; the indifference to which I am required to be attentive is non-manifested. As soon as I wish consciously to think that I am indifferent I perceive the manifested idea of 'indifference' and not the unmanifested indifference. The non-manifested necessarily escapes my dualistic consciousness which comprises a subject that perceives and an object that is perceived, both of which are manifested.

Once I have escaped the snare of this last temptation to act directly, I am brought back to the fundamental law of our evolution towards realisation: *only pure intellectual comprehension is effective.* No useful modification of my inner phenomena can result from a concerted manipulation, no matter how ingenious one may imagine it. Every useful modification, useful in view of intemporal realisation, should come spontaneously from our Absolute Principle, owing to the breach made in the screen of ignorance by intellectual intuition. Each piece of intellectual evidence that is obtained concerning the problem of our realisation is a breach operated in the screen of ignorance; by this breach is accomplished thereafter, without our having to worry about it, the process of our transformation. In the case which concerns us here the intellectual evidence to be obtained is the following: we radically deceive ourselves with regard to our profound emotivity; we believe in the existence of our emotive state only, of our spasm. We do not believe in our profound emotivity except in so far as it manifests itself by a spasm, in so far as it shows signs of life; we misjudge all the rest, we misjudge our emotivity in so far as it does not manifest itself, in so far as it does not show signs of life.

But our emotivity in so far as it shows signs of life is limited, whereas our emotivity in so far as it does not show signs of life is infinite. What is real in my affectivity, at every second of my existence, what therefore is really of importance for me, is not my emotive state, my spasm, my partiality, but on the contrary, behind that, my perfect indifference, my freedom from spasm, my impartiality. That which counts in me, as far as I am a sensitive being, is not what I am in process of feeling but the infinity of that which I am in process of not feeling; in short my emotive state actually manifested is in reality without any interest for myself.

This intellectual evidence, when I obtain it, is a revelation which upsets my whole vision of my inner life. This vision does not immediately destroy my affective partiality for my emotive manifestation but it installs in me a counterbalancing intellectual certitude which affirms my emotive non-manifestation, my serenity relaxed and non-manifested. Thanks to this new intellectual certitude, an attention develops in me to the infinite indifference which dwells in me underneath my limited interests. This attention operates in the Unconscious and gives me no dualistic perception; but it operates none the less (in the degree that I understand), and this invisible action is revealed ultimately and visibly by a progressive diminution of the intensity of my emotive states. Thus it is possible for me to make my way towards the non-emotive state which will permit the release of satori.

The correct operation of our profound attention is revealed in the long run, in the course of our general evolution, by a diminution of our emotive states. But general evolution comprises transitory periods during which the emotive spasm increases. We will see why this is so.

In the case of a man who has not yet understood the distinction between emotions and the emotive states the attention operates in the following manner: the surface attention, on the plane called 'conscious', is fixed on the emotions (or, more exactly, on images of the emotive film); the profound attention, on the plane called 'subconscious', is fixed on the emotive state. The ordinary average man is not conscious of his emotive state (that is why classical psychology ignores this state); he only has a 'subconscious' sense of it, and it is only by inductive reasoning that this man sometimes arrives at the conclusion 'I am very irritable to-day'; he is not directly conscious of his irritability, but only of the images which pass across the background of it.

The understanding of the distinction between 'emotion' and 'emotive state' will produce, in the degree in which it is obtained, a deepening of the task of the attention. The surface attention, which was operating on the conscious plane of the imaginative film, will now tend to operate on the plane hitherto subconscious of the emotive state (that is to say, this man, thanks to his understanding, becomes capable of directing his attention towards his emotive state); and meanwhile the profound attention will tend to operate in the Unconscious, a domain that is infinite and immutable, against which stand out the variations of the emotive state.

If this understanding were complete from the first this shifting of the profound attention would be realised immediately, in its entirety, with stability; this attention would be reinstated in the Unconscious (or Self or Own-Nature of Zen), and satori would take place. But it is far from likely that the understanding would be complete from the first. Between the first moment at which it is conceived theoretically and the moment at which it has acquired, by contact with experience, all the third dimension which it lacked at first, there should elapse a more or less drawn-out period of maturing. The obtaining of theoretical understanding does not sweep away at one stroke all the illusory beliefs which were there before it and which are supported by automatisms, affective and of comportment. Faith and 'beliefs' will coexist for a more or less long time. The maturing of understanding consists in the progressive erosion of errors by means of the truth obtained at last; the good grain grows and stifles little by little the brambles.

In the course of this maturing an antagonism exists between the understanding (or Faith) and the affective automatisms which support the errors. Faith tends to make a man conscious of his emotive state; but his automatisms raise up the obstacle of distress between his conscious vision and this emotive state which is the place of the distress-spasm. The emotive state will lose its illusory poison of distress in the degree in which it is observed; but in the measure in which my automatisms still prevent me from seeing while my understanding directs my gaze towards the emotive state, that is in the degree in which the vision of the emotive state is attempted without success, the emotive state increases. A critical recrudescence of the emotive spasm is therefore to be found on the route to relaxation (the dragons placed on the path to the treasure). The man should be warned in order that he may not let himself be frightened and discouraged; if he knows this he will strive without respite for progress in his understanding, even when his condition seems to be getting worse. When consciousness has courageously penetrated at last to the plane of the emotive state, hitherto subconscious, there will be revealed the penetration of the profound attention into the Unconscious, the domain of Absolute Positivity which dissipates all distress.

We have remembered that only pure intellectual understanding is effective, and that no concerted manipulation can modify our inner phenomena in a direction that is useful for satori. It is important to insist on this point and to reject all the conceptions according to which we think we can *ourselves* effect our metaphysical transformation. However, this being admitted, we will show how a voluntary inner gesture to perceive the emotive state intervenes at a given moment of the liberating evolution.

As soon as my understanding has reached a certain degree, and my major compensatory attitudes have been left behind, my profound emotive spasm increases. My understanding, as I have said above, will then tend to displace my attention towards the depths, it will make clear to me, with evidence, the value of an inner gesture that is neither natural nor automatic, leading to the conscious perception of the emotive state which until then had been subconscious (that is to say the value of no longer running away in the face of distress as I have until now, but on the contrary of facing up to it with a spirit of investigation). This comes from the understanding alone, the decision to make this inner gesture flows spontaneously from the understanding. The gesture is not commended to me by an idolatrous affective attitude ('duty' of 'salvation', 'spiritual' ambition) which would seek to impose itself on me by pushing back other tendencies; the *decision* to make this gesture takes effect in me spontaneously when I see, with evidence, its utility. Then only, after the accomplishment of the long task of necessary understanding, I am able to effect the gesture whose utility has become evident to me; until this moment any attempt at carrying it out would be premature and inopportune. If we now suppose that the required intellectual evidence has been obtained and that the *decision* to make the useful inner gesture flows entirely from a complete certainty, if we suppose then that I am at last capable of successfully executing this gesture, then I realise that this execution cannot flow spontaneously from the understanding alone. The gesture is decided by the pure intellectual intuition, but it is executed on the plane of the concrete inner life on which all my automatic mechanisms operate. This non-natural gesture is executed on the plane of natural mechanisms and against the current of the automatism which unceasingly draws my attention towards images.

We should stress this essential point, we should remember that all inner work in whose undertaking the irrational affectivity has played a part, is by that very fact bound to fail from the point of view of satori. These indispensible oratory precautions having been clearly formulated we can go on to speak of the practical inner task looked at from the angle of this study.

This task consists in making, whenever we can, an inner gesture aiming at the perception of the emotive state. But let us see at once what there is of paradox in this perception. My emotive state affects me, affects my psycho-somatic organism, in so far as that is a totality; it cannot then be the object of a dualistic perception comprising subject and object. It is illusorily objective as long as I do nothing in order to perceive it, but it does away with itself in the measure that I seek to perceive it. *The liberating inner gesture aims at the perception of the emotive state but it could not achieve that; it achieves a certain perception of my total organism, or perception of Self, across the emotive state which covers and hides this Self at the same time that it points out the way. This gesture results then in a moment of real subjective consciousness obtained via the partial annihilation of the emotive state, by 'Looking into one's own nature'.*

The natural man, apart from all inner work, believes that he can perceive his emotive state; but, when he ends up with the observation that he is 'irritable', he only perceives a mental image fabricated in connexion with the illusory objectivity of his emotive state. All his reflexes, all his mechanisms, are conditioned by his emotive state ; the importance of this state is, then, immense;

but this importance is *implicit*, subconscious, and the emotive state in reference to which the man considers everything is never itself consciously considered. The natural man lives uniquely in reference to his Ego, but he never questions himself regarding this Ego. Thus the emotive state, in the functioning of the human-being, plays the rôle of a fixed point round which everything turns; in other words, the natural man is centred round his subconscious (centre of rotation), whereas his real or geometrical centre is the Unconscious.

In reality the emotive state is not a fixed point; and it is its illusory fixity which conditions all the illusions of our egotistical life. When I deliberately direct my attention towards my emotive state (that is to say towards my total coenaesthesis, in reality towards my Ego under this coenaesthesis), then I see that 'this' is not fixed, that 'that' moves, I feel intuitively the intimate pulsation of my life (it is not, therefore, noumenon but phenomena; the Ego cannot be the Absolute since it moves).This partial abolition of the illusory fixity of the emotive state brings my centre of rotation near to my geometrical centre, and I 'normalise' myself.

This vision that 'something moves' at the centre of my phenomenal being is not analogous to my vision that a stone that is thrown moves. In the vision in which 'something moves' in me neither space nor time exist any longer, nor forms; it moves where it is and without changing; I touch there the eternity of the instant.

In practice this work should entail inner gestures repeated, but short and light. It is not a question of laboriously dwelling upon it as though there were there something to seize. There is nothing to seize. It is a question of voluntarily noting, as in the winking of an eye, instantaneous and perfectly simple, that I am conscious of myself globally in that second (through an effort to observe *how* I am conscious of myself in that second). I succeed instantaneously or not at all; if I do not succeed at all I will try again later (this may be a few seconds later, but the gesture should be carried out at one go). It is to my interest to make this gesture as often as possible, but with suppleness and discretion, disturbing as little as possible the course of my dualistic inner life; I have to interrupt the consciousness that I habitually have of my dualistic life by a 'break' that is clean, frank, instantaneous, but without doing anything which modifies it directly. The normalising modification will be carried out by the Absolute Principle through the instantaneous 'breaks' produced by this inner work.

The distinction between emotions and the emotive state allows us to state precisely the nature of the perception which a man has of his affective life. That which is called a sentiment is a complex phenomenon comprising on the one hand an imaginative film and on the other hand an emotive variation.

If I envisage first of all the imaginative film I see that I have an indisputable conscious perception of it. The images which file across my mind are fixed by my memory and stored up in me; they constitute a stock of subtle forms that I can call up, bring back under the notice of my attention, examine at leisure, and describe in words. I have power over my images, I dominate them, I manœuvre them, and I seize them in an active perception in which my consciousness-subject seizes the image-object.

If I now envisage the emotive variation, my sentiment properly so-called, the situation is quite different. In a sense I have a certain perception of it; in fact if my sentiment is sad and someone asks me: 'Are you gay?', I can reply with conviction: 'No, I am sad.' If I had no perception of my sadness I would not be able to reply thus. But if I try to perceive my sadness with an effort of investigation, in order to examine it and know it, I realise that what is presented for my examination is always a film of images, sad or saddenning, but not my sadness itself in its indivisibility. I fail completely in seizing the same active perception of my sadness that I can seize of my sad images. It is completely impossible to me to seize my sentiment in a mental capture and to *know* it as I can my images; I seized my images, decomposed their initial form into partial constituting forms, analysed them, and saw into what elements they were reducible. I simply cannot do as much with my sentiment; I know its existence in me (I am not therefore without knowing something about it), but I cannot know it by means of a similar analysis.

Since I have nevertheless a certain perception of my sentiment, there exists between my surface consciousness and it a certain articulation. But this articulation is manifestly not of the same nature as that which exists between my consciousness and my images since it does not allow me any capture of my sentiment.

In the articulation between my sentiment and my consciousness my sentiment is active and my consciousness is passive. An illustration will help us to understand this. Suppose that in the darkness I seize an object and turn it round in my hand; I have thus an active perception of this object which gives me information concerning it. Let us suppose now that in the darkness an immense giant takes me in his hand, turns me round and presses me; I realise the existence of the giant, I find him more or less agreeable or disagreeable according to whether he caresses me or crushes me, but that is all; I have obtained no information about the giant himself, and it is impossible for me to describe him.

In the course of such a sentiment as I am in process of experiencing I can say, then, that I seize the images which form part of this emotive phenomenon, but that I am seized by the global emotive phenomenon of which the images form part. My consciousness is a seizing-consciousness on the part of the images and a seized-consciousness on the part of the sentiment. Everything happens as if I were conscious of the Images which form part of my sentiment and as if my sentiment were conscious of me.

But this way of looking at it corresponds with the illusory pespective of the natural man, according to which he considers his surface consciousness as constituting him, as being himself. In reality my surface consciousness is not 'me', it does not constitute the principle of all these phenomena by means of which my psycho-somatic organism creates itself, principle which alone can be called 'me'; it is only a certain plane of these phenomena which manifest my principle. Instead of saying that my sentiment seizes my consciousness, I should say then that my subconcious seizes my surface consciousness. My subconscious is still 'me'. If I feel this seizure of my consciousness by my subconscious as an alienation of my liberty, that is not because that which seizes my consciousness is foreign to me, but because that which seizes my consciousness (and which is still 'me') is asleep, and that, because of this sleep, my subconscious acts under the complete determination of the outside world. Everything happens as though, in my sentiment, the outside world seized me. However the outside world confines itself to determining the modalities of the play of my sleeping subconscious, but the real motive-force of this play is not foreign to me, it is my own principle, it is 'me'. In my sentiment

I have been acted upon, certainly, but only because as a result of my actual sleeping state I allow myself to be acted upon.

Arrived at this point of understanding I realise that what I have called my 'subconscious' is illusory, that it forms a part of the dream of my sleep of man-before-satori. That which seizes my surface consciousness and moves it is my first and only motor, my principle, the Absolute Principle which moves me as it moves all created things. This Principle, anterior to all consciousness since it engenders all consciousness by manifesting itself in it, we ought to call here the Fundamental Unconscious (No-Mind or Cosmic Mind of Zen). That which I have called my subconscious is only the illusory manner in which I represent to myself, imaginatively, the action which the sleeping centre of my mind exercises on the superficial phenomena, alone actually awake, of this same mind, that is to say the action which the Unconscious exercises on my surface consciousness. In fact the subconscious, this intermediary stage, has no reality; the Unconscious has an absolute reality (noumenal), the surface consciousness (imaginative film) has a relative reality (phenomenal), but the subconscious has only an illusory reality; it is only an intermediary and hybrid representation which, if one regards it from the point of view of activity, is the acting Unconscious, and which, regarded from the point of view of passivity, is the superficial consciousness that has been acted upon.

Man-after-satori will not then become capable of seizing the sentiment which the man-before-satori was incapable of seizing. For satori, or the awakening of the Fundamental Mind, dissipates the illusory hybrid representation which we call sentiment. *And it is precisely the fruitless attempt to seize the unseizable sentiment which results in the awakening of the Fundamental Mind.* There is no more sentiment for man-after-satori; his surface consciousness is acted upon directly by the Fundamental Mind in a reply that is cosmically harmonious to the excitation of the outside world; this reply takes account of the particular outer circumstances but it is not at all wrought upon, 'in-formed' by it.

Chapter Fifteen

SENSATION AND SENTIMENT

At each given moment of emotion there exists a relation, as we have said, between the images which pass across our mind and our sub-jacent emotivity. This relation is complex; it is interesting to study because it comprises certain very subtle traps which prevent us from paying attention to our emotivity.

It is important first of all to recall the essential distinction which exists between the imaginative film founded on the real present and the imaginative film invented in the mind. When I observe any spectacle in the outer world I observe it by means of an imaginative film which partially reproduces the spectacle outside, a film founded on the outer forms that my attention seized. When I day-dream, in idleness or in the course of any activity, I perceive an imaginative film invented in my mind. Emotivity is connected in very different ways to these two kinds of films. We will study these two cases, using the following terms: the film founded on the outer world we will call the 'real imaginative film' (since it is founded on phenomena which, if they lack absolute reality, have, nevertheless a relative reality); the invented film we will call the 'imaginary film'.

When it is a question of a real imaginative film the relation which exists between this film and emotivity is simple enough: the emotivity varies (quantitative variations of contraction-decontraction) according to the character, affirming or negating, of the images of the film: the images associated with a menace to my existence determine the emotive contraction, those associated with the continuation of my existence determine the diminution of this contraction, that is a relative relaxation. This reaction of the emotivity to the images of the real film constitutes a simple one-way relation: the form of the imaginative phenomena determines the form of the emotive phenomena. From the point of view of form the outside world is active and my inner world is passive. Nothing is motionless; the exterior phenomena change unceasingly, and the reacting emotivity varies unceasingly. There is no motionless emotivity; there are only contractions, no spasm; there is no emotive state, but only emotions.

When it is a question of an imaginary film everything is much more complicated. The relation with emotivity is no longer one-way, it exists in both directions at once. It exists first of all as it existed in the preceding case; the emotivity reacts to the imaginary images as it reacted to the real images (emotivity does not differentiate between these two kinds of images; a jealous man who vigorously imagines a scene in which his wife deceives him is as moved as if the scene were real). But on the other hand the emotive state reacts to the elaboration of the imaginery film; if a real misfortune befalls me and saddens me I start imagining a thousand other misfortunes and I see everything in the same sombre light. Thus there is established a vicious circle of double reactions.

But, in this relation between emotivity and imaginary film, another more important factor intervenes. The imaginary film resembles the real film to a certain extent; the films that I invent are necessarily elaborated with the elements that I have received in the past from the outside world; but there exists an essential difference between these two kinds of films. The real film is invented by the Cosmos, its source is the cosmic source, which is the Primary Cause of the Universe; therefore every real film is harmonic, balanced in the Whole. Its fixed centre is the Noumenon, and there could not be in this film any phenomenal fixity, it is only pure movement. On the contrary the imaginary film is centred on my Ego, on 'myself pretending to be absolutely a distinct individual'; its source, its centre, is not the immutable noumenal centre of the Cosmos, but a false, ex-centric centre. And there is, in this film, at the same time as a continual movement, a certain phenomenal fixity derived from this phenomenal centre. This is revealed by the fact that my day-dreams, if they are made of moving images, are made of images which turn ever more and more round a fixed idea; they are always more or less obsessional. My imaginary scenarios are organised in constellations or complexes, artificially coherent outside the cosmic Whole. To this phenomenal fixity corresponds a fixity in the emotive reaction, an emotive spasm, an emotive state.

The emotive reaction to the real film (a reaction which comprises no element of fixity) is normal or healthy, since it is reaction to the normal relative reality of cosmic phenomena. The emotive reaction to the imaginary film (which always comprises a factor of spasm) is abnormal or unhealthy; it is in fact a reaction to abnormal images since the formation-centre of these images is not the real centre of the Universe.

We have clearly distinguished these two emotive responses, to the real film on the one hand and to the imaginary film on the other. But, with the human-being after earliest childhood, at no moment does the emotivity respond only to a real film; an imaginary film is always there at the same time. The emotions are never pure, there is always an emotive state coexisting, and all the more if the subject is endowed with a need of the Absolute, with a craving to 'be', with 'idealism'. The very young child, in whom the possibility of inventing an imaginary film does not yet exist since his intellectual function is insufficiently developed, still has an emotivity that is nearly pure, quite fluid, without spasm, unstable. But in the degree that the intellect develops, the spasms of the emotive states appear. With the adult, very well endowed with a need of the Absolute, the emotivity presents, under contractions sometimes very unstable, spasms of a slow rhythm; if this man is well able to observe himself he will recognise this duality of rhythm in his emotivity. It will seem to him that he has two distinct emotivities, one which tends to flow and the other to stay put (dreams often contain allusion to this state of things: I want to move, I need to move, and at the same time I remain stuck where I am).

There are, then, two kinds of imaginative film, two kinds of emotive response, and in practice, in our inner phenomenology, two emotivities: one authentic emotivity in response to the real film, and one illusory or false emotivity in response to the imaginary film. The authentic emotivity corresponds with the plane of sensation (sense-perceptions of the outer world), the false emotivity corresponds with the plane of images (imaginary perceptions).

The authentic emotivity, that of the child, operates according to a mobile unstable rhythm and it is quite irrational (it is unrelated with the importance that our reason accords to the images according to our scale of values). The false emotivity operates with a slow rhythm and it is more or less rational (except that at moments of fatigue, a certain instability can be seen there also; but this instability is not a healthy absence of fixity, it is only failure of a spasm which is exhausting itself). This emotivity is in relation with the ideal image that I make of the world and of myself, with my desire to see myself in attitudes that are 'beautiful-good-true' and with my fear of seeing myself in attitudes that are 'ugly-wicked-false'. My authentic reaction to a given circumstance scoffs at the 'ideal', it depends only on my vision of the outer world; but my false emotive reaction can be radically different for it depends on my ideal vision of myself. It is made up of sentiments that I cherish, no longer with regard to the outer world but concerning my attitudes before this outer world. On account of that I can very well be falsely gay (in my imaginary emotivity) while being at the same time authentically sad in my authentic emotivity, or the other way round.

For example: I have amused myself, months beforehand, with the thought of my annual holidays; an image of myself-joyous-at-seeing-Florence has firmly developed in my mind; if I am 'idealistic', strongly 'egotistical', greedy to 'be absolutely', the realisation of this image becomes for me the object of a very imperious need. Once I am in Florence, I find myself very tired and depressed; my authentic state, which mocks at my vision of myself and only responds to the real circumstance, is contracted; at bottom I am unhappy. But my desire to see realised the image of myself-joyous-in-Florence forbids me to realise that I am unhappy; if anyone asks me: 'Well, and this holiday?', I reply: 'Splendid; all these museums are a bit tiring, but what does that matter compared with so much beauty.' If I then direct my attention to my emotivity with an honest spirit of investigation, I see the naked truth: I am unhappy, more unhappy than I usually am in the Underground which takes me to my work; and I see that, without a special effort, I cannot realise it; or else I realised my sadness but I attached it illusorily to an imaginary film which was only the effect of it.

Another example: here is a boy who has been tyranised over for years by an egoistic father; he has been humiliated, interfered with in all his undertakings, negated by a sadistic education which was by way of being devoted to his welfare. The father dies. The authentic emotive response of the son is immense relief. But, if this son is very 'idealistic' he has such a need to see himself as sad that he arrives at the state despite the facts; and the sadness of his imaginary film can prevent to a great extent, or even altogether, the profound relief.

This disaccord between my emotions and my imaginary emotive states is particularly striking from the following point of view: my ideal image, absolute, divine, comprises amongst other 'divine' attributes, stability, immutability; but the Absolute Principle, the fundamental One, from which everything emanates, is immutable, above time and the alterations of time. And so one of the essential attributes of the image that I wish to have of myself consists in evenness of humour, stability of the emotive state. That is why the representation that I make of my emotive states, throughout the day, is enormously deformed in the direction of stability. As soon as I begin to examine with an honest spirit of investigation the variations of my authentic emotivity I perceive that these variations are very much more frequent and more marked that I supposed them to be; a word that someone says to me, an image that passes under my eyes, an intestinal spasm, or the absorption of a little wine or coffee, suffices for peaks or precipices to be drawn on the graph or my emotivity. On the other hand the ideal image that I have of myself requires that my emotive reactions shall be *rational*; as a result of that I pretend that only big things can move me strongly, I pretend that there exists a parallelism between the amplitude of my emotive variations and the importance that my reason sees in the events that affect me. When I observe a young child I am struck by his emotive instability (he passes without transition from laughter to tears) and by the irrationality of his emotions (he shows signs of profound distress when one takes away his rattle); I think of the immense difference that exists between this child's emotivity and my own, so much more stable and rational. In reality the difference only exists between my false emotivity and the emotivity of the child; but this difference depends upon the immense

139

lie which the elaboration of my false emotivity involves. The need
that I have to see realised the ideal image of myself, has little by
little warped my emotivity. As soon as I make honest efforts to
see my emotive variations as they really are I no longer see anything but my authentic emotive variations, and I then perceive
that there is no difference between the young child and myself;
my authentic emotivity is quite as unstable and irrational as his.

The inner work of which we are speaking here (in order to see
directly our instantaneous emotive situation) brings into play an
intuitive and direct inner regard, which passes through the false
emotivity without stopping there. The only emotivity which does
not disappear under this regard is the authentic emotivity, that
which corresponds only with the plane of sensation, or the animal
plane. The plane of images, the 'angelic' or 'ideal' plane, vanishes.
It is a strange revelation to appreciate the unique reality of our
irrational emotive agitation and to see with what constancy we
lie to ourselves on the subject. We then see that the 'animal' has
always persisted integrally in us under angelic imaginary con-
structions and that this animal is all that is actually 'realised' of
our total being; all the rest is unreal. It is to this organism that
we must modestly return in order to obtain the awakening, in its
centre, of its immanent and transcendent principle.

The intuitive inner regard traverses the false emotivity without
stopping there; it traverses the images of the imaginary film, dis-
pelling them as it goes. But, if it dispels this film it does not dispel
the profound spasm in its actual determinism. I can already
understand this theoretically: it is not enough to dispose of the
imaginary film that is joined in the instant to the subconscious,
in order to wipe out all this subconscious itself. And practice
effectively proves to me the persistence of my profound spasm.
This leads me to consider further and to understand that this
spasm, which I have called abnormal (and justifiably in a sense)
is on the road that leads to satori.

In the spasm of my total organism there is an element of immobility which is quite certainly beneficial; our spontaneous evolution will move towards satori if we are 'obedient to the nature
of things', if we cease to busy ourselves with ersatz-forms of satori.
'To do nothing', which is the immobility of our total organism,
the immobility of its phenomenal centre, allows the maturing of

satori. There is then something right and normalising in the profound spasm; it is beneficial in that it tends to immobilise our
centre. If in fact it has not been normalising for me up to the
present that is because I have always defended myself by means of
a reflex against this immobilisation. Let us remember the double
relation which exists between emotivity and the imaginary film;
the images release the spasm and then the state of spasm releases
images. That the images release the spasm is inevitable and is not
to be regretted because that tends towards the desirable immobility. What is regrettable, and avoidable, is that the state of
spasm should release images, entailing perpetual variations in the
spasm, variations which prevent me from profiting by the immobility virtually contained in it. Why is a new imaginary film
released by the spasm, or rather in connexion with it, preventing
me from immobilising myself? Because there exists in me a false
belief according to which immobility is dangerous, mortal; for
lack of Faith in my Principle I still believe that I ought myself to
achieve my salvation, realise by a personal activity my total
accomplishment. As long as this belief operates in me I cannot
prevent my state of spasm from releasing a new imaginary film,
and that is a vicious circle of agitation.

The caterpillar has to immobilise itself as a chrysalis in order to
become a butterfly. When I am agitated in the vicious circle of
emotive states and of imaginary films I am comparable with a
caterpillar who feels himself overtaken by the process of becoming
a chrysalis and who fights bitterly against the immobilisation
which he feels as a danger.

Nevertheless if I understand how absurd it is to fear immobilisation, if I understand that my profound spasm offers me not destruction but only an apparent death (chrysalis) in order to obtain
a life that at last is real (butterfly), then I perceive that the release
of an imaginary film by the emotive state is not by any means
inevitable. Strong in my understanding, in my Faith, I realise
that I am able, and quite easily, to lose myself in my spasm, that
is in my fear, or sadness, or anxiety, without any *image* fearful or
sad or anxious, without thoughts, or inner movements. At the end
of a moment my sadness ceases to be such in order to become
colourless immobility merely. I am then insensible, anaesthetised,
like a piece of timber; an idiot in one sense, but still very well

able to act, to react correctly to the outer world, like a robot in
good working order.

One sees at what paradoxical conclusions our study arrives.
Our first observations condemned the emotive spasm and in-
spired in us a nostalgia for the purely fluid emotivity of childhood.
But it is impossible to go backwards; and besides the state of the
child was the extreme opposite of that of satori. We must go
ahead. The deplorable consequences of our intellectual development arose only from the fact that our intellect was not enlightened;
as a result of our ignorance we were resisting our inner immobilisation ; the resistance to immobilisation caused our variations of
spasm, eddies of distress; we were wounding ourselves on the bonds
which bound us up. But the remedy is there where we saw the
evil; the bonds were only enemies to us when we resisted them.
The emotive spasm was only destructive as long as it continued
to be emotive, that is agitated. As soon as I cease to dread
immobility I free myself from the imaginary film, illusorily
coercive, which was born from the spasm; the spasm ceases to
be emotive, and it ceases forthwith to be spasm in order to become
merely immobility without suffering. The maturing of satori is
then possible.

Our intelligence always ends up with this paradox at the
moment at which thesis and antithesis are resolved in a synthesis.
I was possessed first of all by the unconsidered belief that my
emotive state was my very life (thesis); my considered study
brings me to the belief, diametrically opposite, that my central
spasm is my death (antithesis); and then suddenly my intellectual
intuition discovers that my conscious adhesion to my spasmodic
emotive state delivers me from it, that is this adhesion conciliates
life and death, movement and fixity, spasm and suppleness. The
paradox is only apparent, on the formal plane; behind this appearance there is the conciliation of the contraries.

Our comparison between emotivity and a muscle allows us to
make clear what new kind of relaxation we obtain in ceasing to
struggle against the immobilisation of the spasm; and this comparison, as we shall see, serves us thus at the moment at which it
is no longer applicable. When my muscle goes into a spasm it is
shortened; when it is decontracted it recovers its length and is
ready for a new shortening spasm. When I do not correct inner

work it inevitably happens that my central spasm decreases; this eventuality, as with the muscle, then throws me back into a re-laxation ready for a new spasm. Up to this point our comparison is applicable, but when I adhere consciously to my spasm, what takes place in me is analogous to a phenomenon that is never seen in physiology: a muscle which is relaxed without becoming longer, which could decontract without recovering its original length, and then be at once shortened and supple. Let us suppose that a failure puts me into a spasm of humiliation; if I take no correct inner action my humiliation will pass more or less rapidly and sooner or later I will come out of this state; I shall be no longer humiliated, but then I shall have come back to my habitual pre-tention and in consequence open to an eventual new humiliation. If, on the contrary, in my state of humiliation, I consciously adhere to my spasm, my humiliation disappears without my pre-tention reappearing; my central 'muscle' (as opposed to what can be seen in the case of my material muscles) decontracts without losing its shortening; my *humiliation* is transformed into *humility*.

The comparison with the muscle (with its states of expansion and of diminution) is a good one. When a success exalts me I feel myself to be aggrandised, increased tenfold in volume; physically even, I feel my chest fill out, my nostrils open, I use large gestures. When, on the contrary, a repulse humiliates me I feel myself small, shrivelled, reduced, I have a weight on my chest, my ges-tures are curtailed. The inner action of which we are speaking consists in shutting ourselves up willingly in this reduced volume. There is then produced a sort of condensation of the Ego; the Ego is at once denied in its volume and affirmed in its density. This process is comparable with that which transforms coal into diamonds; the aim of this process is not the destruction of the Ego but its transformation, its sublimation. The conscious accept-ance results in the coal which has become denser, and so blacker and more opaque, being instantaneously transformed into a diamond that is perfectly transparent.

It is evident that we cannot really accomplish this inner gesture of complete adhesion to our shortening spasm the moment we try. For all our previous automatisms push us towards gestures that are radically opposed to this one. The inner work consists in making with perseverence partial performances of the useful gesture; that already brings me a certain calm which progressively increases; I thus move in the direction of the absolute calm which may permit one day the release of satori.

I learn to feel directly in myself my spasm, my uneasiness, under the imaginative film which more or less masks my centre; the acquisition of this new inner sensation conditions all the rest of the work. Then my attention brusquely abandons my film in order to focus, and remain motionless, on this profound uneasiness which I have felt in its purity. I install myself in this uneasiness from which I have always fled till then (the only place where this lion ceases to be dangerous is in his very jaws); at least I make a very sincere effort to install myself there but, as we have understood, in the degree in which my effort succeeds my discomfort disappears and it is in my centre (where my illusory distress seems to have its seat) that I find myself. For a long time my success being only partial my attention does not reach my centre with stability; it only reaches it for a moment that is without duration. The disappearance of my discomfort removes every object from the field of my attention and this attention finds itself again seized by images; then everything begins once more. Our spirit of investigation has to be persevering.

This work implies the correct 'despair' from which Hope is born. Until now I was hoping that the convulsions of my imaginary film would one day wipe out my spasm; when I had a worry I carried out the forced labour of sterile ruminations (because, implicitly, I believed them to be useful); I was in the gaol in which my absurd confidence in my imagination shut me up. Now I have seen imagination for what it is, a sterile camouflage; the hope which I placed in its activity is transformed into Hope placed in its non-activity; the door of my prison opens. I have at last the right to suffer without ruminating, that is to say without perpetuating my suffering; I have at last the right to profit by the essential instability of my suffering, to allow myself to be relieved by the Principle without doing anything. In exempting myself from suffering for no reason, I sacrifice my suffering, I store up, in view of my transformation, the vital energy which I have been wasting up till now.

The description of the inner gesture of which we speak is evidently what should interest us most. Unfortunately our language does not lend itself to the description of things that are altogether 'within'; it loses its efficacity when we approach the limits of the phenomenal, formal world. One can indeed say that what should be perceived, under the imaginary film, is a certain profound sensation of cramp, of a paralysing grip, of immobilising cold (as the cold immobilises the river by freezing it), and that it is on this hard couch, immobile and cold, that our attention should remain fixed; as though we tranquilly stretched out our body on a hard but friendly rock that was exactly moulded to our form. But such a description has only value as an indication; each man should experiment in himself in the light of what he has come to understand.

Chapter Sixteen

ON AFFECTIVITY

WE can enlarge more thoroughly the preceding studies by envisaging the whole of conscious affectivity, that is the whole of the inner phenomena by means of which we experience pleasure or pain in contact with the outer world. Since these two poles, pleasure and pain, correspond with the qualitative variations of a single thing, my consciousness of being-distinct, it will simplify our exposition to speak for the most part of the painful variations. What will be valid for the painful will be valid also for the pleasurable.

First of all it appears that there are two sorts of sensibility, physical (physical pain) and psychic ('moral' suffering). I cannot confuse the pain which an abcess gives me with that given me by the death of someone I love. These two sensibilities seem to correspond with the gross part of me (the somatic), and with my subtle part (or psychic). The physical sensibility comprises *sensations*, agreeable or disagreeable; the psychic sensibility comprises *sentiments*, also agreeable or disagreeable. In practical psychology I necessarily make a clear-cut difference between these two domains of sensibility.

But this duality of soma and psyche only indicates two aspects of a single thing, my psycho-somatic organism; there are therein merely two aspects (distinct only to the outside observer) of this creature which I call 'Self', of this microcosm, synthetic and single, which is a particular manifestation of the Absolute Principle. If I hold, on edge, a sheet of cardboard in front of my left eye, my left eye sees this sheet as a straight line while my right sees it as a surface; but the sheet of cardboard is the same; in one sense it is both a line and a surface; in another it is neither line nor surface; in any case it is only a single sheet of cardboard.

If soma and psyche are thus two aspects of a single thing, the physical and psychic sensibilities are also necessarily two aspects of a single sensibility. Under two aspects there is in reality only one organism; in the same way under two aspects there is in reality only one sensibility.

Since I now conceive a unity of nature under the different aspects of my sensation and my sentiment, I am tempted to conclude that one only of these aspects is real, the other being illusory. First of all, for example, I am going to try to reduce all my sensible phenomena to sensation. There are only, I shall assume, sensations; physical pain is a sensation which affects my soma to a partial extent, in so far as it is an aggregate of organs. Moral suffering is a sensation which affects my soma in its entirety, in so far as it is a totality, through the medium of the global image that I have of myself. But this ingenious attempt breaks down. If I can envisage my soma as an aggregate of organs, that is only an aspect artificially isolated by my analysis in abstracting the conciliatory principle which totalises this aggregate. The concept of an aggregate is not able to define my soma. On the other hand, if I can envisage my soma as a totality, that again is only by an analytical artifice; my soma only exists by virtue of its connexions with the rest of the cosmos, as a particle of the cosmic whole. The concept of totality is not able to define my soma. Since I fail to conceive my soma with precision I cannot take it as a criterion of a unique sensibility which is only made up of sensations.

After the failure of this 'materialistic' attempt I yield to the temptation of trying the opposite, the 'spiritual'. There are only, I shall assume this time, sentiments; there is no physical pain since I can perceive nothing disagreeable except by means of my brain, by means of a representative mental image; every unpleasant impression is ultimately psychic; therefore there is only 'moral' suffering. But if I failed just now to conceive my soma as a fixed entity to serve me as a criterion, I fail now—and in a sense still more absolutely—to conceive the world of my mental images as a fixed entity; if I was not able to define myself by my soma I am not more able to define myself by my psyche.

I fail then to reduce my sensibility to one of its two aspects, as I failed to reduce my psycho-somatic organism to one of its two aspects. I am at once soma and psyche, and I am at the same time neither soma nor psyche. My sensibility is at once physical and psychic, and it is at the same time neither the one nor the other. When it is a question of my psycho-somatic organism I arrive at the concept of the Self or Absolute Principle in so far as it manifests in me; and this concept resolves the dualism of soma and psyche. But how to reduce the dualism of my sensibility? What then is my sensibility in reality under its two aspects? Since I did not succeed in seeing my unique sensibility residing in my gross aspect (my organs) nor in my subtle aspect (my images), where then does it reside?

The study of sensibility, when it started from the distinction between soma and psyche, started badly; it started from an artificial discrimination and it is not surprising therefore that it was not able to arrive at any result. I am going to take it up again in another way, in a way which concerns my physical sensibility as much as my psychic.

Instead of studying the manifestations of sensibility at the end of their development we are going to study this development itself; to that end let us start with a very banal experience. One day I feel, in my arm, a rheumatic pain of moderate intensity; a friend comes to see me, engages me in a conversation that interests me, then leaves me. After my friend has gone, I feel my pain and realise that I had ceased to feel it during the conversation; and I tell myself that my pain was certainly always there during the conversation; it was there but I did not feel it because my attention was distracted from it. If, instead of a rheumatic pain I experience some moral suffering of moderate intensity, as a result of a vexation which saddened me before the visit of my friend, the same phenomenon can arise. The distinction to be drawn here is no longer between two sorts of sufferings developed, but between two stages of development of the suffering whether this suffering be somatic or psychic. What was happening while my attention was distracted? Can I really think that my pain was there but that I was not conscious of it? Certainly not; I cannot state that a pain 'is there' if I do not feel any pain. I am nevertheless not mistaken in thinking that there persisted, during my distraction, something or other which afterwards gave me back my suffering. But what, then? I am led to establish a distinction which will explain my experience; it is the distinction between the painful excitation and the mental consciousness of the pain. While I was distracted the painful excitation persisted but the consciousness of the pain ceased. This distinction once established, I see how I can recover correctly the distinction between soma and psyche; for the painful excitation is a somatic phenomenon whereas the consciousness of pain is a psychic phenomenon. And the two attempts, 'material-istic' and 'spiritual', which failed a moment ago, are now going to turn into something that is valid. The painful excitation is a phenomenon which effects the soma, either partially in so far as it is an aggregate of organs (physical painful excitation) or totally in so far as it is a totality (painful excitation called 'psychic', touching the totality of the soma by means of the global image that I have of myself). The painful excitation can reach me either in passing by my gross aspect (plane of sensation), or in passing by my subtle aspect (plane of images or of sentiment). So, on the side of the pole 'painful excitation', our materialistic thesis is applicable; it is always my soma which is painfully excited in part or in whole. If we go on now to the pole 'consciousness of pain' our 'spiritual' thesis is applicable: it is always my mind which is conscious of the pain, whether the painful excitation has affected my soma in part or in whole.

Let us now envisage these two poles 'painful excitation' and 'consciousness of pain' by asking ourselves in which of these the pain resides. The difficulties begin again: in fact I cannot make the pain reside in the painful excitation alone without conscious-ness of the pain; but neither can I conceive a pain which is pure consciousness, without painful excitation. Where then does the pain really reside? This question in its 'spatial' expression, is the form in which is translated, according to our space-time perspec-tive, the question 'What is the reality of pain?' or, still better, 'What is the cause of the pain?' since the cause is the reality of the effect. The painful excitation is causal in relation to my conscious-ness of the pain; my mind is affected because my soma is affected. But the affection of my soma is itself the effect of a cause. This cause is not the outer world as one might suppose at first sight. Indeed the affection of my soma is reaction to the action of the outer world; if the action of the outer world can be called the immediate cause it cannot be called the efficient cause. The efficient or real cause of the reaction of my soma is in my soma itself, not outside it; it is in my vital principle, in the source of all my manifestation, that is to say in the Absolute Principle in so far as it manifests in me. We find then, in the genesis of conscious pain, three stages: the Absolute Principle first; next my somatic aspect which, activated by the Absolute Principle, develops what we have called 'painful excitation'; finally my subtle aspect which, prompted by the painful excitation, develops the consciousness of pain. The Absolute Principle corresponds to the fundamental Unconscious; the painful excitation corresponds to the 'subconscious' (my suffering, during my distraction, was subconscious); the consciousness of pain corresponds to the conscious.

We see then that pain, in its ensemble, is an uninterrupted flux of energy which disintegrates from the universal centre towards the individual periphery. Reality, or the primary cause, of all this phenomenal current resides in the fundamental Unconscious. In other words the reality of conscious suffering is unconscious. That is to say that we deceive ourselves in seeing our conscious developed sensibility as an entity which is self-sufficient and in relation to which we can correctly direct our life.

One could say: 'No doubt our sensible phenomena, like all phenomena, are not Absolute Reality; at least they are relative reality which is that of Manifestation.' But it is not so at all, for this disintegration of energy which is an effective phenomenon passes from infinity to zero without stopping, without integrating itself at any moment in a form. My organs are a relative reality because they are an integration, in a gross form, of the original energy. My mental images have a relative reality because they are the integration, in a subtle form, of the original energy. But my pleasures, my pains, my joys, my sorrows, are not integrations in forms, either gross or subtle. The painful affection of my soma has a gross form; the painful mental affection which replies to it has a subtle form. The gross manifestation of my pain has a form and its subtle manifestation also has a form; but my pain itself, thus doubly manifested, is in-formal, as in-formal as the Absolute Principle which is its only reality. Let us not be surprised then that we can never, owing to lack of form, seize our suffering itself; we have said above that every effort to seize a sadness only resulted in seizing sad images, and that the sadness itself escaped us. But it is the same where a physical pain is concerned. When I have a pain in my arm and I attempt to seize my pain, I only succeed in seizing, in an active perception, my suffering arm and not its pain; that escapes my capture. It can capture me but I cannot capture it.

These notions will become clearer if we get at them by means of a different approach. My painful somatic reaction to the excitation from the outside world, a reaction which then conditions my consciousness of the pain, only occurs in virtue of the 'need to exist' which is in me. This defence-mechanism supposes that my existence ought to be defended; it implies that that which menaces my existence menaces me. But I only feel myself to be menaced by that which menaces my organism in the degree in which I identify myself exclusively with my organism. On account of this identification the intemporal will 'to be' which is one of the attributes of the fundamental 'Being' is represented in my organism by the will to persevere in existence, by the need to live. The illusory confusion between the Self and the Ego (otherwise, my exclusive identification with my organism or, again, my belief in the absolute reality of my phenomenal existence), gives to the outer world the power to make my energy well up from its source and deliver it to the disintegration of the pain. If I were not ignorant, if I did not identify myself with my organism, if I were capable of saying, like Socrates, 'My enemies can kill me but they cannot do me harm', then I would not feel that which menaces my organism as a real menace to Myself; I would not suffer. I would perceive that my organism is menaced, would recognise that the red-hot iron which burns me burns me, and I could then withdraw myself from this contact if my rational will was to live. But I would not suffer, I would not submit to any inner pressure in order to defend my life; I would choose in full liberty to defend or not to defend my life according to circumstances. I could preserve myself, I would not be constrained, by suffering, to do it.

All affectivity is founded on ignorance, on the implicit illusory beliefs which represent in me the sleep of my Faith in the unique Reality, the sleep of the Cosmic Mind. My perception of the aggressive excitation of the outer world is not illusory, for it informs me correctly about the phenomena which attack my organism. But the affective character, agreeable or disagreeable, of my perception is illusory because founded on illusory beliefs. I do not deceive myself in considering that which touches me as being favourable or unfavourable to my existence; but I deceive myself in considering it as 'good' or 'bad', in considering it with affectivity. The sensation of being burned is not a delusion, but the pain of the burn is. My perceptions are correct in so far as they inform me, they are illusory in so far as they *affect* me. Between my Absolute Principle which 'is' and my organism which 'exists', between my noumenon and my phenomena, my affectivity neither is nor exists. Every affective phenomenon is the interpretive deformation, through ignorance, of non-affective phenomena. All my affectivity is an interpretive delirium resulting from illusory beliefs. My real Self is inaffective.

Besides, at every moment, at the same time as I am affectively sensible to such and such a thing I remain insensible to all the rest of the universe. But as long as my Faith is not entirely awakened, in satori, my attention allows itself to be captured by my fallacious affectivity and turns away from my inaffectivity.

The inner work leaves things in this state, it lets the attention wander towards the affective pseudo-phenomena. But it does more than let it go passively in this direction, it actively pushes it that way. Where I was captured by something incomprehensible, and where this fact of being captured was expressed by suffering, I now project my active attention in order to seize that which seized me, that which I called my suffering. Now that my understanding has neutralised my fear I have the courage to turn round, in a spirit of investigation, towards these hypothetical flames that my flight had stirred up. This inner effort to capture what was seeking to capture me causes my suffering to lose hold; it is thus that we should understand the Zen concept of 'Letting Go'. This inner gesture frees the energy which was tied up, dissolves what was coagulated; it installs me in an anaesthesia which is not just absence of affectivity, but Not-Feeling, the motionless principle of all the affective movements. In destroying affective partiality it prepares the breaking forth of satori; it cures the '*malady of the spirit*', *this malady which consists, according to* Zen, *in 'opposing that which we like to that which we do not like'*.

Chapter Seventeen

THE HORSEMAN AND THE HORSE

THE dualism of the Yin and the Yang, which rules the cosmos under the conciliation of the Tao, exists in man as in all created things. Man is conscious of this dualism, which reveals itself in him by the belief that he is composed of two autonomous parts which he either calls 'body' and 'soul', 'matter and spirit', 'instinct and reason', or otherwise. The belief in this bipartite composition expresses itself in all sorts of common sayings: 'I am master of "myself" ', 'I cannot prevent myself from . . .', 'I am pleased with myself', 'I am annoyed with myself', etc. . . .

But we know that the belief in the autonomy of these two parts is an illusion; there are not in man two distinct parts, but only two distinct aspects of a single being; man is in reality an *individual* artificially divided by an erroneous interpretation of his analytic observation. The error of our dualistic conception does not lie in the discrimination between two aspects in us—for there are indeed two aspects—but in concluding that these two aspects are two different entities, of whom one, for example, may be perishable while the other is eternal. To tell the truth, our observation does not show us that there are two parts in us; it only shows us that everything happens in us as though there were two parts separated by a hiatus. It is our ignorant intellect that takes an illusory leap from the statement 'everything happens as though' to the erroneous affirmation that there are in us two parts separated by a hiatus. In reality it all happens in us thus because we believe that it is thus or, more precisely, because the universal consciousness which alone can reveal to us our real inner unity is asleep in us. An illustration will help us to understand this problem. What man interprets as his two parts he conceives, the one as inferior, instinctive, affective, motor, irrational, the other as superior, rational,

153

directing, capable of deciding what the inferior part should carry out. He conceives himself as a horseman riding a horse.

In reality, as Zen reminds us, we are not horseman and horse, with a hiatus between the two. The true symbolic representation of man, in this connexion, should be the centaur, single creature comprising two aspects separated by no hiatus. We are centaurs but everything happens in us as though we were horse and rider because we believe in the reality of a hiatus between our two aspects, or, more exactly, because we do not see the unity in which the two aspects are integrated.

We will try to define, in our concrete structure, what we see as horse and as rider, and to understand why we have this false vision of ourselves.

We are first of all tempted to trace the boundary between the horse and the rider starting from a morphological standpoint: the horse would be our gross manifestation, or soma, the rider our subtle or psychic manifestation.

But this morphological point of view does not suit the angle from which we are studying man at this moment. We are studying, at this moment, not only the modalities of the functioning of the human machine, but the problem of the determination of this functioning. Going beyond the consideration 'how our life works' we are studying the orientation of this working Looked at from this higher perspective, the two parts of man are no longer two modalities of phenomena, some physiological the others psychlogical, but two ways of being, two styles, two different rhythms of the manifestation of our being.

The horse represents my way of being when my thought does not function in an independent, impartial manner. It is my personal life, egotist and partial, that which I live when my intellect works geared to my desires, my fears, my affective re-actions in general. It is my life when there operates in me only the inferior conciliatory principle, the Demiurge who rules over the metabolism of the temporal plane. It is Nature willing herself in me, achieving her ends through my organism. It is I in so far as I wish to be distinct, in so far as I wish to be Self beside, and op-posed to, the Not-Self.

The rider represents my way of being when my thought, un-geared from my affective life, works in an independent, impartial manner. It represents my Independent Intelligence, impartial reason, or pure, objective, or universal, thought. It is I in so far as I think without wishing to be distinct, outside all opposition between the Self and the Not-Self.

The rider, understood in this sense, is not a motive-power. It is the principle of direction in the movement of my machine, but it is not the motor. It is the principle of my 'acting', itself 'non-acting'. In consequence, if the horse and the rider are two ways of being, the horse alone is a way of *living*; the rider is not a way of living—since living implies movement and the rider is 'non-acting'—it is a way of thinking that is independent of my life. In my actual state my life is necessarily egotistical, partial, natural, affective; when my thought functions independently of my affectivity it is independent of my personal life, of my life itself. In other words the horse represents my life, accompanied by partial thought; the rider represents my thought, pure, non-acting. I am the horse when my attention is seized by my life, I am the rider when my attention, escaping from this domination, arouses my Independent Intelligence.

My conscious attention, which is a unity, could never be focussed at once on my life and on my pure thought that is above my life; it is necessarily focussed on one or the other of these two aspects of my being. The moments alternate during which, by means of my attention, I identify myself with the horse (when I feel and act), or again with the rider (when I think impartially). And it is because my surface consciousness alone is actually awakened in me—and that thus I can only be alternatively horse and rider— that I believe in the existence of a hiatus between these two parts although this hiatus does not exist in reality. The illusory hiatus between horse and rider is not a hiatus between two parts operating at the same time, but a false interpretation of the fact that I cannot be conscious at the same time of my partial life and of my impartial reason. If I had no memory this interpretation would not exist; it exists because I have a memory and because, thanks to this faculty, my imagination can evoke at once the two ways of being of which I am never conscious at one and the same time. In memory I picture myself imaginatively at once as horse and as rider, and thus I can see simultaneously the image of these two aspects of myself which never operate simultaneously for my surface consciousness; but because these two aspects never operate simultaneously for my surface consciousness the image which brings them together does not succeed in uniting them. It cannot be the image of a centaur; it is necessarily the image of a horseman mounted on a horse, with a hiatus between the two of them.

Since the horse and the rider, defined thus as two ways of being, never operate consciously at the same time, the horse is never guided. We mean by that that the rider never guides the movement of the horse while this movement is taking place. Nevertheless the play of the rider has a directive action on the movements of the horse; but it is an indirect action and displaced in time. At the moment at which the rider is awakened (and at which the attention which animates him cannot be upon the horse), he sees, thanks to memory, how the horse has functioned the moment before and evaluates this functioning in relation to the ideal norm which he is able to conceive. This judgement, favourable or unfavourable, constitutes an image, affirming or negating, which flatters or wounds the horse in his need of affirmation. Thereafter, when the attention comes back to the horse, his functioning will be affected by this judgement, by the caress or the blow that it constituted; the horse preserves the memory of it marked in him as a conditioning factor of his reflexes. In this state of things, in which horse and rider cannot operate at the same time, the only guiding action that the rider can have is one of *schooling*, of elaboration of automatisms; it is a mediate action, a consequence of the illusory hiatus, entirely comparable with what happens when a man schools a real horse. By caresses or by little blows of his crop, he conditions the automatisms of the horse, but he and he alone executes each movement that the horse carries out. The horse depends mediately upon the man, but immediately he does not depend upon him at all.

So in my actual state, before satori, my 'life' can only be an ensemble of conditioned reflexes and not of directed movements; and my Independent Intelligence cannot really conduct my life but only have on it a mediate action that is relative and limited. In my actual state, all self-direction can only be a training, an elaboration of this or that automatism. In speaking of automatisms one means necessarily fixed, stereotyped movements. However numerous, however fragmented the automatisms may be, the fixity that they imply prevents any automatic demeanour from being really adapted to the outer world. It is like a broken line; however frequently broken one may imagine it, this line can only cover a curve approximately, it cannot coincide. As long as I believe myself to be horseman and horse, and in consequence, as long as everything happens in me as though I were horseman and horse, I can only achieve a schooling of my horse without being really adapted to the outer world.

But man's veritable realisation is something very different from a training. It takes place as a result of a flash of consciousness by the centaur in which the illusory hiatus between the rider and the horse is abolished. Then there is no longer trainer or trained, no longer reflection in which 'I' consider 'myself' (subject and object); the 'I live' and the 'I think' are conciliated in a unique 'I am'.

The majority of men do not even envisage this realisation; they do not envisage the disappearance of the illusory hiatus. And so they conceive realisation as a training that has succeeded; that is, they confound intemporal realisation with temporal realisation. We will see shortly how absurd it would be to condemn the training; we will even see the necessity of this in the course of the work which prepares satori. What we wish to show at this moment is the error in regarding realisation as the accomplishment and success of a training; if the realisation chronologically follows such training it should not on any account be regarded as engendered or caused by it. If it is true that satori is released after such and such phenomena and on the occasion of such phenomena, it could not be released or caused by any phenomenon.

The error which consists in considering realisation as the success of a training is epitomised in the adhesion given by so many men to systematic methods: the conception of this or that 'ideal', yogas of one kind or another, 'moral systems' proclaiming that such automatisms should be installed and such others eliminated, in short any kind of discipline to which one attributes an intrinsic efficacity for realisation. *The error is not in doing and putting to the test what these methods require, the error does not consist in following these methods; it consists in believing that these methods can result by themselves in satori as roads issue at the end of a journey.* All training, since it implies the illusory hiatus between him who trains and him who is trained, is powerless to dissipate the illusion of the hiatus; but only this destruction of the illusion will be realisation.

Another current error, which follows directly from the preceding, consists in estimating the position in which a man is, with reference to the eventuality of realisation, basing himself on the degree of harmony of his training. Only the degree of understanding can give us information about this, and not the degree of harmony of the training. Such and such a man can be a master for me if I sense in him an understanding capable of enriching mine; no matter the kind, perhaps mediocre, of schooling of his horse. At the same time I have no reason to disturb myself, as far as I myself am concerned, if my horse has very unharmonious reactions, more so perhaps than at an epoch of my life when my understanding was inferior; for, if the schooling is very important from the point of view of inner comfort, the only thing that counts from the point of view of realisation is understanding.

We have seen that all training consists fundamentally in the fact that I evaluate my life, in that I judge it good or evil; every appreciation of my phenomena, exterior or interior, is a caress or a blow given to my horse. And Zen reminds us with insistence of the importance of passing beyond this partiality: 'As soon as you have good and evil confusion results and the mind is lost.' Zen shows us that this evaluation, this training, constitutes the inopportune inner manipulation which is our habit and of which we ought to rid ourselves; there is the regrettable 'doing' to which Zen alludes when it tells us that we have nothing to do, that we ought to learn no longer to 'do' anything.

But this advice is hard to understand in the right way. If I see in it a condemnation of training I am mistaken, for this condemnation does not free me from evaluation; it only results in an inversion of training. In this false understanding I would train myself to train myself no longer, which would change nothing; I would be believing, without escaping from my error, in the efficacity for realisation of a counter-training which would still be a training. Zen tells us not to lay a finger on life: 'Leave things as they may be.' It is not for me to modify directly my habits of training myself. It is only indirectly that I can obtain the disappearance of these habits, by means of my understanding, ever more profound, that these attempts at training, which I continue to make, have in themselves no efficacity for realisation. It is a question, in short, of obtaining the devalorisation of these compensations which are my attempts at training; and this implies the defeat of the attempts and the correct interpretation of this defeat. I am not obliged to concern myself with the defeat; that will flow from the very nature of things; but I am concerned with the correct interpretation of this defeat. If I believe in the intrinsic efficacity of a discipline, I attribute its failure to all kinds of things but not to the discipline itself; so that does not devalorise itself. If, on the contrary, I have understood the intrinsic inefficacity of the discipline, while not by any means forbidding myself to practise it if I feel the need to do so, a profound lassitude will develop little by little in me which will detach me from this discipline in a real *transcendence*. I neither can nor should forbid myself the indiscrete interventions which it is natural to me in this moment to operate in my inner life; but, if I have clearly understood the sterility of these interventions, the affective belief that I have in their usefulness will disperse little by little in the course of the experience. Beliefs may be compared with wheels set going at a high speed; if the intellect ceases to keep my beliefs going by admitting that they are right, they will end up some day by exhausting themselves.

Satori, as we know, is not the crowning of an ultimate success but of an ultimate defeat. The consciousness of always having been free appears in us when we have exhausted all the attempts, all the training, that we believe may be capable of liberating us. If the disciplines could not be 'paths' resulting in satori, that does not mean that they may not be paths to be followed; they are paths leading to blind-alleys, all leading to a unique and ultimate blind-alley; but they are to be followed just because satori cannot be obtained unless we have come up against the end of this last blind-alley. They are to be followed with the theoretical understanding that they lead nowhere, so that experience may transform this theoretical understanding into total understanding, into this clear vision which is the arrival in the blind-alley and which lays us open to satori.

Let us cite here a dialogue between a Zen monk and his master. The monk, Tsou-hsin, has just had satori. 'Tsou-hsin went towards the master Houeï-nan, and, as he was about to make his bows, the master smiled and said: "You have now come into my room."

Tsou-hsin was very pleased about it and said: "If the truth of Zen is what I possess now, why do you make us swallow all those old tales and exhaust us in efforts to find out the meaning of them?" The master said: "If I did not make you fight in every possible way in order to find the meaning and lead you finally to a state of non-fighting and of no-effort from which you can see with your own eyes, I am sure that you would lose every chance of discovering yourself." '

I am not then obliged to refuse to see myself actually as a horseman on horseback, nor to refuse to act as a horseman who schools his horse. But I do not forget, despite this optical illusion, that I am in reality a centaur, and that all schooling which allows the illusory hiatus between horseman and horse to persist keeps me away from my true nature. However fine, however exalting, may be the result of my schooling, it keeps me away from my true nature. Little does it matter to me in reality that my horse is schooled to be a 'saint' or a yogi with spectacular powers, or to experience inner states felt as transcendent; my true nature is not there, it consists in no longer being other than one with my horse; then the smallest gesture of my life, however apparently banal one may suppose it, will participate in Reality.

But at the moment in which the illusory hiatus is abolished, the centaur, this formal symbol of which my understanding made use before realisation, is abolished at the same time that it is realised. 'In not being two', says Zen, 'everything is the same and everything that exists is included therein.' The horseman and the horse are united, but they unite in the in-formal All; so that there is no longer either horse or horseman, and the centaur is transcended as soon as he is reached. It is this that is demonstrated by the admirable Zen text entitled: 'The Ten stages of the Training of the Cow.' In that Zen affirms the necessity of passing through the training; but it affirms also that the ultimate aim is by no means a trained cow. 'Mounted on the cow, the man is at last back at home. But behold here there is no longer a cow and with what serenity he is sitting all by himself.' Then the man himself disappears also: 'Everything is void, the whip, the cord, the man and the cow; who has ever contemplated the immensity of the sky? On the incandescent furness not a flake of snow can fall. When one has arrived there, manifest is the mind of the old Master.'

Chapter Eighteen

THE PRIMORDIAL ERROR OR 'ORIGINAL SIN'

IN the preceding study we have spoken of discipline, or of the 'schooling of our horse', including in this idea all the particular modalities of training. From this point of view we have distinguished between man before satori, with whom there must necessarily be training, and man after satori, with whom there is no longer training.

It is interesting now, for me as man before satori, to remark that there are various kinds of training and that these various kinds are ranged, in my eyes, as is everything that is phenomenon, according to a hierarchy stretching from the very gross to the very subtle. This hierarchy evidently *is* not *absolutely*, phenomena as such do not participate *more or less* in Absolute Reality; it exists relatively, in proportion to my affective partiality. It should not be symbolised by a ladder sloped obliquely (as my affectivity suggests), but by a road which, on the horizontal plane, runs towards the point from which the vertical axis strikes off. It corresponds with all the inner work by means of which man chronologically approaches satori but which could not bring him near to it really, in the sense that no creature could approach its Principle since it has never been outside it.

To this horizontal hierarchy of disciplines there corresponds a gradation in the functioning of our Independent Intelligence. In this connexion we must establish the distinction which exists between the principle of our pure thought, which is Infinite Wisdom, Objective Knowledge, the *Buddhi* of the Vedânta; and the relative, limited play of this unlimited intelligence. For that we will take a concrete psychological example. One day I am in anger and I manifest this anger impulsively; another day I am equally in anger, but I hold back the manifestation of it because I am conscious of an ideal image of myself that I wish to realise and which necessitates the control of my manifestations (because this attitude is more aesthetic, or more comfortable ultimately or more favourable to my plans and to the general conduct of my life, or because I expect from this meritorious attitude a 'spiritual' reward, etc.). In the first case my mind is geared with my most immediate affective movement, with my affectivity limited to the very moment, with my 'quality' of the moment. In the second case this gearing is thrown out, but my mind this time is geared with my love for my ideal. That is with a generalised affective movement, operating in duration, hovering over the smaller particular affective movement which is that of the moment itself. I am set free from the affective quality of the moment, but bound to a quality which participates in the fourth dimension, in time, and which in a sense lies above an indefinite multitude of moments. There is, in this second case, operation of the Independent Intelligence since I am independent of the quality of the moment itself, but this operation is imperfect since I am not independent of a new quality that lies in duration. Participation in the fourth dimension is deliverance from the limitations of the third, but subjection to the limitations of this fourth.

What then is this Independent Intelligence which participates in the Absolute Impartiality, in the Objective or Divine Reason, and so in the Infinite, and which we see, in our example, as imperfect, limited, relative? The apparent difficulty of this question comes from the confusion that we make easily between a principle and the manifestation of this principle, beneath the words Independent Intelligence we are tempted to confound Buddhi and the manifestation of Buddhi. There is in me a possibility of thinking completely with perfect impartiality; that is Buddhi, or the Independent Intelligence-principle. But, before satori, this possibility is not entirely realised; it is manifested only by a relative impartiality. But this relative impartiality is in reality the *relative manifestation of an absolute impartiality*. There is no imperfect Buddhi, there is incomplete appearance of the perfect Buddhi. My Independent Intelligence, such as it is manifested to-day, has two aspects that I ought not to confound. In it resides its principle, Buddhi (immanence of the principle), and it participates there in the nature of Buddhi; but before satori, my manifested Independent Intelligence is not Buddhi (transcendence of the principle). As soon as my mind escapes however little from my affective movement of the moment (that is as soon as there is a certain passage from the particular to the general), Buddhi is manifested in this mind, but at the same time I would be deceiving myself if I identified this functioning of my mind with Buddhi itself or the 'vision of things as they are'. The Independent Intelligence necessitates throwing the affectivity out of gear with the mind, but there are degrees in the execution of this process; in so far as there is throwing out of gear it is perfectly thrown out of gear, but this qualitatively perfect process is only incompletely effected quantitatively.

From this quantitative gradation of the functioning of the Independent Intelligence flows the whole horizontal hierarchy of disciplines of which we have spoken; and this quantitative gradation conditions, in the eyes of my affectivity, a qualitative gradation of the kinds of training, from the most gross to the most subtle. The purpose of our discussion here is not to study the whole hierarchy itself, but that which constitutes the summit of it. It is important to study the most subtle modality of the operation of the Independent Intelligence, the primordial training, that which gives rise to all the inferior kinds of training, in order to find therein the primordial insufficiency of the manifestation of Buddhi in us, the ultimate error which, in our return to the beginning, we have to transcend.

We have seen that all training consists in an evaluation of the functioning of our horse, in a judgement of this functioning; and that this judgement is in reference to an ideal norm conceived by the rider. Each man, at each moment, has a certain conception of the manner in which in his view his horse ought to work, and this conception expresses itself in an image. The more this image is personal, gross, the more the corresponding training is felt as being 'low' in the affective hierarchy of the modes of training; the more the image is general, subtle, the more the corresponding training is felt as being subtle or 'high'.

But in the degree in which my understanding becomes richer and more precise my lucidity dissipates idolatries, my ideal image of myself becomes poorer and blurred. I end by understanding that Reality is 'up-stream' of all form and that every ideal image is in consequence illusory; I have no longer any theoretical reason to wish that the functioning of my horse should have one form rather than any other.

One might think, then, that this disappearance of all ideal images causes the disappearance of this judgement of myself which took for reference an ideal image. For lack of criterion to which to refer, the judgement would no longer exist; I would cease to judge myself, total impartiality would reign in me and I would then be the man of satori.

It would be thus if the ideal image were the cause of the judgement, that is if I judged myself in function of a pre-existing ideal image. But the opposite is the truth: I construct an ideal image in order to be able to pronounce a judgement the need for which I feel beforehand. The suffering which my temporal limitation inflicts on me awakens in me a doubt concerning my 'being', and releases the need of evaluating myself, of judging myself; and thereafter this need of judging myself releases the process of constructing an ideal image-criterion that I shall be able to copy, hoping thus to obtain my absolution. And the suffering experienced within my temporal limitation was itself the consequence of the profound and implicit belief that I ought not to be temporarily limited. And this belief itself represents the erroneous interpretation, projected on to the phenomenal plane, of the intuition, altogether primordial, unconscious and correct, that 'I am of the nature of Buddha'. All this inner genesis can be resumed thus: in the original Unconscious (universal source), I know that I am Buddha; in my 'subconscious' (first personal plane) I pretend to Temporal non-limitation, I pretend that I should never be denied by a Not-Self; in my consciousness I painfully doubt my subconscious pretention, I have need to judge myself in the hope of dissipating my doubt, and I construct an ideal image that I can copy in order to obtain my absolution.

That is why, when I reach a sufficient degree of understanding to dissipate all idolatrous images, my need to judge myself is not, itself, dissipated. It persists because my doubt of myself persists, and this doubt persists because its profound causes persis Every personal ideal image on which a personal training could depend disappears, but the implicit general image which gave rise to all the personal images persists (the primordial image that 'I should never be denied') and it continues to control a kind of training, primordial training which tends to obtain from my horse that he shall never be denied, that is that he shall triumph always and completely over the Not-Self.

One can see that my inner situation becomes more serious, in one sense, in the degree in which my understanding abolishes in me all personal formal ideals. As long as I had a personal formal ideal I found therein a refuge which affirmed me; a negation could come to me from the outer world in the form of a set-back or of some threat of a set-back; I could soften the blow, compensate it, and even overcompensate it, by imitating my ideal. There existed for me a 'place' where I could, by my effort, by my control exercised over myself, procure for myself as much affirmation as I needed in order to neutralise the negation of the outside world. As my understanding develops, this comfortable artifice becomes impossible to me. The disappearance of personal disciplines thus results not in the absence of all discipline, but in the general, primordial discipline which obliges me, without protecting trickery, to face up to the antagonism of the Not-Self, to the spectacle of my personal non-divinity. And this ultimate discipline cannot be exceeded as easily as have been the personal disciplines; the ideal form which it comprises is no longer a conscious form, valorised by my consciousness, and which my consciousness can easily revoke. It is a subconscious, subterranean form, which I cannot seize and devalorise directly, but whose slow devalorisation I am obliged to await with an ardent patience, in a vigilant impartiality, by really living the idea of Zen: 'Let go; leave things as they may be.'

Let us examine attentively in what consists this primordial discipline and the subconscious ideal image on which it is founded. Let us remember what we said just now. In the universal, original Unconscious I know that I am Buddha; on my subconscious, or primary personal plane, I pretend to be Buddha as a distinct being, in so far as I am face to face with the Not-Self, I then pretend that I never ought to be denied by the Not-Self, that I should triumph always and completely over the outer world; then, in my consciousness, I doubt the legitimacy of my subconscious pretention and I experience distress in face of the redoubtable Not-Self (one understands why the feeling of guilt is attached to every defeat). As long as I had a personal ideal I escaped from the subconscious obligation of succeeding always and absolutely; a personal domain was chosen to represent the whole, and my success in this chosen domain kept me immune from all negation experienced elsewhere. But here my understanding has devalorised all conscious ideal form; then there falls on my shoulders the primordial obligation of triumphing always and completely over the Not-Self. But this primordial obligation is subconscious. At the same time my judgement of myself withdraws into the shadow; my conscious observation is no longer on myself to evaluate myself; but fixed on the outer world, on the episodes of my struggle to live and to succeed, insisting on being affirmed and refusing to be denied. My 'states of mind', positive or negative, affirmed or denied, no longer depend on the form of my mechanisms (beautiful or ugly according to whether it resembles or does not resemble a particular ideal form), they depend on my psycho-somatic fluctuations, my successes or my failures in the outside world, and on my coenaesthetic states of well-being or of discomfort. According to the circumstances affecting my psycho-somatic organism I am arrogant or abashed before the Not-Self, but without consciously feeling in these attitudes a judgement of myself; I have the conscious impression that I no longer exact anything from myself, that my exigence is turned uniquely towards the outside world. Nevertheless, as we can understand, my exigence that the outside world admits is only the expression of my subterranean primordial exigence in seeking to triumph over the world. There lies the fundamental claim, the first personal manifestation of my universal Identity with the Absolute Principle, and so the first egotistical dualistic error, the 'original sin'. One can see the importance of the point that we touch on here; we are at the very root of this Ignorance from which flows all our illusory distress.

Let us analyse in detail the situation created by this primordial training. The horse desires to feel himself affirmed in his opposition to the outside world. The rider exacts from the horse that he succeed in feeling himself always affirmed. It can appear at first that horse and rider tend thus towards the same end. In reality it is quite the contrary; the nature of their respective tendencies and the orientation of these tendencies are radically opposed.

The nature of the horse's tendency is *relative*; the horse belongs to the plane of manifestation, to the relative plane of phenomena; he desires to feel himself affirmed as much as possible, not without limits, for the limitless is not in his domain. He prefers affirmation, but supports negation and adapts himself to it as best he can. Besides the desire of the horse is oriented towards the outer world; the horse desires such and such an object that belongs to the Not-Self.

The nature of the tendency of the rider is *absolute*; my identity, in the Unconscious, with Buddha-the-Absolute engenders, in my subconsciousness, not a relative desire that my Self triumph over the Not-Self but an absolute exigence that it shall do so. My rider is the representative of the Self, of the Absolute Principle of my being; however ignorant my consciousness may be in fact, my rider is none the less the representative in me of the Absolute Self; the independence of my intelligence, however incompletely manifested it may be, is none the less absolute by nature. Directly issuing from the Absolute and representing it, my rider is therefore, in the temporal plane, like a mathematical infinity which multiplies everything by an unlimited coefficient; the absolute exigence of the rider towards the horse is manifested by an unlimited claim, that is it has power to mobilise in my organism all the energies that are available at each moment. Therefore the absolute nature of the rider's tendency is radically opposed to the relative nature of the tendency of the horse.

Besides, the tendency of the rider is not oriented towards the outer world, but towards the horse. The rider does not exact such and such an object belonging to the Not-Self, he exacts that the horse shall obtain this object (one knows the familiar expression, 'it is not for the thing itself, it is for the principle'). The rider is quite indifferent to that which concerns the horse; the horse does not interest him at all for himself (this is seen at its maximum in the case of suicide; when the rider sees the horse to be definitely incapable of satisfying his exigence he condemns him to kill himself). The rider only considers the horse as an instrument capable of incarnating in a false manner, in a total phenomenal triumph of the Self over the Not-Self, the noumenal superiority of the Absolute Principle over its manifestation. Therefore the orientation of the rider's tendency is radically opposed to the orientation of the tendency of the horse; the horse strives against the outer world, against the Not-Self, while the rider strives against the horse, against the Self.

The situation created by the primordial training carries then a radical antagonism between my two parts. This is not surprising since this antagonism is one of the aspects of the dualism of Yin and Yang. But, in the equilibrium of the Tao, the two poles Yin and Yang, if they are antagonistic, are at the same time complementary. What I can deplore is that, on account of my ignorance, the antagonism of my two parts is radical, I only live the antagonism of my two poles and not their complementary character. What I live is not to be destroyed, but to be completed.

This achievement will come through understanding and can only come through that. Understanding, which has freed me from personal ideal images and has thus purified in me the radical antagonism which was making these idolatrous illusions, will go deeper in its work. The clear theoretical conception of the ideas expressed in this study will penetrate little by little my concrete inner life, my inner experience. In the degree in which I recognise theoretically my subconscious pretention of triumphing always and completely over the Not-Self, and the implied subconscious exigence of my rider towards my unfortunate horse, in this degree a new inner attitude appears with regard to the old and neutralises it little by little. This new attitude is indulgence towards the horse, acceptance that he feels himself denied; I cease to bear myself ill-will each time I fail, each time that I am unhappy or unwell. I regard my horse as a friend and no longer as a simple instrument of my limitless claims. I make it up with my brother before going into the temple, as the Gospel has it.

But this new attitude does not appear consciously; and so it must not be confused with the banal conscious self-satisfaction which is the comfortable result of personal training. It is like a base that one throws into an acid; scarcely present in the mixture, the base ceases to exist as such, and its presence is only represented by a diminution of acidity. No friendly partiality is apparent in me for my horse, but only a diminution of my unfriendly partiality against him. No absolving judgement is apparent, but only a diminution of judgement in general, which always condemns when all is said and done.

My horse works well in the degree in which I leave him alone. Zen says: 'When the cow is properly looked after she becomes pure and docile. Even without a chain and attached by nothing, she will follow you by herself.'

Chapter Nineteen

THE IMMEDIATE PRESENCE OF
SATORI

My primordial demand to be a distinct being conditions all my desires and, by my desires, my hopes and my beliefs. Bearing this claim, I am the bearer of an aspiration, of an expectation: believing myself to lack something, I await that which will be able to fulfil my need.

This general aspiration manifests itself in the fact that I await a 'true life', different from my actual life in that I shall then be totally, perfectly affirmed, no longer in a partial and imperfect manner. Every human being lives, whether he realises it or not, in the expectation that there shall begin at last the 'true life' from which all negation will have disappeared.

What this 'true life' may be each of us represents to himself differently, according to his structure and the moment. More exactly, each man represents to himself that which, according to him, might inaugurate a new era in which the imperfections of his present life would be abolished. Voices arise in me in order to tell me that it would definitely be marvellous if at last I had this . . . or if at last I were like that . . . or if such and such a thing were to happen. Sometimes I think I see very clearly what could inaugurate the 'true life'; sometimes it remains vague, I merely await 'something' which, I am persuaded, would settle everything. Sometimes this expectation remains dumb in me, but it is only a passing drowsiness from which there will arise again very soon my aspiration for a life at last perfectly satisfying. Everything happens in me as if I believed myself exiled from a paradise which exists somewhere and as if I saw, in such and such a modification of the outside world or of myself, the key capable of opening the door of this lost paradise. And I live in the quest of this key.

While waiting I kill time as I may. One part of my vital energy can devote itself to the effective preparation of the key: I struggle to achieve this or that success, material or subtle. But I can only put into that one part of my energy; the rest I devote to an imaginative elaboration, to reveries concerning the famous inner trial the successful issue of which should be obtained for me by the key. I feel myself obliged to invest my energy somewhere, to fidget, externally or internally. I cannot remain motionless in my expectation. Besides, without movement, there could not be expectation, tension towards that which should come, aspiration; and without this aspiring movement I would be dead. In the measure in which I cannot fidget externally in order to obtain the expected key I fidget internally by fabricating images which relieve my expectation.

Like everything that I can observe in my natural structure, this expectation is sound in itself but wrongly directed. It is sound in itself because it manifests my deep need of this vision-of-things-as-they-are which will usher in for me a *true* life. But it is wrongly directed because my aspiration is turned towards things as I see them in actuality. As long as my understanding has not been awakened by correct instruction I necessarily let my aspiration direct itself towards what I know, towards what I can picture to myself, to the dualistic world of phenomena. Searching for the key of the lost paradise in what I can picture to myself, it is inevitable that I picture this key either as something already experienced by me (at least partially), or as something not yet exactly experienced but of the same general nature as what I know. Even when I do not see the key clearly, formally, I picture to myself my return to the lost paradise as an inner state that is perfectly positive, perfectly happy, analogous to, but better than, the happy states I have already experienced. The 'natural' orientation of my aspiration is necessarily situated on the horizontal plane of temporal dualism; it does not tend towards anything new, outside this dualism, but towards an amelioration of that which I know.

There is therein a manifest error. In effect I expect thus, from an amelioration, something that is perfect; but no amelioration of something imperfect, however unlimited one may suppose this amelioration, could succeed in reaching perfection. No 'evolution', no 'progress', can reach that which Zen calls 'the asylum of rest'.

Let us note, besides, that my aspiration, turned towards the dualism of satisfaction and unsatisfaction, joy and sorrow, has no right to hope for the dissociation of this inseparable dualism which can only be conciliated in the Tao. Aspiration, turned towards this dualism, can only bring about the dualism itself, with its two poles. The stronger my aspiration thus directed, the stronger becomes my own inner dualism, whether I am conscious of it or not. When my thirst is thus directed the water which comes to me is like salt water which increases my thirst after a moment of apparent quenching. The man who expects the true life from the world of manifestation, from the world which he knows, waits for it in vain until his death.

What is correct in my aspiration itself is revealed in the following manner. In expecting something other than my life of the moment, I escape complete identification with this life, I save my consciousness from being completely swallowed up in the forms that are actually present. But at the same time, on account of the false orientation of my aspiration, I founder in another identification; I identify myself with something that I imagine, more or less clearly, as being absolutely desirable; and this thing, since I imagine it, also has a form (however subtle one may suppose it) in which my consciousness loses itself. If my dream concerning the paradise to be regained saves what I have at my disposal among the circumstances momentarily lived, it abdicates this precious power of disposal in the process of imagining a chimerical phenomenal perfection.

This false direction of my aspiration creates for me the illusion of *time* and the painful impression that time is unceasingly escaping me. When I conceive that to which I aspire as an amelioration of what I know (which is phenomenon, conditioned by space-time), I necessarily project my perfect satisfaction into the future. Thus there is created for me the illusory absolute reality of time, time which seems to me to stretch out between the present imperfect moment and the future perfect moment to which I aspire.

In face of this time illusorily endowed with an absolute value, my attitude is ambivalent. When I look back I bitterly deplore the passage of time, I would like to make it come back or at least prevent it from flowing on further; when I look ahead I would like to see it flow on with infinite rapidity, because I am impatient for the opening up of the lost paradise. When I evoke some epoch of my past life I feel it quite differently from the way in which I felt it when it happened: in fact, when I evoke it, I am freed from this vertiginous aspiration towards a better future which was then possessing me, snatching me from the moment itself and preventing me from living it. Thus is explained in me my regret for a passage of time which, however, I did not appreciate.

In the degree in which my understanding awakens as a result of correct instruction, a change takes place in me. I understand that my primordial unlimited aspiration has nothing to expect from the phenomenal world, however universally and subtly one may envisage this. I understand that what I have always been waiting for, while incarnating it in an illusory manner in one kind of representation or another, is that which Zen calls *satori*. I understand that this satori could not be conceived as an amelioration, however fantastic one may suppose it, of that which I know actually; there could not be dissociation of an inseparable dualism, progressive purification of a 'good' cleansed of all 'evil'; rather is it access, beyond dualism, to 'something' which conciliates the dualism in a trinitarian Unity. This 'something' I cannot evidently picture to myself, I can only conceive it as indescribable, un-imaginable, entirely different by its very nature from anything I know to-day.

My understanding, if it is really exact, does not result in a new conscious expectation oriented towards something unimaginable; for there cannot be operation of our consciousness without imagination, and the imagination of something unimaginable is another image. Exact understanding does not result, then, in a new conscious expectation different from the last. The new expectation is not born in the surface consciousness, but in the depths of the psyche in which it balances and neutralises the old expectation oriented towards the imaginable. Correct understanding brings to birth and nourishes, in the depths of me, an aspiration antagon-istic and complementary to my natural aspiration; as though a demand no longer to expect any restrictive affirmation of myself-as-a-distinct-being were born in face of the natural demand for this affirmation. That which is thus born is as insufficient by itself as that which was before; but a moment will come when these two poles, insufficient by themselves, will be in equilibrium in the

'Great Doubt' of which Zen speaks and in which this state of equilibrium will allow us to experience satori. It is just as though we came into the world with only one eye open and we were obliged to work in order completely to open the second—so that we may obtain at last 'the opening of the third eye'.

If this new expectation, born of understanding, resides in our subconscious only, wherein lies the natural expectation from which aspirations spring, we are not forbidden (nothing, for the matter of that, being forbidden to us) to make a conscious mental effort to try to conceive this new expectation. (It should be well understood that we are not advising this mental effort as a systematic method in view of realisation.)

This new expectation, or expectation of satori, is an aspiration oriented towards 'something' unimaginable, radically new, not resembling anything that I know. When I try to put myself into this state of expectation, my mind comes up against various kinds of imaginable perception which offer themselves to it and which it turns down. The rejected perceptions, as aspects of the outer world or inner states, being situated outside me or within me, their disappearance leaves my expectation between these two situations. My expectation is neither outside me nor within me, nor attached to an object eventually perceived, nor to an I-subject eventually perceiving: it is focussed on the perception itself which joins subject and object. But this perception is itself imperceptible to me, like a point without dimension or situation. There is then virtual liberation from space, which is accompanied, as we shall see, by a similar liberation from time. In my old expectation I awaited something which was not given me at the time but which nevertheless existed for me in the world of possibilities. In my new expectation I await something which does not exist at all for me since it is unimaginable. This something which is outside my possibilities, I can no more imagine in the future than I can evoke in the past; it is outside time as it is outside space (which is not surprising since space and time are two aspects of the same system). When I await this consciousness that is entirely new and unimaginable, of the world, of myself, of their relationship, I await something which, existing neither in space nor in time, is at the centre of my expectation and at the very moment of this expectation, at the point which engenders the whole Universe and in the eternity of the instant, *hic et nunc*. Besides, my expectation ceases to be an expectation since that which I await is separated from me neither by space nor by time. I understand then the mistake that I made when I pictured to myself the state of satori as a future state; my effective becoming-conscious of the state of satori can be seen as a future eventuality, but not the state of satori itself which is from the present moment my state, has always been my state, and is my eternal 'being'. And as for this becoming-conscious of the state of satori, I ought not to believe that it will be offered to me in the future; it is offered to me from this moment, at every moment. Only my acceptation can be regarded as situated in time, in a negative manner, that is to say that I can say at each moment that I have not yet accepted satori, but without rejecting the possibility that I may accept it the next moment. I am comparable with a man in a room, where the door is wide open whereas the window is protected by bars; since my birth I have been fascinated by the outside world and have been clutching the bars of the window; and my keenness for the images outside makes my two hands violently contract. In a sense I am not free since this contraction prevents me from going out of the room. But in reality nothing else shuts me in but this ignorance which makes me take the imaginative vision of life for life itself; nothing shuts me in but the crispation of my own hands. I am free; I always have been; I will realise it as soon as I 'let go'.

It is interesting to compare with these thoughts resulting from Zen the parable of the ten virgins in the gospel. Five of them, the foolish virgins, did not supply themselves with oil; the wise virgins supplied themselves with it; and all slept until the coming of the bridegroom. The sleep of the virgins symbolises the identification of my egotistical life with all the dreams of my hopes and of my fears. The oil symbolises the expectation of the unimaginable, of satori. As long as I have not this oil in me, this new expectation born of understanding, I am the foolish virgin who cannot receive the bridegroom. And, at the end of the parable, the bridegroom says: 'watch, for ye know neither the day nor the hour'; it can be at each moment, it is offered at each moment.

A Zen anecdote illustrates this conception of the *pure expectation* (pure from time and from space), which is *pure attention*, attention without an object:

'A man of the people one day asks the bonze Ikkyou: "Bonze, will you write for me some maxims of high wisdom?"

'Ikkyou took up a brush and wrote the word "Attention".

' "Is that all?" said the man, "won't you add a few more words?"

'Ikkyou then wrote twice: "Attention. Attention."

' "All the same," said the disappointed man, "I don't see much depth or subtlety in what you have written there."

' Ikkyou then wrote the same word three times.

'Slightly irritated, the man said: "After all, what does this word 'Attention' mean?"

'And Ikkyou replied: "Attention means attention." '

Chapter Twenty

PASSIVITY OF THE MIND AND DISINTEGRATION OF OUR ENERGY

WE wish in this study to carry our reflections deeper on the subject of satori and on the inner phenomena which precede it. It is necessary first of all to establish a clear distinction between the intemporal satori-state and the historic satori-occurrence. We have already shown that the state of satori should not be conceived as a new state to which we have to obtain access, but as our eternal state, independent of our birth and of our death. Each one of us lives in the state of satori and could not live otherwise. When Zen speaks of satori within time, when it says for example: 'Satori falls upon us unexpectedly when we have exhausted all the resources of our being', it is not speaking of the intemporal state of satori but of the instant at which we realise that we are in this state, or, more exactly, of the instant at which we cease to believe that we are living outside this state.

This distinction between the satori-state and the satori-occurrence is very important. If I only conceive the satori-state I fall into fatalism. If I only conceive the satori-occurrence I fall into spiritual ambition, into the greedy demand for Realisation, and this error enchains me firmly to the illusion on which all my distress is founded.

The satori-occurrence is an event that is very special in that it ceases to be seen as such as soon as it happens. The man of satori no longer believes that he lives exiled from the Intemporal; living in the Intemporal and knowing it, he no longer makes any distinction between a past in which he believed himself to be living outside satori and a present in which he knows that he is living in it. This does not mean that this man has lost the memory of the

177

time lived before the satori-occurrence; he can remember every-thing, his distress, his weaknesses, the inner phenomena which obliged him to act against his reason; *but he sees that all that was already the state of satori*, that nothing has been, is, nor will be out-side the state of satori. Past, present, and future bathing for this man in the same state of satori, it is evident that the satori-occur-rence ceases to exist for him as a particular historical date. The satori-occurrence only exists for us to whom this event has not yet happened, it only exists in our illusory actual perspective. For us the man of satori is a *liberated* man, but he does not see himself as liberated, he sees himself as *free*, free from all eternity. Thus is explained what Hui-neng says 'I had satori at the instant at which I understood such and such an idea', and that he can also say, 'There is no liberation, there is no realisation'.

The state of satori, an intemporal state, is evidently uncon-ditioned; in particular it is not conditioned by the satori-occurrence. But our actual perspective only allows us to envisage the satori-occurrence, and we necessarily envisage it as conditioned by such and such inner processes concerning which we question ourselves.

This conditioning of the satori-occurrence demands first of all certain precisions of a general nature. The idea of conditioning ought not to be understood as causality here least of all; no event is caused by a previous event, but is conditioned by it according to the Buddhist formula. 'This being so, that happens.' We will not, therefore, seek to know what inner processes are capable of causing or of engendering the satori-occurrence, but what processes neces-sarily precede it.

Besides we shall see that this conditioning, even freed thus from all idea of causality, is a notion of most inexact approximation. Indeed the very special functioning of the attention to which satori succeeds is not, properly speaking, a process but brings about the abolition of a process inherent in our actual condition. In reality it is my non-perception of the state of satori which is conditioned by certain processes; and the 'conditioning' of satori is only negative, is only the cessation of the conditioning of my non-perception of the state of satori.

All our study will then be devoted to analysing the inner pro-cesses which now condition our illusion of not living in the state of satori. We will see that they are our imaginative-emotive processes—in which our vital energy is disintegrated—and we will try to define clearly what incomplete functioning of our attention conditions in its turn these imaginative-emotive processes.

To that end let us start with a concrete observation. A man annoys me; I become angry and I want to hit my adversary. Let us analyse what takes place in me in the course of this scene. We will see that my inner phenomena are divided into two different reactions that we will call primary reaction and secondary reaction.

The primary reaction consists in the awakening, in me, of a certain amount of vital energy; this energy was lying, latent, in my central source of energy until it was awakened by my perception of an energy manifested in the Not-Self against Self. The foreign aggressive energy stirs up in me the manifestation of a reactive force which balances the force of the Not-Self. This reactive force is not yet a movement of anger, it has not yet a precise form; it is comparable with the substance which is going to be poured into a mould but which has not yet been released. During an instant, without duration, this budding force, mobilised at my source, is not yet a force of anger; it is an informal force, a pure vital force.

This primary reaction corresponds to a certain perception of the outer world, to a certain knowledge. It corresponds therefore to a certain consciousness, but quite different from what is habitually so called. It is not the mental consciousness, intellectual, clear, evident. It is an obscure consciousness, profound, reflex, organic. It is the same consciousness which presides over the release of the knee-cap reflex; every reflex corresponds to this organic consciousness which 'knows' the outside world in a non-intellectual manner. Besides, this is corroborated by an inward observation: I feel anger *going to my head* where it will proceed to build up a thousand images; I feel it rising from below, from my organic existence. This primary reaction is extremely rapid and it escapes my observation if I am not very attentive, but if, after my anger, I examine in detail what has happened in me, I realise that, during a short moment, a pure anonymous organic force, coming from an organic consciousness, has preceded the play of my intellectual consciousness, formulator of images of anger.

Let us note that my organic consciousness releases my energy-reaction against the Not-Self when it perceives it. That is, the play of this consciousness implies the acceptance of the existence of the Not-Self in face of the Self: it is in accord with the cosmic order, with things as they are. It presides over exchanges of energy between Self and Not-Self, it conciliates these two poles; it is in accord with the Tao.

Let us now study the secondary reaction. The dynamic modification of my being constituted by the primary reaction, this mobilisation of my energy in response to the energy of the outside world, will release a second reaction. Just as the movement of the outside world released the reactive play of my organic consciousness, this play in its turn—the inner movement which manifests this play—will release the reactive play of my intellectual consciousness; and this secondary reaction will tend to re-establish in me the original immobility by disintegrating the mobilised energy. Why? Because, in contradiction to my organic consciousness, my intellectual consciousness does not accept the existence of the Not-Self. Let us recall what we have called our primordial demand, or divine fiction, or claim to be-absolutely-as-a-distinct-being, to exist-absolutely. At the bottom of our intellectual understanding of the Universe, there is the irreducible discrimination between Self and Not-Self, there is an assumption that 'I *am* and that, in consequence, the Not-Self is not'. It is this discrimination that one evokes when one speaks of the Ego, when one speaks of identification with our psycho-somatic organism. In so far as I am an organic consciousness I do not discriminate, but, in so far as I am an intellectual consciousness, I discriminate. In my organic consciousness I am as much identified with the Not-Self as with the Self; in my intellectual consciousness I am identified with the Self, I affirm that only my Self exists. My intellectual consciousness only knows Self. When I think that I have an intellectual knowledge of the outside world, I only have knowledge in reality of the modifications of my Self in contact with the outside world. Philosophers call that 'the prison of my subjectivity', disregarding my organic consciousness which does not discriminate between subject and object and thanks to which I am already virtually free.

My intellectual consciousness being what it is, let us see what results in my inner phenomena. In the course of the primary reaction my organic desire to exist was thwarted by the outside world; from which there was born in me a force that balanced the exterior force. In the course of the secondary reaction, my intellectual need to 'be' is thwarted by this mobilisation of energy in me, for this mobilisation implies the acceptance of the outside world and so tears me from the immutability of the Principle. Everything happens as though, in so far as my intellectual consciousness operates, I were claiming, for the source of energy of my organism, the attributes of the Absolute Principle: immutability, non-action, permanence, an unconditioned state. My secondary reaction to the mobilisation of my energy can only be, therefore, a refusal opposed to this mobilisation. But this opposition to the cosmic order could not succeed; the force which is mobilised in me could not return to non-manifestation. My refusal of the mobilised energy cannot result, therefore, in anything but the destruction of this energy by its disintegration.

The law of equilibrium of the Tao comes into play in these two reactions. The primary reaction balances the force of the Not-Self by a force of the Self. The secondary reaction balances the mobilisation of my vital energy by the disintegration of this energy. The primary reaction aims at maintaining the equilibrium between Self and Not-Self; the secondary reaction aims at maintaining the equilibrium in the interior of the Self, between the constructive manifestation and the destructive manifestation, between Vishnu and Shiva.

The disintegration of the energy mobilised is realised by the imaginative-emotive processes. These, as we have said elsewhere, are veritable short-circuits during which the energy is consumed in producing organic phenomena and mental images. These mental formations are what Buddhist philosophy calls *samskaras.* The samskaras have substance and form; their unique substance is my vital energy in process of disintegration. Their form, on the contrary is not mine, it is foreign to my form, to the form of my organism, and consists of mental images of infinite variation. On account of these foreign forms the samskaras are comparable with foreign bodies that my organism ought to reject. They are formations in some degree monstrous, heterogeneous, lacking in inner architectural harmony, non-visible: and this is by no means astonishing since they manifest the disintegration of energy.

The appearance of these images in my mind starts a vicious

circle. They excite, in fact, my organic consciousness, as did a moment ago the images perceived in the outside world, and thus release a new primary reaction that mobilises my energy. And this new mobilised energy is disintegrated in its turn. Thus there is born a prolonged imaginative-emotive rumination which only exhausts itself progressively, as a pendulum set going only comes to a standstill after a certain number of oscillations.

On the other hand my imaginative-emotive rumination is kept going by the renewed perception of the outside world, of the man who is annoying me. Thus is explained the tendency that I feel to hit this man. My secondary reaction, which tends to wipe out my mobilised energy, wishes to neutralise, owing to the image of myself injuring my enemy, the inverse image which releases the mobilisation of my energy. This aggressive exterior reaction would not occur if the disintegration of energy did not give birth to images which establish the vicious circle of which we have spoken. In this case the secondary reaction would be entirely occupied internally by a process of satisfying disintegration. It is because the process of disintegration is not satisfying (since it releases by itself fresh quantities of energy to be disintegrated) that the secondary reaction overflows the inner domain and pushes me to wipe out also the external object which denies me. But my aggressive tendency towards the external object is accessory, and the fundamental process which aims at disintegrating my mobilised energy is the imaginative-emotive process. This assertion ·may appear paradoxical; let us observe, however, that the external gestures of anger can be contained, suppressed, whereas there could not be anger without the corresponding imaginative-emotive processes. Sometimes I will not touch my enemy but I will break the first vase that comes to my hand, and by this representation of Self injuring the Not-Self I neutralise the representation of the Not-Self injuring the Self. Little does it matter after all that my external enemy is not touched; *the real aim of my secondary reaction is not without, it is in me; in reality what this reaction aims at wiping out is my energy mobilised outside my source.* We need not be astonished since we know that we have no really objective perception of particular objects; the particular exterior object does not exist for me in itself and I am never really concerned with it. Even in the course of the primary reaction I am not concerned with this particular external object; the force which is mobilised in me is certainly reactive to the outside world, but this force is still informal, anonymous, it is a pure vital force. This force animates me in contact with the world, but if it comprises an objective knowledge of the Universe in its generality it comprises none of the particular external object.

If, in the course of the scene that we have imagined, a third person says to me: 'Why be angry?' my anger redoubles. That is because this remark increases my mental perception of the mobilisation of my energy; and my secondary reaction increases with the perception that releases it. This proves once again that my secondary reaction is uniquely directed against the internal mobilisation of my energy and not against my external enemy; for the allusion that has been made to me does not concern my enemy and in no way affects the excitation which comes to me from him.

What we have just seen in connexion with anger is equally true for all our contacts with the outside world. It matters little from this point of view whether the contact be negative or positive. If the outside force is positive, bringing an affirmation of Self, a primary reaction replies to it which again entails the mobilisation of a certain amount of pure energy; then the secondary reaction comes into play, aiming at the disintegration of this mobilised energy in an imaginative-emotive rumination whose images and emotions this time are positive, agreeable.

It matters little also whether the contact with the outside world reaches me by the psychic or the somatic medium. In our example of anger it was the psychic medium that was in question; but the mobilisation of my energy follows as regularly from contacts which affect my centre via the somatic medium. A toothache is a negation of the Self by the Not-Self. The disappearance of this pain is an affirmation of the Self. Both the one and the other are accompanied by a mobilisation of my central energy and by disintegration of this energy in imaginative-emotive processes pleasant or unpleasant.

The process of the double reaction is altogether general; it presides at all our vital metabolism, the primary reaction representing anabolism and the secondary reaction catabolism. The primary reaction corresponds to the reflex, it is centrifugal. The secondary reaction corresponds to *reflection* (not in the ordinary sense that one gives to this word), it is centripetal. This secondary reaction is directed against an internal phenomenon in myself, and the energy-wave is there reflected towards my centre. Physiologically one can relate the primary reaction to the functioning of the central grey-matter of the brain, the secondary reaction to the functioning of the cerebral cortex. Certain recent surgical operations, by destroying a part of the connexions which exist between these two centres of the brain, greatly reduce the secondary reaction, emotivity, imagination, and the distress which depends thereon. Let us note also that the primary reaction corresponds to the life-instinct of Freud, the secondary reaction to his death-instinct. The mobilisation of my energy is in fact life; and the need to disintegrate this mobilised energy represents a resistance to life, a refusal of life, and so a tendency towards death. If, leaving aside the distinction of Freud, we envisage the distinction that we have established between 'existing' and 'living'—'existing' that man despises and 'living' that he esteems—we see that the primary reaction corresponds to 'existing' and that the secondary reaction corresponds to 'living'. The natural man particularly esteems as 'living' the processes by which his vital energy is disintegrated; he does not attribute value to his vital energy itself but he accords a unique value to the sparks that produce the disintegration of this energy.

To the two reactions correspond, as we have said, two different consciousnesses, to the primary reaction my organic consciousness, to the secondary my mental, or intellectual, or imaginative consciousness (that which one means habitually when one says 'my consciousness' without further precision). My imaginative consciousness is dualistic, the imaginative-emotive processes which take place therein being affirming or denying, pleasant or unpleasant. My organic consciousness, on the contrary, is not dualistic since the vital force which wells up in it is informal, anonymous, always the same, independent of the dualistic forms which it will animate thereafter. This organic consciousness plays, then, with regard to the imaginative consciousness, the rôle of an hypostasis, of a conciliating principle. We have seen, on the other hand, that the organic consciousness does not discriminate between the Self and the Not-Self, that its play implies an essential identity between these two poles and in consequence a really objective knowledge of the Universe in general, in its unity. These characteristics, added to its profound, abysmal situation lead us to conceive this organic consciousness as the first personal manifestation of the original impersonal Unconscious. To the play of this consciousness is linked our possibility of perceiving one day that our actual state is already the state of satori. To the recognition of this consciousness in us is linked our Faith that the state of satori is from the present moment our state.

In short, my organic consciousness alone knows the Universe; its action is released by the Universe and it reacts by the mobilisation of my energy. My mental consciousness only knows my personal inner world, my mobilisations of energy; its action is released by my inner dynamic modifications and it reacts by imaginative-emotive processes, by *samskaras*. Contrary to what one might expect, the notion of organic consciousness is easy, satisfying, whereas what I habitually call simply 'my consciousness' is difficult to conceive, and consequently to name. I have called it intellectual, psychological, mental, imaginative, but none of these words is satisfying. The continuation of this study will enable us to understand the reason. It will show us that this consciousness presiding over the secondary reaction is not strictly speaking a consciousness; it is a simple resistance to the action of the organic consciousness (which is the unique real personal consciousness), it is the manner in which the incomplete functioning of the organic consciousness manifests itself. The incomplete character of the functioning of the organic consciousness is comparable with a spanner in the works of my machine. My 'mental' pseudo-consciousness is that to which Zen alludes when it says that satori is 'withdrawing the spoke'. This pretended consciousness designates the ensemble of inner phenomena by which is revealed the fact that my organic consciousness, before satori, is not fully operating as No-Mind.

These observations, so contrary to the notions habitually accepted, help me to understand better the curious machine that I am. If I envisage in an impersonal, universal manner the processes that I have described, I see that all is perfect, perfectly balanced. Each of the two reactions establishes an exact equilibrium, even if the balancing of the secondary reaction can imply terrible distress and result in suicide. Besides, the two reactions balance one another exactly. My energy, after its mobilisation, is disintegrated, completing a perfect spiral turn in the course of which I am linked to the Not-Self by an interaction of energy, thus participating in cosmic creation with its two aspects, constructive and destructive.

But these processes appear to me, on the contrary, imperfect if I envisage them in a personal manner, that is from the point of view of my subjective affectivity. In the course of its journey between Self to Not-Self, the energy ceases for a time to be pure, informal; between the moment at which it wells up in my source and the moment at which it is restituted to the outside world after disintegration, it takes on mental forms that are foreign to my form, and these foreign bodies, rough, wounding, make me suffer in the course of their expulsion; I experience these samskaras, these complexes, these coagula, as a negation of my 'being'. These monstrous forms, participating at once in the Self (since it is my force which animates them) and in the Not-Self (since their elements come from the outside world) represent, for my subjectivity, a fusion of the two poles Self and Not-Self which seems to contradict and deny the trinitarian unity. From which there comes an apparent Nullity contradicting the Being.

My inner processes are then imperfect for me, for my affectivity; and I seek a means of no longer suffering. I ask myself where lies the pain. I see it in the imaginations-emotions, the *samskaras*. I then seek a means of eliminating them, a means of allowing my energy to pass from my source into the outside world without hurting me, and to that end I wish to understand more exactly what conditions the formation of the samskaras. I have already understood that it is the fact of identifying myself only with my organism and not with the rest of Manifestation. But that is not enough; it is necessary that I discover by what intimate process is revealed this identification with my organism which results in the formation of the samskaras.

This intimate process is the passive mode according to which my attention functions. It is because my attention is passive that it is alerted by a mobilisation of energy already produced, at a late stage at which there is no longer anything else to be done but to disintegrate this energy. My attention is not, actually, in a state of autonomous, unconditioned vigilance; it is only awakened by mobilisations of energy which are produced in my organism, and its awakening is conditioned by these mobilisations. Thus I am always faced with a *fait accompli*. As soon as the moment-without-duration is passed in which my energy wells up, still informal, from non-manifestation, this energy is as though snapped up by the formal world; the chance has been missed of storing it up, informal, with a view to the future explosion of satori. The disintegration into imaginative-emotive forms is inevitable. My energy is now in the domain in which my egotistical identification reigns, and it bumps up against this wall in disintegrating itself. Everything happens as though, finding myself faced with my mobilised energy, I were afraid to keep it. In my exclusive identification with my organism I implicitly consider this as 'being', permanent, immutable, invariable. The mobilisation of my energy, on the contrary, shows me my organism as moving, impermanent, limited. I therefore refuse the mobilised energy which this intolerable vision proposes to me; for my exclusive identification with my organism acts in such a way that, paradoxically, I refuse to be this limited organism (Saint Paul: 'Who will deliver me from this body of death?'). I claim not to feel this organism. (Note that, in psychic and medicinal extasies, the body seems to lose its density.) The mobilised energy which fills my organism, which gives it substance, I hasten to disintegrate.

The disintegrating processes are then inevitable when my attention, functioning in the passive mode, is alerted by my already mobilised energy. These processes should on no account be considered as 'bad', as something 'that should not be'. They do not reveal a 'bad' condition of my manifested being, but only an imperfect condition, incomplete, unfinished. Thus it is in my identification with my organism on which these processes depend; and this identification is not mistaken, but is merely incomplete in that it excludes my equal identification with the rest of the Universe. The egotistical illusion does not consist in my identification with my organism but in the exclusive manner in which this identification is realised. The explosion of satori will not destroy my identification with my organism—what is already realised in my egotistical condition—it will destroy the sleep which now affects my identification with the rest of the Universe, what sleeps in me to-day beyond the illusory limits of the Ego.

Then my identification with the totality of Manifestation will awaken.

These ideas are necessary in order to understand the correct doctrine and to avoid adhering to vain 'methods' of realisation. As long as I considered as 'bad' my imaginative-emotive processes and the exclusive identification with the Self, I was necessarily led to struggle against the Ego, and so against my egotistical condition, and so against my own machine concerned in this condition; from which resulted a perpetual inner disharmony. As soon as I understand, on the contrary, that my condition identified with the Self is not 'bad' but merely incomplete, I understand ar the same moment that I must live fully this stage of development in order to pass beyond it. My present misfortune is not that I am living this stage but that I am not living it to the full integrally.

Let us see how all this is applicable in a concrete manner to the object of our study. When I see the wastage of energy that takes place in my imaginative-emotive processes I am tempted to suppress these; and since these processes are linked with the refusal of my mental consciousness to accept the mobilisation of my energy I am tempted to make an effort not to refuse this mobilisation. But such efforts do not upset my inner situation, they merely complicate it; for these efforts to stop refusing are in fact the refusal of a refusal, and this contraction opposed to a spasm could not result in a relaxation. Inversely to what is true in algebra, this 'no' said to a 'no' does not result in a 'yes'. The suppression of the refusal of the mobilisation of my energy is therefore impossible. Besides, this suppression is undesirable since, as we have seen, this refusal forms part of a process which is not 'bad' but merely unfinished.

What is regrettable is not that I refuse the mobilisation of my energy, but that I refuse it incompletely, too late, and in consequence ineffectively. My present refusal is not a true and effective refusal but a vain protestation in face of a *fait accompli*; and that because it *succeeds* the inner phenomenon that I refuse. My mental consciousness functions actually in a reactive and not an active manner, its action does not balance the action of the organic consciousness for it merely replies to the manifestations of that consciousness.

My mental consciousness is not made, in reality, to operate in this reactive manner, which is female, but in an active manner, which is male. The organic consciousness, on the other hand, is female; she is made to react to the excitations of the outside world (primary reaction). But the mental consciousness is not made to react against this primary reaction by a secondary reaction. My refusal of mobilisation of my energy ought not to succeed this mobilisation, but should be effected in the very instant at which my energy comes out of non-manifestation. The action of my mental consciousness, male, should directly balance the action of my organic consciousness, female, and not its consequences in energy. Only then will occur the conciliation between the two antagonistic and complementary consciousnesses; and this conciliation will be revealed by the fact that the energy will be mobilised without being seized by the formal domain. When the refusal of mobilisation of energy, entirely accomplished, is re-placed at the very instant at which this mobilisation occurs, it does not suppress this mobilisation (which would be death), but it exactly balances the organic will which produces it, and this equilibrium results in the production of an energy which remains informal, which escapes the imaginative-emotive disintegration, and which is accumulated right up to the explosion of satori. When my refusal of the mobilisation of my energy ceases to be passive in order to become active it remains a refusal in the sense that it effectively opposes the leakage of my energy in formal disintegration, but at the same time it ceases to be refusal in the sense that it does not prevent the actualisation of the informal non-manifested energy.

But of what in fact does this transformation consist? Is it a transformation of the reactive-female functioning of the attention into active-male functioning? We have said that my attention comes into play too late with regard to the mobilisation of my energy. Must one then wish that it succeed in coming into play sooner, in reacting more quickly? No; however rapid might be the reaction, it is always late because it is reaction and not action. Besides, the expression 'too late' should not be understood here in the usual sense. Between the primary reaction and the secondary reaction that we have described, no time passes, no duration, no matter how brief one may imagine it. Our expression 'too late' does not indicate a second or even a minute fraction of a second, but the fact that the reaction of the mental consciousness, even though immediate, is belated *because it is reaction whereas it ought to be an action.* My attention ought not to be awakened by the mobil-isation of my energy, but before that; and this is realised when, instead of seeing the imaginative-emotive processes which are being produced, I regard the processes which are about to be pro-duced. This is realised when, instead of being passively attentive to my mobilised energy and to its disintegrating future, I tend actively to perceive the very birth of my energy. A new vigilance now superintends the mobilisation of energy. To put it more simply, an active attention lies in wait for the advent of my inner movements. It is no longer my emotions which interest me, but their coming to birth; it is no longer their movement that interests me, but this other informal movement which is the birth of their formal movement.

This active functioning of my attention, so contrary to my auto-matic nature, cannot be in any degree the object of a direct effort, of an explicit 'discipline' effected in view of Realisation. We will develop later this important idea; we merely wish to point it out now in order to forewarn the reader against the tenacious and illusory search for 'recipes' for realisation.

First we wish to show that our attention, when it functions in the active mode, is pure attention, without manifested object. My mobilised energy is not perceptible in itself, but only in the effects of its disintegration, the images. But this disintegration only occurs when my attention operates in the passive mode; active attention forestalls this disintegration. And so, when my attention operates in the active mode there is nothing to perceive. Energy is mobil-ised nevertheless; the female organic consciousness continues its work; but the energy remains informal, un-disintegrated, non-manifested. Thus is realised the advice of Zen: 'Awaken the mind without fixing it upon anything;' we can even understand that, if the mind is awakened in itself instead of being awakened by the organic energy-reactions, there is not necessarily anything on which it can fix itself. This phrase of Zen could therefore be modified thus: 'Awaken the mind in itself, and it will not then be fixed on anything.'

It is easy for me to verify concretely that active attention to my inner world is without an object. If I take up, in face of my inner monologue, the attitude of an active auditor who authorises this monologue to say whatever it wishes and however it wishes, if I take up the attitude which can be defined by the formula 'Speak, I am listening', I observe that my monologue stops. It does not start up again until my attitude of vigilant expectation ceases.

This suppression of the imaginative film will perhaps be feared by some as a suppression of 'life'. In reality the imaginative film is not life. Produced by the disintegration of my energy, which on the contrary ought to be stored up for the birth in the future of the 'new man' in satori, the imaginative film is in reality an abortive process; the birth of that which I call my inner world is in reality the repeated miscarriage of the 'new man'. The suppression of this abortive process is not therefore contrary to my veritable life and growth. To watch the birth of the pretended 'living' in myself and to suspend thereby this 'living' is to prepare the blooming of the consciousness of 'existing', or perfect existential felicity.

We have spoken of feminine functioning and of masculine functioning of the mental consciousness, clearly separating these two modes. But let us see now that these two ways of functioning really coexist in us.

It would be altogether illusory to try by direct effort, by exercises of active attention, to set ourselves expressly to supervise the birth of emotions; efforts whose success would result in the perception of nothing whatever. We are at present attached to our imaginative film, *which is even our primordial attachment*, and death terrifies us because we see in it the cessation of our precious 'consciousness'—and such exercises would aim at directly destroying this attachment. The complete 'virilisation' of our attention realises total detachment in satori, the bursting of the limitations of the Ego. To make direct efforts towards this total virilisation would therefore be a direct striving to catch, to acquire at last total detachment; and this attempt comprises an evident inner contradiction which condemns it to failure.

As we have said on several occasions, there are no recipes for Realisation. The processes which condition the satori-occurrence, or more exactly the suppression of the processes which condition our ignorance of our intemporal state of satori, are uniquely a matter of *comprehension* (what the Tibetans call 'the penetrating vision'). Comprehension acts by devalorising images for me, not such and such images and then such and such others but the imaginative-emotive process as a whole and in general. For many years my credulity has been great as regards my inner cinema; I 'played up' as one might say; I believed in it; I believed in the so-called reality of what my disintegration-process showed me. According as my intellectual work and my understanding advance my credulity diminishes, I fall less and less into the trap, I believe less and less that it is what matters for me. In this degree is reduced the fascination that my images exercised on my attention maintaining it in a passive mode of functioning. And my attention, in the measure in which it detaches itself from my imaginative world, returns spontaneously, following its normal orientation, towards the source of my being, towards the informal energy which is the reality of my life (and no longer towards the formal images which represent the continual miscarriage of my life). This movement of conversion is unconscious, since my attention is without an object in the measure in which it operates in the active mode. All that I observe in myself is a progressive diminution of the apparent reality of my inner imaginative world (the evolution towards the satori-occurrence is, as we have said elsewhere, an apparent descent, an apparent involution).

We find again here an idea that we have already expressed above, the idea that the 'reflexive' consciousness, psychological, intellectual, mental, is not a consciousness properly speaking, and that the organic consciousness alone is real in us. When the attention functions in the active mode it is without an object, unconscious, and its mental manifestation is abolished; then what I called my mental consciousness disappears, and the male mental principle which was behind it (the *Buddhi*) is linked to the female mental principle of my organic consciousness, in the trinitarian unity of No-Mind or Fundamental Unconscious.

The accounts of the Zen masters who have had satori make it possible for us to picture to ourselves the ultimate stage of this evolution. A moment arrives at which the male functioning of the mind equals in importance its female functioning; there is as much incredulous lucidity as credulous blindness. It is the 'Great Doubt'. The organic consciousness can be compared with a first eye (which is open from our birth); the mental consciousness is a second eye; the female functioning of this consciousness (consciousness which in its essence is male) will be represented in our illus-

tration by a spasm which closes this second eye. In proportion as
the male functioning of this consciousness balances its female
functioning a relaxation of the eyelid counteracts its spasm. At the
moment of the 'Great Doubt' this equilibrium is exactly realised.
An instant later and the 'Great Doubt' is annihilated; the second
eye opens; and the conjoined vision of the two eyes, vision that is
entirely new and giving access to an unknown depth, to a new
dimension, is what is called the 'opening of the third eye'. The
interest of this illustration lies in that it shows that there is not
really a third eye to open, a third consciousness that is 'supra-
normal'. No new 'thing' has to appear in us. The satori-occurrence
is the instant at which our dualistic being, such as it is from now
on, discovers at last its normal method of functioning by awakening its attention to an autonomous, unconditioned activity.

Chapter Twenty-One

ON THE IDEA OF 'DISCIPLINE'

OUR reflections, in the light of Zen, have enabled us to understand that there cannot be recipes for the attainment of Realisation. No systematic manner of living can release the synthesis of all possible manners of living; no conscious activity can reintegrate us in the original Unconscious. No training, no discipline comprising a struggle can make us pass beyond the dualism in which such struggle takes place. And we arrive thus at the conclusion that understanding alone can dissipate our present illusion and obtain satori for us.

Besides, we understand that the explosion of satori supposes the accumulation in us of energy, which is not disintegrated and that this accumulation supposes, in its turn, not only theoretical understanding but the practical utilisation of this understanding in a very special activity of our attention. Thus we see that, if nothing else but understanding can obtain satori for us, this understanding should not be realised under the single aspect of a directing theory but also under the aspect of inner phenomena which actualise in a practical manner this theory. These phenomena could not be correctly produced without the understanding of which they are a simple practical prolongation—and this is why they do not constitute a recipe for realisation sufficient in itself—but they constitute nevertheless a certain practical inner task, in the course of life, distinct from the abstract vision obtained during moments of retreat within the ivory tower of the intellect.

We reach thus two certitudes that are apparently contradictory. On the one hand no intervention methodically imposed upon our way of living, on our phenomena external or internal, can be effective in obtaining satori; on the other hand obtaining satori necessarily implies a practical inner task in the course of our daily life. We have arrived at these two certitudes by different routes, but these routes have both left us with the impression of evidence which makes us believe that the idea is true.

Every contradiction of this kind is for us an occasion for a precious deepening of our understanding; it pushes us towards the discovery of a larger view of things, which conciliates the two preceding views and in which their apparent opposition is resolved.

In this particular case we have to understand the inner task in such a way that it is not an intervention methodically imposed on our way of living. This may be decomposed into two propositions: we have first of all to understand the inner task in such a way that it is not an intervention with regard to our life; thereafter we have to understand it in such a way that it does not comprise any methodical constraint. This second point is the one on which we will spread ourselves most fully since we have never dealt with it hitherto. But we will recall, first of all, on the subject of the first point, certain ideas already expressed.

The inner task in view of satori ought not to be an intervention in our life. The word 'intervention' indicates what happens when, among the elements on a certain plane, something comes between these elements, modifies the relations that they would otherwise have had, troubles the essential arrangement of the plane. Zen proclaims: 'Do not trouble the course of life'; and the master gives as an example to his disciple the torrent which flows without hindrance. There will be satori for us when we cease at last to place ourselves in opposition to the nature of things, to our own nature at the same time as to the nature of the cosmos in general. The inner task designed to obtain satori could not comprise an indiscreet and pretentious interference in the outlet of our phenomena. That is not to say that no change should occur in these phenomena as we approach chronologically the satori-occurrence; but that which alone can produce adequate changes is our Absolute Principle, the Unconscious in us, and not our pretentious consciousness. When there is intervention, that which comes between the elements of the plane is of the same kind as these elements; any intervention in my comportment consists in the action of a new comportment, but it is always a comportment; every intervention in my inner life, in my psychic mechanisms,

195

consists in the action of a new mechanism, but it is still a mechanism. When there is intervention on a certain plane nothing comes into play which does not belong to that plane. But the harmonious synthesis of the being implies the simple action of the Conciliatory Principle which does not belong to the plane of phenomena, which is transcendent with regard to this plane; and the harmonising manifestation of the Principle on this plane should not in any way be understood as an intervention. Only the Principle can modify our phenomena, our life without troubling that life.

We have spoken several times of this gesture of inner decontraction which is not an intervention since it results in the suspension of the mental film—and not in its modification—without causing any particular image to intervene. We have said that this gesture is produced on a plane that is superior to that of our habitual inner phenomena, as the cerebral plane which decontracts our muscles is superior to the medullary plane which contracts them. The 'doing' of this gesture corresponds with a 'not doing' of our habitual phenomena. If this gesture of decontraction tended to result directly in the suspension of the imaginative film by using a particular image—such as the image of this suspension itself—there would be indiscreet intervention which, besides, would not result in the suspension of the film but in the fixed idea of this suspension (an exercise of concentration resulting in a sort of auto-hypnosis, or of catalepsy, or syncope). The gesture of decontraction correctly executed only indirectly results in decontraction, it does not aim at it directly, it does not utilise the evocation of the mental image of decontraction. *It consists, on the contrary, in an authorisation, total, impartial, unconditional, given to our mental consciousness, to all its powers perceptive and active.* In this gesture which is momentary cessation of any particular direction given to my life, everything happens as though I were trying to open myself to my very existence, immutable under my vital movements. But I do not even evoke the image of 'existence'. It is like a look which, cast on the full centre of my inner world, transpierces the plane of this world towards that which is unknown to me. This look, because it does not prefer any object, because it is sent, without preconception, towards no matter what, meets nothing and so results, without my having wished it, in the suspension of my imaginative film. It is a total interrogation without particular formal expression, which remains without answer since it does not carry any. It is a challenge which neither aims at nor meets anybody; it is an attention to everything, which has no object. The suspension of my imaginative film, thus obtained without having been sought, is instantaneous; it is without duration, an intemporal flash of lightning in the heart of time; it in no way resembles the states into which, on the contrary, exercises of concentration can put me. On account of this absence of duration, this gesture of looking into my own nature does not result in the vision of the 'third eye', it only prepares it. These gestures are repeated set-backs—which should be condensed into an ultimate set-back—which some day will bring about the disappearance of the illusion in which I am living at present of not being in the state of satori.

If the gesture of instantaneous decontraction prepares the satori-occurrence, that is because the instantaneous suspension which it obtains in the unfolding of the imaginary film breaks on each occasion the vicious circle which exists between our images and our emotions. This vicious circle that we have called 'imaginative-emotive rumination', which corresponds also with what we have described as the 'emotive state', or 'inner spasm', or as 'gearing of the affectivity with the intellect', is an inner automatism animated by a great force of inertia. Our imaginative rumination does not function continuously with the same effective power, but in each stage of our evolution it has a certain possibility of power. This possibility is used, mined little by little by the instants of decontraction. This progressive diminution of the solidity of the vicious circle of images and emotions is revealed by a progressive modification of our inner life, of our vision of things in general. Not that we are able, before satori, to have the least little atom of 'vision of things as they are'; but our present vision of things-as-they-are-not loses its clarity, its relief, its colours.

In order to make clear the modifications that the inner work obtains indirectly in our vision of things we will make use of an illustration. We will compare our imaginative film with the projection of a cinematographic film comprising a projector, a screen, and the luminous cone which connects them. When the projection is well focussed on the screen I see clear images thereon, in which the blanks and whites are well-contrasted. If, without changing anything in the projector, I progressively bring the screen nearer to it, the images will gradually lose their clearness and their contrasts. A moment will come when I recognise them with difficulty and when the blacks become grey. Then there are nothing but pale and vague shadows accompanied by an increase in the general luminosity of the screen. Finally, when I am in contact with the projector, the screen is completely white and sparkling.

The projector here symbolises the original Unconscious or No-Mind, source of our consciousness; the luminous beam symbolises the subconscious; the screen the consciousness. The screen of our consciousness is set, by our personal egotistical determinism, at the distance at which the images are in focus. It is there that our claim-to-be-distinct fixes our attention. That corresponds with the partial inner attitudes by which I oppose with a clear contrast that which I like and that which I do not like. The images, in this bright contrast of light and shade, stir up strong emotions which release new images, and the clear unfolding of the film represents my imaginative-emotive rumination.

In the instant of decontraction, of attention without an object, the screen is in contact with the projector, bathed in pure light without images. I do not perceive this light as pure because this happens in an instant without duration and because, all perception being memory, I can perceive nothing except in duration. But, as a result of this instant without images, the force of the vicious circle which kept the screen far from the projector is reduced; the screen is brought nearer. If the gesture of decontraction is repeated with enough perseverance the screen is brought nearer and nearer. The shadows and the lights of the imaginative film lose their clearness; the formal contours which separate them become less precise and the blacks become grey. This does not mean that my thought loses its precision, but that my evaluations, my opinions, my beliefs, have less rigidity and compelling force. The increase in the total luminosity on the screen represents a diminution of my fundamental distress, a relief in the ensemble of my affective condition.

The 'Great Doubting' which precedes satori corresponds with the ultimate stage of this evolution. The screen is then very close to the projector. The inner conscious state is very luminous, without distress; the fundamental negativity of our affectivity is almost entirely neutralised; distress is no longer there, although positive existential felicity is not yet conscious. The mental forms, the samskaras, have disappeared, and so the subject says that he is then 'like an idiot, like an imbecile'. The disappearance of shadows is indicated by the impression that the world is transparent, like a crystal palace; 'the mountains are no longer mountains and the waters are no longer waters'. One degree further and the attention, already so near the source of the Unconscious, is installed there definitively; it is the 'asylum of rest'. During an instant all distinction is abolished between the screen, the projector and the beam of light. Then all that exists afresh but it now functions in a simple manner, perfectly harmonious, unimaginable to us to-day.

This illustration allows us to understand how the metabolism of vital energy is modified in us in the course of the inner work. The nearer the screen approaches the projector, the less the luminous energy is disintegrated in black and white forms. At the limit, at the point at which the light-beam leaves its source, it is only whiteness, pure light. We have said that our energy wells up, still informal, from the source where it is unmanifested; we have then affirmed the existence of an energy at once manifested and informal. This seems to be a metaphysical absurdity, since manifestation cannot be conceived without form. But this absurdity only comes from words which appear to immobilise the movement of the birth of energy; in speaking of energy at once manifested and informal, we would, by these disputable words, evoke the instant without duration in which the energy leaves its source. We would point it out on the frontier that we suppose to lie between non-manifestation and manifestation, in the instant at which, envisaged with regard to the source, it is already manifested, and at which, envisaged with regard to the manifestation, it is still informal. And the accumulation of informal energy of which we have spoken should be understood as a possibility, unceasingly increased, of sparing the energy the imaginative-emotive vicious circle.

After this reminder of the inner task understood as a 'letting-go', as an instantaneous and total decontraction of our conscious being, we reach the essential point of this study; when is it desirable that we execute this 'not doing', this letting-go? A trap is set for us here: if I incorrectly conceive satori as an accomplishment of myself-as-a-distinct-being, in the illusory perspective of a 'superman', I shall *covet* satori, desire it positively, I shall wish for it in the usual sense of this phrase. If I thus demand satori, and if on the other hand I have understood the efficacity of a letting-go in view of satori, it is going to be necessary for me to carry out this letting-go. A compulsion of my primordial spasm, the logical result of my claim to be-as-a-distinct-being, forces me to impose on my organism, whether it likes it or not, the gesture of decontraction. It is very clear that no real decontraction is possible thus and that what will be achieved will only be the contracted mental evocation of the image of decontraction.

This is not to say that there is no discipline in the inner task correctly carried out; but it must be clearly understood. In all inner discipline 'something' directs the functioning of my psychosomatic machine; but what should this something be, in order that the inner task may be correctly carried out?

To reply to this question we will first of all show what this something should not be, and analyse to that end the usual notions of 'self-control', of 'self-mastery' and 'will'.

We will neglect, to begin with, the examination of this famous and illusory 'Will-power', and we will use this word in its usual sense in studying 'self-control'. The control of self can be control of the outer behaviour—'good' deeds or 'good' abstentions (asceticism); or control of the inner behaviour—'good' sentiments or 'good' thoughts or mental exercises to achieve a 'good' manner of making the mind function (concentration, meditation, mental void, etc.) If one analyses deeply what happens in the course of such efforts, one always finds, as an initial mechanism, the voluntary mental evocation of an image or of a system of images. That is evident when it is a question of meditation (even if the mental image evoked is that of the absence of images); and it is the same if it is a question of external action since the decision governing all action is controlled by the conception of its mental image. All self-control consists therefore essentially in a voluntary mental evocation, an imaginative manipulation in the course of which there is actualised my partiality for one image to the detriment of all other possible images. This partiality for such and such a form of my manifestation, and consequently against the opposite forms, prevents the control-of-self from working towards a synthesis of all my manifestation; I can only 'do' thus by refusing what I do not do; no unification of my being is then possible. The preferred images are samskaras as much as the refused images. This method cannot modify the imaginative-emotive process as a whole; the forms fabricated by the process alone are modified. The preferred samskaras are reinforced; they tend to become encysted; imaginative habits are acquired. I can thus train myself to feel sentiments of love for the whole Universe at the expense of my aggressiveness. A form has been modified but there can be no passing beyond form, no transformation.

We have already said that these kinds of training are not in themselves an obstacle to the obtaining of satori. The reinforcement of certain samskaras to the detriment of others should not be able to make man's inner situation worse with regard to an eventual transformation. That which does not work for satori is limited to not working for it; but nothing should be able to work against it. Ignorance has no active reality against the Intemporal nor against the eventual realisation of the Intemporal. It is merely time that is lost with regard to the satori-occurrence.

An objection offers itself: the corrct inner gesture of letting-go is carried out under a general authorisation given to no matter what image; it is no longer a question, therefore, of evoking a preferred image; there is no longer partiality in face of my inner world. That is true, but if I wish to make myself perform the gesture of letting-go in a systematic manner because I covet satori, if I wish to do it each time that I think of it, without taking into account my actual inner condition, I will be obliged to evoke the *preferred* mental image of the authorisation given to no matter what image; and I will fall back again thus into the same absurdity.

We meet for the first time the capital notion of taking into account my actual inner condition. That which places the usual conception of discipline in opposition to the correct conception that we are trying to define, is precisely that fact that the usual discipline does not comprise the idea that one should take account of the actual inner condition.

Let us analyse exactly what happens in the course of 'self-control'. Every effort of self-control is a struggle between two tendencies. One man will fast in order to slim, for aesthetic reasons; there is a struggle between the tendency to satisfy the appetite and the tendency to be less fat, more beautiful. Another man fasts in order to progress 'spiritually'; this case does not differ, basically, from the former; the desire to progress 'spiritually' is evidently personal; it is then, like the desire to eat, a tendency to affirm oneself as-a-distinct-being. In the two cases we see the struggle between two tendencies of the same nature. It is like two men hauling on the two ends of the same rope, or pushing both ends of the same pole.

One must clearly distinguish this struggle, this opposition, from the composition of tendencies which represents their normal working. Every kind of behaviour that I may have, without effort imposed on myself, does not express a unique tendency. To each of my perceptions multiple tendencies react in me; the simple unique manifestation, which is then realised by my effortless behaviour, results from the subconscious composition of my tendencies, and represents the resultant of a parallelogram of forces. Whence come then these differences in the ways in which my tendencies can operate? Why do they compose themselves sometimes without my even realising it, while at other times they fight with one another, tearing me to pieces?

It is here that partiality intervenes. There is struggle in me when I am partial to one tendency against the opposite tendency. The affective preference that I feel for the working of such and such a tendency conditions, in my mind acting passively, an intellectual partiality, a judgement of value. This amounts to 'believing' that this tendency 'is', and so should exist, and that the contrary tendency 'is not', and so should not exist. Thus is produced identification with the preferred tendency (transfer of my 'being' on to the tendency that I see as 'being').

Here as elsewhere the mistake does not lie in the identification with such a tendency but in the exclusive character of this identification, in the disavowal of the opposing tendency. We may remark that this inadequacy of identification in my microcosm is in relation to the inadequacy of my identification in the macrocosm. As soon as I am identified with the Self while excluding the Not-Self, I cannot be identified with the whole of Self; my microcosm is divided in its turn into Self and Not-Self, for example, in

202

tendencies that I make my own and in tendencies that I regard as foreign. One can break up indefinitely the loadstone; each fragment will always have two poles. Every dualism engenders unlimited dualisms.

This identification with a tendency, with disavowal of the opposite tendency, is revealed by the fact that the subject has the impression of *himself* struggling against the disavowed tendency. The subconscious composition of forces has given place to their conscious opposition. The complementary character of the dualism has disappeared, there only remains the antagonism. The two forces can no longer operate as belonging to a harmonious whole; partiality makes them work as though they belonged to two different wholes. *'As soon as you have Good and Evil confusion results and the spirit is lost.'*

The illusory notion of a 'will', such as man habitually understands it, 'will' representing a special inner power, distinct from the tendencies and capable of exercising a kind of police supervision over them, results fatally from the identification with a preferred tendency. Let us take up again our example of the man who fasts in order to slim. He identifies himself with his aesthetic tendency, and so he ceases to become conscious of this tendency. If he has failed to stick to his diet he does not say 'My greed was stronger than my wish to be beautiful'; he says 'My greed was stronger than I was.' In the opposite case he will say 'I have triumphed over my greed.' As the tendency which has triumphed has then ceased to exist for this man, and as he feels clearly nevertheless that a force has conquered his greed, he calls this force his 'will'. Sometimes one observes a more complex case which in the end comes back to the same thing. Such and such a man, proud to have seen his 'will' triumph or ashamed to have seen it defeated, conceives the desire to have more and more 'will-power'; thus is born a partiality for the tendency to counteract the action of no matter what other tendency. The ambition for 'self-mastery' is nothing else. One might say that to control the working of one's tendencies is not necessarily to counteract them; but one must admit that all control, even when it authorises the action, comprises an eventual opposition. If someone controls my acts, I feel reasonably enough that it is a denial of my liberty. This man who, for example, is going to fast in order to prove to himself that he is capable of doing so, will say that he has imposed this fast on himself in a disinterested manner, and that it is not a tendency which has struggled in him against his greed; he does not see in himself this tendency to drive his inner world with a whip, the tendency to tyrannise by which he is himself tyrannised. He wished to cease being the slave of his desires, but he has concentrated his slavery on the unique desire to be free from all his other desires. On the whole the inner condition remains the same, neither improved nor worsened from the point of view of an eventual satori. The 'self-control' can lead to 'holiness', to the harmonious unification of a positive part of the being alone authorised to act, but not to the unification of the totality of the being or satori. From the point of view of intemporal realisation this 'will' can be of no use whatsoever.

Let us note that in these 'wilful' efforts of self-control the subject does not take account of his actual inner condition; he makes his effort each time that he thinks of it. When he does not do it, that is only because he forgets his task. If, sometimes, he thinks of the effort that should be made and does not make it nevertheless, it is not that he takes account of his inner condition. The fact of envisaging the effort he has conceived as systematically good is already, by itself, a release of the effort; and if this release some-times misses fire that is because the opposite tendency has been stronger from the beginning.

When I have thus clearly seen the inefficacity of 'self-control' I am tempted to admit that the man is right who lives as he likes, who makes no demand on himself, who only makes demands on the outside world in order to obtain what suits him. But I perceive, first of all, that my reaction depends upon false reason-ing; if efforts at self-control made the state of mankind worse from the point of view of eventual satori, the man who ceased to make these efforts would bring himself nearer the eventual satori. But, as we have seen, these efforts could not in themselves constitute an obstacle. The fact of no longer exerting oneself in that way cannot, therefore, remove an obstacle which never existed.

The principle refutation of the quietist attitude is much more important. In reality the man who does not make efforts of self-control seems to live as he likes, but he does not do so. If his mind does not consciously disturb the play of his tendencies, it disturbs them subconsciously. If there is no conscious opposition to the tendencies, if there is apparent composition of the tendencies, this apparent composition masks to a great extent a subconscious opposition. This man has not a theoretical, conscious 'ideal', but he has a practical, subconscious one. From the fact that his tendencies have procured him affirmations or negations, practical judgements are pronounced in him on these tendencies, approving or condemning them. The man necessarily sees a certain relation of causality between his tendencies and their practical results; his attachment to the results necessarily carries with it a partiality for or against his tendencies, that is a secondary tendency to control his primary tendencies. Even the man who appears to struggle only to control the outside world conceals an inner struggle under the tyranny of his practical 'ideal'.

What takes place in this man is more complex than what takes place within the partisan of 'will-power'. For the partisan of 'will-power' the inner control is visible all the time, for a conscious examination of the tendencies presides as much over their authorisation as over their repression. In fact, for this man, a tendency is never merely authorised; if it is not repressed it is activated by the secondary controlling tendency. In the man who, consciously, only struggles against the outer world, the inner control is only perceptible in its repressive aspect. When the controlling tendency does not repress a primary tendency it does not activate it either, it lets it work; it disappears itself. The mechanisms of this man enjoy from time to time a certain spontaneity.

In short, the man who performs no conscious inner task does not let-go on that account. Impartiality does not reign in his inner world. Even this relative spontaneity that we have just seen is not a real spontaneity. When I act impulsively my subconscious attitude in face of the inner world of my tendencies, of my Self, is not a 'Yes' said to the totality of that world; it is a 'Yes' spoken to the only tendency which is acting, but a preferential 'Yes' which is accompanied by a 'No' said to all the rest of my 'Selves', that is to say it is a 'No' said to my machine as-a-totality.

What should one think now of the method which consists in supervising all my tendencies but in consciously approving the present tendency? It is the attitude at which the man logically arrives who, after having cherished in the past a conscious 'ideal', or several, has completed the task of comprehension which devalorises every ideal. This man understands that, from the only real point of view of intemporal realisation, all the inner mechanisms are of equal value; he is detached from the aesthetic or in-aesthetic character of his tendencies. This relative impartiality confers on him a relative liberty. The withdrawal of partiality in face of the tendencies does not prevent these from existing but it takes from them all compulsive value, Dream and reality are more and more divided; I feel in accordance with my dream, but I behave in accordance with my reason.

This method, then, which consists in consciously approving each present tendency, confers on me a relative outer liberty. But it is not the 'letting-go' of Zen. Consciously to authorise is not to let-go, it is only an imitation of it. The letting-go, as we have seen, is realised when I authorise the totality of my tendencies *before* the conscious appearance of any one of them; and then none of them appears. When, on the contrary, I authorise my present tendency, I only let-go with regard to this tendency; all the rest remain held. Observation of my inner phenomena that is impartial and approbatory cannot have by itself any efficacity for an eventual satori.

Let us return now to the letting-go as we have understood it. The question is no longer for us to define the gesture of the correct inner task, but to know when to make this gesture. It is thus at least that the question is at first presented to us, in a form which would only be suitable if an ordinary gesture were in question, a gesture of contraction. If I have decided to do some physical culture I can ask myself 'when shall I do it?' because if some moment of the day is more propitious than another for a good result from the exercises, I can impose them on my muscles at that moment. It is not the same for the inner gesture which decontracts all the tendencies by authorising them all in a moment of impartiality. This gesture can be tried no matter when, but not effected at random. My consciousness can demand this gesture from my machine, but cannot impose it. The realisation of the gesture supposes that two factors are united—that my thought proposes the gesture and that my machine accepts it. If, meeting in me a resistance to the gesture of decontraction I try to overcome this resistence, I prevent myself by that very fact from succeeding, for then I graft a contraction on to a spasm.

Let us examine the two factors that we have just mentioned. It is necessary that my thought propose the gesture. This assumes the vigilance of the mind operating in an active manner; and this vigilance assumes a clear understanding of the inner task and of its interest. In this vigilant invitation by the active mind resides the veritable *will*, will which, as Spinoza said, is nothing else but the understanding. Next it is necessary that my machine accept the invitation of the mind and open itself to it in full consent. This good-will of my machine is realised when it feels that my thought seeks its collaboration with perseverence but without the least constraint, when my machine feels itself the subject of *consideration* on the part of my thought.

We can now understand what is the correct inner discipline. We asked ourselves just now: 'Since, in all inner discipline, "something" directs my machine, what can this "something" be?' Shall we say that it is the active mind? Yes, in one sense, but not in another sense, since the effective directing action of this mind depends on an accord between it and the machine, accord over which the mind has no immediate power. The direction from which the machine benefits, in the course of the letting-go, passes through the active mind, but it comes in reality from the Conciliating Principle which reconciles my two parts. *The correct inner discipline can only be assumed by the Principle itself, and it comprises no kind of constraint, no inner struggle.* The only effort that we have to make consists in forgetting as little as possible that our true advantage is conditioned by letting-go, by attention without object, by 'mental presence of mind in face of nothing' and never to impose on our machine—but only propose to it—this decontraction, this common opening to the Principle.

The decontraction so proposed is accepted from time to time by the machine, when it is tired of refusing the invitation, but as we have said, in a flash without duration. Everything happens as though I were afraid of the bursting of my Ego. If I wish to tame a frightened child I hold out my arms to him without approaching too near, by inviting him without constraint. One day perhaps he will throw himself into my arms, but for a long time I shall only see in his eyes fugitive flashes of relaxation in the course of which he accepts for a moment the idea of coming towards me; after which fear takes possession of him again. It is in this sense that my gestures of decontraction, my letting-go, are in reality only infinitely short glimpses of the real letting-go which would be satori. All the gestures to which my inner discipline leads, even correctly understood, are set-backs; they constitute those very special set-backs, felt by the whole of my being, which condition by their accumulation the ultimate set-back of my actual condition, with the passing-beyond, in satori, of all the dualism of success and failure.

One sees how this conception of discipline conciliates the ideas of 'training' and of 'non-training'. There is non-training in the sense that no part of me constrains any other to that end. There is training however in the sense that my understanding obtains from my machine a decontractoin that this machine would never have effected by itself. The trainer makes the trainee do that which is good for both of them, in the moments during which the trainee consents voluntarily; and this is possible because trainer and trainee become one in the conciliation of Absolute Reality.

Satori can be understood as a letting-go which lasts. In this instant there is established a definitive double decontraction. The machine opens itself to the active mind which is united with it, and the couple so formed opens itself to the Principle which is united with it, in a trinitarian Unity. Only then man sees with evidence that there has never been separation between machine, mind and Principle.

Chapter Twenty-Two

THE COMPENSATIONS

THE man who has not attained realisation, animated by the need to be absolutely as-a-distinct-being, cannot accept his existence such as it is. This impossibility is not due, as one might suppose at first, to the fact that individual existence is passed under a constant menace of partial or total destruction, for man's essential need is a need to 'be' absolutely and not to 'exist' perpetually; it is a need of infinite eternity and not of indefinite duration. Were illness and death definitely avoided man would be not less constrained by his need to be absolutely, to refuse his existence such as he knows it. What is inacceptable to man in his existence is not that the outer world menaces this existence, but that everything he perceives is not conditioned by his individual existence while that remains unconditioned. Man, because he is virtually capable of living his identity with the Absolute Principle, cannot accept the sleep of this identity; he cannot allow that he is not the First Cause of the Universe. But he cannot perceive his real and essential unity with the First Cause of the Universe as long as he lives in the belief that he is only his psycho-somatic organism, as long as he is identified only with this organism.

However, man accepts his existence, in fact, since he forces himself to maintain it. He accepts it, in fact, because, if he knows that his organism is not the motor centre of the Universe, his imagination preserves him from feeling it by recreating in his mind a universe centred on himself. The imaginative film masks the intolerable vision, saves the man from this vision. But it only saves him from it during the moments in which it functions; the danger remains and has to be conjured incessantly by a continuous imaginative activity. Imagination mitigates the distress without being able to destroy it.

THE COMPENSATIONS

Our imagination, this function which creates in us an imaginative film that is not based on the real present, is therefore our compensating function ; it is the function which fabricates our compensations. Our compensations are systems of images which we borrow from our sensory and mental perceptions—from the material of images stored up by our memory—and which we arrange as we please, in accordance with the structure of our individual psycho-somatic organism. These constitute our inner personal world. Evidently they could not be a pure creation; they are recreation, with non-personal elements, of a personal representation of the world, according to a personal order which is like a special section cut in the volume of the Universe (for this personal order does not result, either, from a personal creation; it is a particular aspect, chosen according to our personal structure, from among the indefinite number of aspects of the cosmic order).

One can compare the universe personally recreated, which our compensations constitute, to a design imagined by an artist. No designer could create a form of which the prototype did not already exist in the Universe and which he has not perceived himself by the intermediary of a personal image based on outer reality. The creation of the designer only consists in choosing a form in the outer world by neglecting all others and, sometimes, in assembling as he wishes forms he has never seen assembled in this way in reality. Thus the personal element in the recreation of our imaginary universe does not reside in the elementary forms used, but first in using such and such a form rather than any other, and second in assembling universal forms in accordance with a personal style. The elaboration of a compensation is an imaginary artifice.

Our compensations correspond with what one currently terms our scale of values. Each man sees certain things as particularly real, particularly important, and it is these which give a meaning to his life. If I wish to know my compensations it is enough for me to ask myself: 'What gives a sense to my life?'

Before going further let us return to the question: 'What do our compensations compensate?' They do not compensate, as one often thinks, the particular negating aspects of existence. If it were thus our compensations would always be affirming, positive images; but we shall see that they can just as well be negative.

The essential character of a compensation is not that it should be agreeable to me but that it should represent the universe to me in a perspective such that I am the centre of it. Only that matters, and not the fact that this universe centred on me is affirming or negating. Our compensations compensate our illusory belief that we are separated from Reality, that is the subjective non-appearance of our essential identity with the Absolute Principle. In other words, the recreated imaginary personal universe constituted by our compensations compensate the sleep of our vision of the Universe as it is in its total reality. It is because we do not yet see things as they are that we are obliged to see them in an imaginary way which is a partial way.

Our compensating vision of the world is not false, therefore it is merely partial; what is false is our belief that this vision is totally adequate for that which is seen. The importance that we attach to certain aspects of the world is not false, it is not illusory; what is illusory resides in the exclusive character of this vision, in the fact that it denies the same importance to the rest of the world. The vision of things as they are would attribute an equal importance to all aspects of the Universe; everything would be important and in consequence nothing would be important in the preferential sense that we usually give to this word 'important'. It is only in the partiality of our imaginary vision that the illusion resides, not in the vision itself. Let us establish then clearly, from the beginning of this study, that our compensations are not to be deplored as obstacles to satori, to the vision of things as they are. Our compensations are not illusory in themselves and are not opposed to satori; the idol is not an obstacle to Reality; the reality that we see in the idol is not opposed to our reunion with Reality. The obstacle is only the ignorance through which we deny to that which is not the idol the same reality that we see in the idol. *The only obstacle is ignorance, and ignorance is partiality.* Our compensatory vision of the world is not, then, a bad thing, to be destroyed; it is something incomplete, to be extended, to be accomplished, by dissipating restrictive ignorance that is exclusive and partial. Adhesion to that which is only a part is not bad but only 'partiality', that is ignorant belief in the total character of that which is only a part.

This should be well established before entering into a detailed study of compensations. When one speaks of the subjection in which a compensation places us it is really a question of the subjection in which we are placed by the ignorant partiality by which we deny implicitly what we are not affirming. A compensation is never enslaving in itself; what enslaves us is the partiality with which we consider it. Subjection does not lie in seeing Reality in the evocation of Jesus or of the Buddha, but in only seeing it there by denying it to the rest of creation.

Our compensations are necessary to our total realisation since without them we could not accept existence and we would destroy ourselves at once; they are on the way of our correct evolution towards satori. But the obtaining of satori assumes that some day we shall pass beyond our compensations. This passing-beyond should be understood not as a loss of the vivifying substance contained in our compensations, but as a bursting of the formal and exclusive circumference which was limiting this substance. The reality seen in the idol is not wiped out but is diffused outside the idol whose restrictive circumference has burst.

Compensation is at once favourable and unfavourable to the evolution towards satori. It is favourable by its affective aspects, which are nourishment to me and save me from suicide. It is unfavourable in the measure in which it comprises an intellectual belief in the Reality—or absolute value—of the compensating image. For example; one of my compensations is to have a healthy child. The joy which I find in this situation (the image of myself possessing this healthy child) is favourable to my evolution towards satori, for it forms part of that which helps me to accept existence. What is unfavourable to my correct evolution is my belief that this situation is *absolutely* good whereas the death of my child would be *absolutely* bad; it is the belief according to which my adhesion to the compensating situation excludes my adhesion to the eventuality of the contrary situation. In fact this exclusion limits what I perceive of cosmic reality and even prevents me from correctly perceiving what I perceive of it by cutting it off from its connexion with all the rest. I cannot perceive anything as it is in reality as long as any one of its connexions with the rest of the Universe is cut; and all the connexions of anything are concentrated in its relation with the opposite thing, antagonistic and complementary.

Hui-neng refutes the deplorable 'belief' which resides in our compensations when he proclaims: 'From the beginning not a thing is.' In speaking thus he does not condemn my compensating joy; this joy is a moving phenomenon which 'exists' merely and does not pretend to 'be'; *he refutes my belief in the Reality of a fixed image which pretends to 'be' by the exclusion of the contrary image. Hui-neng does not condemn the affective point of departure of the idolatry, but he refutes the idolatrous intellectual belief.* This belief, in isolating an image by the exclusion of the image which depends upon it in the cosmic equilibrium of the Yin and the Yang, attempts illusorily to confer on the isolated image the immutable Unity of the Absolute Principle. The image thus artificially isolated becomes a compensating 'idol', and it is not the image itself but this manner of seeing it as an idol that Hui-neng aims at when he reminds us that 'not a thing is'.

The declaration of Hui-neng does not at all advise us not to live our compensations, to feel that there is value in particular things. It merely invites us to pass beyond these compensations in breaking, by means of understanding, the enslaving exclusivity of our idolatrous 'opinions'. This breaking aims only at limiting intellectual forms, not at all at the living affective substance contained therein. It is possible for me, by means of understanding, to continue to feel value in this or that particular thing without persisting in implicitly proclaiming the anti-value of the contrary thing. My understanding shows me in fact that, from the only real point of view of my intemporal realisation, there is not value and anti-value, but that all things are fit to be used for this realisation.

The phrase of Hui-neng is not, therefore, a malediction on all particular things, but, very much on the contrary, a blessing, undifferenced, impartial, on all particular things. The same thought is found in many passages of a remarkable Zen text known by the title of 'Inscribed on the believing mind':

> The Perfect Way knows no difficulties
> Except that it refuses all preference.

> If you would see the Perfect Way manifest
> Take no thought either for or against it.
> To oppose what you like and what you dislike,
> That is the malady of the mind.

THE COMPENSATIONS

Do not try to find the truth,
Merely cease to cherish opinions,
Tarry not in dualism.

As soon as you have good and evil
Confusion follows and the mind is lost.

When the unique mind is undisturbed
The ten thousand things cannot offend it.

When no discrimination is made between this and that
How can a biassed and prejudiced vision arise?

Let-go, leave things as they may be.

If you wish to follow the path of the One Vehicle
Have no prejudice against the six senses.

Whereas in the Dharma itself there is no individuation
The ignorant attach themselves to particular objects.

The enlightened have no likes or dislikes.

Gain and loss, right and wrong,
Away with them once and for all!

The ultimate end of things, beyond which they cannot go
Is not subject to rules and measures.

Everything is void, lucid, and self-illuminating
There is no strain, no effort, no wastage of energy.
To this region thought never attains.

In not being two all is the same
All that exists is comprehended therein.

It matters not how things are conditioned,
Whether by 'being' or by 'not being'.

THE COMPENSATIONS

That which is is the same as that which is not.
That which is not is the same as that which is.

If only this is realised,
You need not worry about not being perfect!

All compensations are idolatries, attempts to see Reality incarnate itself in a particular image illusorily immobilised outside the cosmic whirlpool. The passing beyond compensation is not destruction of the image but of its artificial immobilisation; the image, devalorised as an idol, is replaced in the middle of the multitude of other images in the ceaselessly-moving flow of cosmic life such as it is in reality.

Passing beyond compensations, the devalorisation of idols, is a process which takes place in my intellectual intuition. This process supposes first of all the acquisition of a correct theoretical comprehension which demasks in the abstract the illusory idolatrous belief. It assumes on the other hand that I have experienced, by suffering, the unsatisfactory character of compensation. This painful dissatisfaction is inevitable; indeed the compensation, as we have seen, only mitigates my distress in the moment during which it functions, but I expect in the depth of my being, that it will definitively remedy my distress; and so I am necessarily led, more or less rapidly, to realise the deceptive character of my compensation in comparison with what I expected of it. It is then, in the suffering of deception, that my understanding will manifest itself by a correct interpretation of my suffering. Abstract comprehension and concrete suffering are both necessary; neither one nor the other is sufficient alone. We will return later to this question of passing beyond compensations, it is in fact impossible to deal with it without knowing how the various compensations are constituted.

Every compensation is essentially constituted by an image involving my Ego, by an image-centre around which is organised in a constellation, a multitude of satellite images. The image-centre is bi-polar, like everything that belongs to the domain of form. This explains why there are positive and negative compensations. Man has an innate preference for the positive—the beautiful, good, true—and tries always at first to build up a positive compensation; but failure can release the inversion of it into antagonistic negative compensation. For example, I begin to hate the being with whom I have tried in vain to establish a love relationship; and this hatred can give a sense to my life as love had. After pointing out this process of the possible inversion of our compensations, we will limit ourselves to describing the principle positive compensations that the observation of human-beings and our own inner world reveal to us.

The image-centre can represent me as receiving the service of the outside world, which is the compensation of being loved. It can represent me as actively seizing my nourishments in the outside world, which is the compensation of enjoyment (the affirmation of myself eating the outside world; the love of riches, which is a potential means of eating the outside world).

The image-centre can represent me as serving the outside world, as nourishing it, and very many compensations proceed from this image: 'to love', 'to give pleasure', 'to give life', 'to help', 'to serve' (one's Country, a political cause, a cause regarded in general as just, humanity, the oppressed, the weak, etc.). There also should be placed the joy of doing one's duty, of doing well what one does, the joy of being faithful to a moral code, of being at the level of such and such an 'ideal'.

In other compensations the image-centre no longer comprises action linking the Self with the outer world, but a simple perception. The compensating image is of the Self perceiving the outer world (joy of thus participating in beauty, in art, in intellectual truth, in knowledge in general). Or again, an image of Myself perceived by the outside world: the joy of attracting attention, of being admired, of being feared.

The image-centre can be the image of Myself as 'creator' of some work in the outside world, of a modification which I impose on the surrounding world and which I see as a distinct entity: the 'creation' of a work of art, a scientific or intellectual work, a political movement, a social organisation, religious order, etc. . . .

It can be the image of Myself creating something in myself: 'developing myself', 'realising myself', 'discovering who I am', 'developing my gifts', 'showing what I am capable of', 'cultivating myself', 'making efforts or experiments which make me rich', etc. . . . This category of compensation is very vast and important;

it groups all the ambitions, either in the material or the subtle sphere, or in the sphere that is called 'spiritual' (the obtaining of 'superior' states of consciousness, of 'spiritual powers', the cult, more or less disguised, of the 'superman'. We will come back more particularly to this question of 'spirituality'.)

Finally there is a very remarkable compensation in which the constituting elements of all the compensations already enumerated are found in fusion and so abolished as distinct (as all the colours are found together and abolished in white); that is *adoration*. In adoration I am dealing with my own Ego projected on to an exterior form that is more or less gross or subtle. The dualisms Self and the outer world, act and acted upon, nourish and to be nourished, perceive and to be perceived, create and to be created, disappear on account of the identity existing between the subject and the object. These dealings, besides, are reduced to the utmost simplicity; joy no longer comes to me from acting nor from seeing myself perceiving, *but simply from perceiving in a unitive contemplation*. It is a simple glance in which I believe that I see my Principle in the image on to which I have projected myself in an exclusive identification.

These various compensations can evidently be combined among themselves. Adoration in particular is combined, more often than not with loving and being loved, in the sense of affirming and being affirmed, serving and being served.

Every compensation, or imaginative constellation, constitutes in the being an element of fixity; but it is a dynamic fixity, like a stereotyped gesture of which I have the habit and which represents a fixity in my movement. The fixed compensation tends towards a certain ensemble of moving, living phenomena. Each compensation is a certain stereotyped form of living. I must therefore distinguish such compensation—which tends to make me live in such and such a manner—from the fact that I live, or not, in that manner; for it may happen that I have in myself such compensation and that nevertheless I do not live according to it, according to the bargain towards which it tends. This is clearly seen in neuroses; and the neurotic can be defined as a being who is badly compensated, incapable of living in accordance with his compensations. Let us imagine a being in whom exists the compensation 'loving and being loved', 'participation in the collective life by an exchange of services'. This being comes up against the wickedness of the outside world, a mischance unjustly wounds him. If the compensation were entirely inverted he could live in accordance with it so inverted: his life could find a sense in hatred and vengeance and he would be compensated in that way. But often the inversion only partially takes place, in its practical and not its theoretical aspect; the subject refuses his participation in the outside world in each particular eventuality, but continues to wish to participate in general. He would like to hit someone else, to wound him, in a particular practical action, but he cannot act thus because he persists in wanting to love, to serve, in general.

One often says that such persons have not found their compensations, but that is not true because each person always finds his compensations. These people have found their compensations but they are not able to live in accordance with them. The neurotic has split, divorced compensations in which he cannot live. He is paralysed between hatred and love of the same object. The impossibility of investing his vital energy therein entails a perturbation of the inner metabolism of his energy. The aggressiveness of the individual acts against itself; there is distress. This distress, felt up-stream of compensations that the subject does not succeed in using in his life, is of the same nature as the distress felt in the compensations that are lived-with when these exhaust themselves without comprehension. In the two cases there is 'de-compensation', but the happy issue of these two kinds of crisis is different. For the man who lives in accordance with his compensations it is desirable that he should come out of this stage; for the man who cannot live in accordance with his compensations it is desirable that he should enter this stage.

When a man succeeds in living his compensatory life the functioning of his psycho-somatic machine is harmonised, made flexible thereby. The man who thinks he has found Reality in one thing or another—whether it be money, or honours, or power, or any kind of exalting undertaking—possesses a point of orientation which allows his life to be efficiently organised. The apparent concentration of Reality on an image confers on the man an apparent inner unity by means of simplification of his dynamism. This *simplification*, which assumes the putting to sleep of a part of the world of his tendencies, clearly should not be confused with the *simplicity* of the man of satori in whom all is united without distinction in a total synthesis. But they resemble one another as the plane projection of a volume can resemble that volume. If a compensation of the 'adoration' type is pushed to a very high degree of subtlety, the inner simplification which it entails can actualise, in the psycho-somatic machine, rare powers which seem to be 'supernatural' (such as thought-reading, clairvoyance, psychic influences upon others, unconscious actions exactly adapted, power of healing, etc.).

The well-compensated man is, in the exact sense of the word, an idolater in the measure in which he 'believes' that the harmonising effects of his compensation come from the compensating image itself, the measure in which he identifies this image with Reality. This belief, which renders objective the subjective value of an image, evidently drives the idolater to think that all men ought to see as he does. If the idolater is of a positive type this results in proselytism, in apostleship, in a mission; if he is of a negative type it results in intolerance, in the persecution of unbelievers. The belief in the Reality of a form also entails the need of formal manifestations; the rite, which in reality is only a facultative means of expression, becomes where the idolater is concerned a constraining necessity.

Compensation forms an integral part of the period of human development which stretches from birth up to satori. Until satori, man is in unstable equilibrium, and this equilibrium is conditioned by the compensations. Therefore he should not totally pass beyond the compensations before satori, for satori alone constitutes this complete passing-beyond. But before the transformation (passing beyond form) which represents an inner event that is unique and instantaneous, there are produced in the human-being modifications and changes of form. These changes reveal the progressive elaboration of the inner conditions necessary for satori, and it is in this sense that we will speak of passing-beyond compensations as a progressive process. An illustration will make this point clear. It is said that the fox, when he wants to rid himself of his fleas, seizes a piece of moss in his mouth and enters the water backwards; the fleas leave the parts that are immersed and take refuge on that which still remains above water. Little by little the fox carries his fleas on an ever smaller part of his body, but this reduced surface is ever more and more infested with fleas. Ultimately all the fleas are concentrated on his muzzle, then on the piece of moss, which the fox then lets go into the flowing stream. Up to the instant at which the fox abandons the totality of his fleas he is not freed from a single one of them; nevertheless a certain process has modified the distribution of the parasites and prepared their complete and instantaneous disappearance.

Progressively passing beyond the compensations, thus understood as a reduction of extent and an increase of intensity, corresponds to a purification of the compensating image which evolves from the particular towards the general. All compensation being an image of the Universe centred by my Ego—a constellation of which the Ego is the central star and certain images the satellites—the purifying process of which we speak consists in the satellites becoming more and more subtle, whereas the central star increases in density. But then occurs something very particular which no illustration can demonstrate: the Ego having no reality, either absolute or relative, the density which accumulates there remains without any manifestation. Progressive *detachment* is a purification of that attachment to oneself which is at the centre of all attachments in general; but this central attachment to an illusory hypothetical image can purify itself and condense itself again and again without manifesting itself by anything perceptible. When St. John of the Cross passes beyond his mystical compensation, when he detaches himself from the image of 'God' after this image has been as far as possible rendered impersonal, he does not feel attached to the image 'Ego' from which the image 'God' drew its apparent Reality; he does not feel attached to anything. He no longer feels anything; it is the 'Night' in which nothing exists any longer in connexion with what can be felt or thought. But there is still an ultimate attachment to the Ego which links together all the powers of the being, an ultimate and invisible compensation. It is passing-beyond this invisible compensation which is the veritable detachment, total and instantaneous. To the Night succeeds what St. John of the Cross calls the theopathic state, that which Zen calls Satori.

Detachment, or passing-beyond the compensations, is often imperfectly understood; people believe that it is a question of destroying the affective preference that is felt for the compensating image, or that it is a question of tearing desire out of oneself. One forgets that attachment does not lie in desire but only in the claim to satisfaction of the desire. Desire need not disappear, but only the claim resulting from it. And the abandonment of the claim does not result from an inner struggle; it results from the correct interpretation of the deception that is inherent in the claim, whether it be satisfied or not. Distress, revendication, belief that the image claimed is Reality—these are the pieces of faulty scaffolding which is undermined by understanding and which that will one day bring crashing to the ground. Detachment is not a painful inner occurrence but, on the contrary, a relief.

Sometimes our too feeble understanding does not allow us for a long time to pass beyond such and such a compensating situation. Our inner growth seems to bump up against this obstacle. But, let us repeat, that which we love, to which we are attached, is never in itself an obstacle; the obstacle is only in the false identification of the loved image with Reality, the obstacle lies only in ignorance.

Our chances of passing beyond such and such a compensation depend then on the power of our intellectual intuition. They depend also on the degree of subtlety of our compensatory image. First of all, the more subtle this image the less the chances that it will deceive us; every image loses its value in course of time, but the more subtle the image the stronger it is and the slower in exhausting itself. Then, if nevertheless fatigue and deception occur the correct interpretation of this deception is as much more difficult as the compensating image happens to be subtle. Instead of throwing doubt on the Reality of this image I am tempted to consider myself inadequate, maladroit, idle, or cowardly, in the dealings that I have with it. It is useful, from this point of view, to draw special attention to a species of compensation that is very subtle and that one ordinarily designates by the word spirituality. In 'spiritual' compensation man loves and serves a very high cause; an infinitely just and good 'God' of whom he tries to obtain a unitive knowledge: 'superior' 'elevated' states of consciousness, which he wishes to attain; a total realisation conceived as something that ought to be conquered; or an 'ideal' aimed at the reign of love and justice among men, etc. . . .

What in fact are these 'spiritual' values? One often hears three kinds of values distinguished: material, intellectual, and spiritual. These spiritual values evidently form part of Manifestation, since one can indicate them, love them, and serve them; but if Manifestation presents a gross or material aspect and a subtle, psychic or intellectual aspect, it is hard to see what could constitute a third aspect called 'spiritual'. The adorers of the 'spiritual' say that it is the Absolute (every idolater says that of his idol); it is assumed to be the 'Spirit' dominating and conciliating 'soul' and 'body'. But the Absolute cannot be conceived as opposed to any other values existing in Manifestation, for this opposition assimilates it with Manifestation. And the Absolute could not be indicated, nor loved, nor served, like an object placed in front cf our Self-subject. 'Spiritual' values cannot be the Absolute. Under the different forms assumed by these values there is always the conception of something perfectly positive which represents in short the positive principle of 'temporal' dualism. One can call it God or the Constructive Principle of the World, or the Principle of Good opposed to the 'Devil', the Destructive Principle of the World, or Principle of Evil; it is the Principle of Light opposed to the Prince of Darkness. It is normal that man should love construction and detest destruction, that he should love 'God' and detest the 'Devil'. The idolatry of 'spirituality' only begins when 'God' is illusorily identified by the intellect with the Absolute or Reality or the Intemporal. When this error is committed 'God' is identified with the Absolute Principle and the 'Devil' with Manifestation; 'Satan' becomes the Prince of this World; 'spiritual' goods are opposed to 'temporal' goods. This forgetfulness of Metaphysical Unity results in an inner dualism, in the impossibility of the synthesis of the being; as one sees, besides, in all idolatrous compensation.

We have insisted on drawing attention to these compensations called 'spiritual' because they are the most subtle of all. The mental image of 'God', of the positive principle of temporal dualism, is the most powerful compensatory image, the most resistant to devalorisation; consequently the most difficult to pass beyond. It is not in our power to choose our compensations; if our psychic structure is such that we have the 'sentiment of holiness', the 'love of God', it just happens that we are thus.

But we have then a very special interest in reminding ourselves that nothing that is conceivable can be Reality. Our 'own nature' is the Absolute itself; nothing of that which we can conceive, contemplate, love, lies beyond the domain of the images created by ourselves, by us as the Absolute.

Zen is categoric on this point and could not in any way be considered as a 'spiritual' doctrine. It is radically atheist if, by the word God, one means Reality assumed to be conceivable by our mind. 'From the beginning not a thing is.' Rinzai said also: 'IF ON YOUR WAY YOU MEET THE BUDDHA, KILL HIM . . . O YOU, DISCIPLES OF THE TRUTH, MAKE AN EFFORT TO FREE YOURSELVES FROM EVERY OBJECT. . . . O YOU, WITH THE EYES OF MOLES! I SAY TO YOU: NO BUDDHA, NO TEACHING, NO DISCIPLINE! WHAT ARE YOU CEASELESSLY LOOKING FOR IN YOUR NEIGHBOUR'S HOUSE? DON'T YOU UNDERSTAND THAT YOU ARE PUTTING A HEAD HIGHER THAN YOUR OWN? WHAT THEN IS LACKING TO YOU IN YOURSELVES? THAT WHICH YOU HAVE AT THIS MOMENT DOES NOT DIFFER FROM THAT OF WHICH THE BUDDHA IS MADE.'

Chapter Twenty-Three

THE INNER ALCHEMY

HE who would understand Zen should never lose sight of the fact that here it is essentially a question of the *sudden* doctrine. Zen, denying that man has any liberation to attain, or has to improve himself in any way, could not admit that his condition can improve little by little until it becomes normal at last. The satori-occurrence is only an instant between two periods of our temporal life; it may be likened to the line which separates a zone of shade from a zone of light, and it has no more real existence than this line. Either I do not see things as they are, or I see them; there is no period during which I should see little by little the Reality of the Universe.

But if the idea of progression bears no relation to Realisation itself, if the transformation is rigorously sudden, Zen teaches that this transformation is preceded by successive changes in the form of our inner functioning. We have said successive and not progressive as a reminder that this evolution which precedes satori does not correspond with a gradual appearance of Reality, but with simple and gradual changes of the modalities of our blindness.

This point having been clearly recalled, it is interesting to consider this gradual but not progressive evolution which precedes satori. In the degree in which our understanding, our 'penetrating glance', grows deeper, we observe that our spontaneous inner life—emotions and spontaneous imaginations—are modified. 'You become, according to what you think,' says Hindu wisdom. This evolutive modification is comparable with the distillation which, applied to any sort of body, purifies it, renders it subtle. When one distils fermented fruits and draws alcohol from them, the modification of the original product consists in a quantitative rarefaction and a qualitative exaltation.

There is less material, but the material is finer, less power of a gross nature (for example alcohol is lighter than the fruit from which it has been extracted), but more power of a subtle nature (the ingestion of alcohol produces effects that the ingestion of fruit could not produce). The alchemy of the Middle-Ages, with its retorts and alembics, its search for the quintessence, was a symbolic representation of the inner process which we are studying at this moment. The more a substance is thus rendered subtle, the less its essential characteristics are perceptible to the eye. The visible aspect of the fruit clearly evokes the idea of that which its consumption will give; alcohol, on the contrary, although possessing greater force, appears in an aspect that is less obvious. The word 'subtilise', in current language, means to cause to disappear. Subtilisation is also, as we have said, a purification, the subtler substance is at the same time simpler.

Evolutive understanding represents a distillation of our inner world, of our image-material. There is purification, subtilisation, simplification of this material and, correlatively, of all our imaginative-emotive processes. Let us give an example of this. As a child I believe in the Infant Jesus as in a perfect child who loves me and wishes me well, who watches me living and feels about me sentiments similar to my own; and this image is crude, very visible, charged with concrete details. As an adolescent I arrive at an understanding of God whom I represent to myself as a Being still personal, but without visible body, still having thoughts and sentiments, but vaguer, less easily imagined. The image is subtilised, it has lost some of its manifest clarity; it is more non-manifested and at the same time vaster, more powerful in the sense that it embraces more things. My age and my understanding again increasing, there forms in me the abstract idea of an impersonal Principle that I see as only good, constructive. At the next stage I arrive at the conception of this Principle as being above the dualism of construction and destruction, Non-Action dominating all phenomena, but I distinguish this Principle from its Manifestation, believing in the reality of this distinction. I understand that the Principle is my Principle, I perceive my identity with it, but I distinguish my Principle from my manifestation, believing in the reality of this distinction. At last I succeed in understanding that the distinction between Principle and Manifestation is a simple analytical artifice which my mind needs in order to express itself; I understand that I deceive myself as soon as I oppose among each other the elements that I have distinguished. The mental image of Reality, which at first had been the concrete image of the Child-Jesus, has been subtilised until it has become the abstract image of the Void of traditional metaphysics, Void which includes all the imaginable plenitudes. Parallel with this imaginative distillation it is evident that my affective reactions to my conceptions of Reality are subtilised also; the interior and exterior operation of my machine is modified when I cease to believe in a personal God, an object of love and of dread, and when I arrive at conceiving abstractly my Buddha-nature as being above all thought and all sentiment.

This process of distillation, due to the work of intellectual intuition, corresponds to the idea, often expressed in this work, that *our correct inner evolution destroys nothing but fulfils everything.* The apparent death of the 'old' man is not in reality a destruction. When I extract alcohol from fruit I do not destroy the essence of the fruit, but rather purify it, concentrate it, and fulfil it. In the same way I fulfil my conception of Reality when I evolve from the image of the Child-Jesus to the image of the Void. There is apparent death because there is a diminution of the visible, of that which is perceptible by the senses and the mind; but nothing has been destroyed just because the belief in the Reality of a perception ceases to exist. The fulfilment of the human-being carries with it the disappearance of the illusory Reality of images perceived by the senses and the mind.

The condition of man, at his birth, is to feel himself fundamentally unsatisfied; he believes that he lacks something. What he is and what he has does not suit him; he expects something else, a 'true life'; he seeks a solution of his pretended problem, claiming such and such situations in existence. This revendicative attitude, which engenders all our sufferings, is not to be destroyed, but to be fulfilled. We have seen, in studying the compensations, how our claim and attachment are subtilised. All our personal attachments derive from our central attachment to the image of our Ego, to the image of ourselves-as-distinct, by means of identifying association between a personal image and this general image. The more my understanding deepens, the more these associations are abolished; my attachment is thus purified, subtilised, and concentrated; it becomes less and less apparent, more and more non-manifested. The attached revendication is not reduced by an atom before satori, but it purifies itself, and fulfils itself according as the instant approaches of the sudden transformation when attachment and detachment are conciliated.

My amour-propre is an aspect of my revendicatory attention. It also is purified in the extent to which I understand. To the people who observe me from outside, I appear to be more modest. But I feel clearly that it is not so. My amour-propre becomes more and more subtle and concentrated, so that one sees it less; it fulfils itself, tending in one sense towards the zero of perfect humility, and in another towards the non-manifested infinite of my absolute dignity.

The distress which is associated with the egotistical claim is subjected to the same gradual modification. It is a serious mistake to believe that understanding can increase the anxiety of man. False information, by implanting in our mind constraining 'beliefs', can increase our distress. But the intuition of truth on the contrary subtilises distress, reducing its manifested aspect and increasing its non-manifested aspect. Profound distress, from which derives all manifested personal distress, is not reduced by an atom before satori; but it remains more and more non-manifested, so that the adept of Zen, in the measure in which he evolves (without progressing) feels distress less and less. When distress has become almost entirely non-manifested, satori is near.

The inner agitation of man reveals the conflict which exists between the vital movement on the one hand, and on the other the refusal of the temporal limitation which conditions this movement. Placed face to face with his life such as it is, man wants it and at the same time does not want it. This agitation purifies itself in the measure in which understanding entails a decrease of the refusal of the temporal limitation. The vital movement is not touched, whereas that which was opposed to it is reduced; and so this movement is purified, agitation disappears, our machine ticks over ever more smoothly.

The evolution that we are studying comprises before everything, as we have said, the subtilisation of our image-material. Our images lose little by little their apparent density, their illusory objectivity; they become more subtle, vaster, more general, more abstract. Their power of causing our vital energy to well up in emotive spasm decreases. The whole imaginative-emotive process loses its intensity, its violence. Our imaginative film presents less contrast; our inner dream is lightened.

One can consider satori as an awakening, our actual condition in relation to this awakening being a kind of sleep in which our conscious thought is the dream. There is truth in this way of looking at it, but it contains a trap into which our understanding risks falling. I always have a tendency to wish to represent things to myself and to forget that satori, an unimaginable inner occurrence, cannot be assimilated by analogy with anything that I know. Thus I have a tendency to assume an analogy between satori, ultimate awakening, and that which I experience every day when I pass from the state of sleep to the state of wakefulness. In this illusory analogy there reappears insidiously the progressive conception; just as my ordinary awakening seems to me to be a progress in relation to my sleep, so satori should be a 'super awakening', a 'veritable' awakening, a supreme progress in relation to my actual waking state. Just as my ordinary awakening gives back to me a consciousness which was lacking to me while I slept, so satori should give me a 'supra-consciousness' which is lacking to me now. This false conception (it is false since I am from all eternity in the state of satori and since, in spite of appearances, I lack nothing) entails erroneous ideas concerning the inner process which precedes the satori-event. Between profound sleep and the state of wakefulness, I pass by the state of sleep with dreams. The appearance of conscious activity, in the course of sleep, is in the direction of awakening, and the more my dream is striking, moving, urgent, illusorily objective, the nearer I am to awakening myself. In following my false analogy of progress I begin to think that satori will be preceded by an exacerbation of my conscious thought, of my imaginative film; I believe that mental hyperactivity, in extasy or in nightmare, attaining a critical point of tension, will obtain the bursting of the last barrier and entrance into a state of cosmic supra-consciousness. All that is in complete contradiction with the 'sudden' conception of Zen. Let us note how there is found again, in this progressist chimera, the egotistical identification which entails the illusory adoration of our consciousness. Our imaginary inner universe, centred on our person, pretends that it is the Universe; the consciousness which fabricates this universe is thus assimilated to the Cosmic Mind; and it is not astonishing after that that we should depend on this conciousness in order to conquer Realisation.

In reality, whether I sleep or remain awake, I am from this moment in the state of satori. Sleep and waking are steeped equally in this state; the state of satori, with regard to sleep and waking, plays the rôle of a hypostasis which conciliates them. Steeped in the Intemporal, sleep and waking are two extreme modalities of the functioning of my psycho-somatic organism, extremities between which I oscillate. Between profound sleep and the waking state, sleep with dreams represents a middle stage, the projection, on the base of the triangle, of its summit. From this the transcendental wisdom of the dream is derived. The symbolic thought of the dream, in which are expressed the situations of our personal microcosm, stripped of all the illusory objectivity of the outside world, is actually the only thought in us capable of seeing certain things as they really are; that is why dream-thought expresses itself in symbolic fashion, things-as-they-are being impossible to express adequately in a direct manner.

In this correct perspective let us try to conceive how, in our waking dream the gradual non-progressive evolution which precedes Satori is revealed in our consciousness. Our waking dream, like everything in us, is fulfilled gradually by subtilising itself. Far from becoming more striking, more apparently real, more deluding, it becomes lighter, less opaque, less dense, more volatile; it is less attaching, less viscous. The affective charges, which certain images carry, decrease; our inner universe evens up. Under this waking dream that is ever lighter we fulfil more completely the sleep of our actual egotistical condition. In short the fulfilment of our conscious thought brings it nearer in a sense to profound sleep. And, at the same time that our conscious thought approaches sleep, it differentiates itself from it by developing to the maximum its subtle intellectual possibilities. There is a real approach in the non-manifested, and apparent separation in the manifested. One remembers the hermetic aphorism: 'That which is above is like that, which is below, that which is below is like that which is above.'

The imaginative activity subtilises itself and tends towards non-manifestation, although the mind remains awake, and continues to function. A 'concentration on nothing' develops below the attention that is always held by images. My state then resembles that of the absent-minded scholar; but, as opposed to the scholar who is absent-minded because his attention is concentrated on something formal, I am absent-minded because my attention is concentrated on something informal which is neither conceived nor conceivable.

The whole imaginative-emotive process is lightened. This is revealed by the fact that I feel myself happy without apparent motive; I am not happy because existence seems good to me, but existence seems good to me because I feel myself to be happy. The evolution which precedes satori does not comprise an exacerbation of distress, but on the contrary a gradual relief from manifested distress. A neutralising balancing of our fundamental distress precedes the instant at which we will see directly and definitively that our distress has always been illusory. This links up with the idea that our nostalgia for fulfilment disappears in the measure in which we approach the 'asylum of rest'.

The Western mind often has difficulty in understanding the term 'Great Doubt' which Zen uses to indicate the inner state which immediately precedes satori. It thinks that this Great Doubt should be the acme of uncertainty, of uneasiness, therefore of distress. It is exactly the opposite. Let us try to see this point clearly. Man comes into the world with a doubt concerning his 'being', and this doubt dictates all his reactions to the outer world. Although I do not often realise it, the question 'Am I?' is behind all my endeavours; I seek a definitive confirmation of my 'being' in everything that I aspire to. As long as this metaphysical question is identified in me with the problem of my temporal success, as long as I debate this question within Manifestation, distress dwells in me on account of my temporal limitation; for the question so posed is always menaced with a negative reply. But, in the measure in which my understanding deepens and in which my imaginative representation of the universe is subtilised, the identification of my metaphysical doubt with the eventuality of my temporal defeat falls asunder; my distress decreases. My question concerning my 'being' is purified; its manifested aspect wears thin; in reality it is not reduced but becomes more and more non-manifested. At the end of this process of distillation the doubt has become almost perfectly pure, it is 'Great Doubt', and at the same time it has lost all its distressing character; it is at once the acme of confusion and the height of obviousness, obviousness without formal object, having tranquillity and peace. 'Then the subject has the impression that he is living in a palace of cristal, transparent, vivifying, exalting and royal'; and at the same time he is 'like an idiot, like an imbecile'. The famous and illusory question 'Am I?', in purifying itself abolishes itself, and I shall at last escape from its fascination not in a satisfying solution of the problem, but in the ability to see that no problem ever existed.

Let us observe at last how this evolutive process which subtilises our inner world modifies our perception of time. We believe in the reality of time, as we have said, because we are expecting a modification of our phenomenal life capable of supplying what we illusorily lack. The more we feel the nostalgia of a 'becoming', the more painfully this problem of time harasses us. We reproach ourselves with letting time go by, with not knowing how to fill these days which are passing. In the measure in which my urge towards 'becoming' is subtilised in me, growing more and more non-manifested, my perception of time is modified. In so far as it is manifested in my anecdotal life, time escapes me more and more and I let it escape me in attaching to it less and less importance; my days are ever less full of things that I can tell, which I remember. Side by side with this I feel a decrease in my impression of lost time; I feel myself ever less frustrated by the inexorable ticking of the clock. Here as elsewhere, the less I strain myself in order to seize, the more I possess. Let us specify however that it is not a question here of a positive possession of time but of a gradual lessening of the keen impression of not possessing it. At the time of the Great Doubt we do not possess time at all, but it no longer escapes us for we no longer claim it. And this suspension of time announces our reintegration with the eternity of the instant.

Let us see now why this gradual process of simplifying subtilisation necessarily precedes satori. When we read the accounts that certain Zen masters have left us of their satori, we note that this inner occurrence happens in connexion with a sensory excitation that has come from the outer world, in connexion with a visual or auditive impression, or with a fall or a blow received. The impression can be of slight intensity but it has always this character of suddenness which awakens our attention. Just as a sudden perception habitually awakens the attention of our passive mind, this time the sudden perception conditions the awakening of the active autonomous functioning of the mind and renders conscious the vision of things-as-they-are.

The interpretation of this fact lends itself to two errors. If I am very much attached to the notion of causality I may believe that the sound of a bell has caused the satori of the Zen master, and I ask myself how the thing can be possible. I may be tempted to believe that there exist special bells, producing special sounds capable of revealing to a human being his Buddha-nature. Or again, leaving aside this infantile interpretation, I may believe that the sound of the bell has played no part and that the Zen master has perceived it entirely independently of what was then taking place in his inner world.

In reality the perception of the outer world plays a necessary rôle at the instant of satori, but as perception of the outer world in general without the particular kind of perception being of the slightest importance. In fact, every perception, at every moment of our lives, contains a possibility of satori. A Zen disciple one day reproached his master for hiding from him the essence of the doctrine. The master led the disciple into the mountains; the oleanders were in flower there and the air was enbalmed by them. 'Do you smell them?' asked the master; then as the disciple

232

answered in the affirmative, he added: 'There, I have kept nothing hidden from you.' Every perception of the outer world contains a possibility of satori because it brings into existence a bridge between Self and Not-Self, *because it implies and manifests an identity of nature between Self and Not-Self.* We have said many times that our perception of an outside object was the perception of a mental image which is produced in us by contact with the object. But behind the exterior object and the interior image there is a single perception which joins them. Everything, in the Universe, is energy in vibration. The perception of the object is produced by a unitive combination of the vibrations of the object and of my own vibrations. This combination is only possible because the vibrations of the object and my own vibrations are of a single essence; and it manifests this essence, as one under the multiplicity of phenomena. The perceptive image is produced in me, but this image has its origin in the Unconscious, or Cosmic Mind, which has no particular residence, and dwells as much in the object perceived as in the Self who perceive it. The conscious mental image is individually mine, but the perception itself which is the principle of this conscious image neither belongs to me nor to the image. In this perception there is no distinction between subject and object; it is a conciliating hypostasis uniting subject and object in a ternary synthesis.

Every perception of the outside world does not, however, release satori in me. Why not? Because, in fact, my conscious mental image occupies all my attention. This purely personal aspect of universal perception fascinates me, in the belief in which I live that distinct things *are.* I have not yet understood with the whole of my being the declaration of Hui-neng: '*Not a thing is.*' I still believe that *this* is essentially different from *that*; I am partial. In this ignorance, the multiple images which are the elements of my inner universe are clearly distinct, one opposed to another; each of them is defined in my eyes by that in which it differs from the others. In this perspective no image can anonymously represent, equally with any other image, the totality of my inner universe. That is to say that no image is 'Self', but only an aspect of Self. In these conditions everything happens as if no union is realised, in the process of perception, between Self and Not-Self, but only a partial identification. The Self, not being integrated, only partially identifies itself with the Not-Self. The revelation of the total identity, or satori, does not occur.

This revelation only becomes possible at the end of the process of simplifying subtilisation. The more my images are subtilised, the more their apparent distinction is effaced. I continue to see wherein they differ one from another, but I see less and less these differences as oppositions; everything happens as though I foresaw little by little the unity underneath the multiplicity. The discriminative oppositions become more and more non-manifested. No veritable unity is realised, in my inner universe, before satori; but in the measure in which multiplicity becomes non-manifested, my inner state tends towards simplicity, homogeneity, mathematical unity (which must not be confused with metaphysical or fundamental Unity). Impartiality in face of my images, in fulfilling itself, accomplishes the integration of the Self. The partial identification with exterior objects decreases; I feel myself more and more distinct from the outer world. The process which precedes total identification does not consist in a progressive increase in the partial identification but on the contrary in its gradual disappearance. To use a spatial expression, the manifested Self is more and more reduced and tends towards the geometrical point that is without dimension. In the measure that I tend towards the point, my representation of the outer world also tends towards the point; everything happens as though an intermediate zone of interpenetration were purifying itself between Self and Not-Self, as though Self and Not-Self were more and more separated at the same time that their apparent opposition decreased. Thus two men who are enemies, in the degree in which their hatred disappears, feel themselves more and more strangers to one another while their opposition is disappearing.

At the end of this gradual evolution my inner universe reaches homogeneity in which not forms but the opposition of forms is abolished. Everything is equalised. Then any image can represent adequately the totality of my inner universe. I have become capable of experiencing, in a perception, no longer only a partial identification with the Not-Self, but my total identity with it. Still it is necessary that the Not-Self shall manifest; that is what happens at the time of this releasing perception of which the men of satori tell us. Before the Self, integrated in a non-manifested totality, the Not-Self appears totally integrated in a phenomenon which represents it; then perception flashes out, in which without any discrimination the totality of the Self and of the Not-Self are manifested together. The totality of the Self becomes manifest, but in the unity in which all is conciliated and in which this Self seems to be abolished at the very instant at which it fulfils itself.

Chapter Twenty-Four

ON HUMILITY

WE would like to end this book by insisting on a capital aspect of this theoretical and practical comprehension which alone can deliver us from our distress. It is a question of understanding the exact nature of humility and of seeing that in it is to be found the key of our liberty and of our greatness.

We are living from this moment in the state of satori; but we are prevented from enjoying it by the unceasing work of our psychological automatisms which close a vicious circle within us. Our imaginative-emotive agitation prevents us from seeing our Buddha-nature and, believing therefore that we lack our essential reality, we are obliged to *imagine* in order to compensate this illusory defect.

I believe that I am separated from my own 'being' and I am looking for it in order to reunite myself with it. Only knowing myself as a distinct individual, I seek for the Absolute in an individual manner, I wish to affirm myself-absolutely-as-a-distinct-being. This effort creates and maintains in me my divine fiction, my fundamental pretension that I am all-powerful as an individual, on the plane of phenomena. This task of compensating my psychological automatisms consists, in my imaginative representation of things, in refusing my attention to evidence of my impotence, in giving it to evidence of my power, and in withdrawing my pretension whenever the spectacle of my impotence cannot be eluded. I train myself never to recognise the equality between the outside world and myself; I affirm myself to be different from the outside world, on a different level, above whenever I can, below when I cannot. The fiction according to which I should be individually the Primary Cause of the Universe requires that it

236

shall only be a question of the conditioning of the world by me: either I see myself as conditioning the outer world, or I see myself as not succeeding in conditioning it, but never can I recognise myself as conditioned by it on a footing of equality. From which arises the illusion of the Not-Self. If I condition the outside world, it is Self; if I do not succeed in doing so, it is Not-Self; never can I bring myself to recognise it as Itself, because I lack knowledge of the hypostasis which unites us.

The impossibility in which I find myself to-day of being in possession of my own nature, of my Buddha-nature, as universal man and not as distinct individual, obliges me unceasingly to invent a representation of my situation in the Universe that is radically untrue. Instead of seeing myself as equal with the outside world, I see myself either as above it or below, either on high, or beneath. In this perspective, in which the 'on high' is Being and the 'beneath' is Nullity, I am obliged to urge myself always towards Being. All my efforts necessarily tend, in a direct or a roundabout manner, to raise me up, whether materially, subtly, or, as one says, 'spiritually'.

All my natural psychological automatisms, before satori, are founded on amour-propre, the personal pretension, the claim to 'rise' in one way or another; and it is this claim to raise myself individually which hides from me my infinite universal dignity.

The pretension which animates all my efforts, all my aspirations, is at times difficult to recognise as such. It is easy for me to see my pretension when the Not-Self from which I wish to be distinguished is represented by other human-beings; in this case a little inner frankness suffices to give its true name to my endeavour. It no longer works so easily when the Not-Self from which I wish to be distinguished is represented by inanimate objects or above all by that illusory and mysterious entity that I call Destiny; but it is, at bottom, exactly the same thing; my luck exalts me and my ill-luck humiliates me. All perception of positivity in the Universe exalts me, all perception of negativity in the Universe humiliates me. When the outside world is positive, constructive, it is as I want it, and it then appears to me as conditioned by me; when it is negative, destructive (even if that does not directly concern me), it is as I do not want it, and it appears to me then as refusing to let itself be conditioned by me. If we see clearly the profound basis of our amour-propre, we understand that all our imaginable joys are satisfaction of this amour-propre and that all our imaginable sufferings are its wounds. We understand then that our pretentious personal attitude dominates the whole of our affective automatisms, that is the whole of our life. The Independent Intelligence alone escapes this domination.

My egotistical pretension towards the 'on high' has to express itself in an unceasing process of imagination because it is false, and in radical contradiction with the reality of things. If I look at my personal life as a whole with impartiality I see that it is comparable with the bursting of a fireworks-rocket. The shooting upwards of the rocket corresponds with the intra-uterine life during which everything is prepared without yet being manifested; the moment at which the rocket bursts is the birth; the spreading-out of the luminous shower represents that ascending period of my life in which my organism develops all its powers; the falling back of the shower in a rain of sparks which expire represents my old age and death. It appears to me at first that the life of this rocket is an increase, then a decrease. But in thinking about it more carefully I see that it is, throughout its duration, a disintegration of energy; it is a decrease from one end to the other of its manifestation. So is it with me as an individual; from the moment of my conception my psycho-somatic organism is the manifestation of a disintegration, of a continual descent. From the moment at which I am conceived I begin to die, exhausting in manifestations more or less spectacular an original energy which does nothing but decrease. Cosmic reality radically contradicts my pretension towards the 'on high'; as a personal being I have in front of me only the 'beneath'.

The whole problem of human distress is resumed in the problem of humiliation. To cure distress is to be freed from all possibility of humiliation. Whence comes my humiliation? From seeing myself powerless? No, that is not enough. It comes from the fact that I try in vain not to see my real powerlessness. *It is not powerlessness itself that causes humiliation, but the shock experienced by my pretension to omnipotence when it comes up against the reality of things.* I am not humiliated because the outer world denies me, but because I fail to annul this negation. The veritable cause of my distress is never in the outside world, it is only in the claim that

I throw out and which is broken against the wall of reality. I deceive myself when I complain that the wall has hurled itself against me and has wounded me; it is I that have injured myself against it, my own action which has caused my suffering. When I no longer pretend, nothing will injure me ever again.

I can say also that my distress-humiliation reveals the laceration of an inner conflict between my tendency to see myself all-powerful and my tendency to recognise concrete reality in which my omnipotence is denied. I am distressed and humiliated when I am torn between my subjective pretension and my objective observation, between my lie and my truth, between my partial and impartial representations of my situation in the Universe. I shall only be saved from the permanent threat of distress when my objectivity has triumphed over my subjectivity, when the reality has triumphed in me over the dream.

In our desire to escape from distress at last, we search for doctrines of salvation, we search for 'gurus'. But the true guru is not far away, he is before our eyes and unceasingly offers us his teaching; he is reality as it is, he is our daily life. The evidence of salvation is beneath our eyes, evidence of our non-omnipotence, that our pretension is radically absurd, impossible, and so illusory, inexistent; evidence that there is nothing to fear for hopes that have no reality; that I am and have always been on the ground, so that no kind of fall is possible, so that no vertigo has any reason to exist.

If I am humiliated, it is because my imaginative autonomisms succeed in neutralising the vision of reality and keep the evidence in the dark. I do not benefit by the salutary teaching which is constantly offered to me, because I refuse it and set myself skilfully to elude the experience of humiliation. If a humiliating circumstance turns up, offering me a marvellous chance of initiation, at once my imagination strives to conjure what appears to me to be a danger; it struggles against the illusory movement towards 'beneath'; it does everything to restore me to that habitual state of satisfied arrogance in which I find a transitory respite but also the certainty of further distress. In short I constantly defend myself against that which offers to save me; I fight foot by foot to defend the very source of my unhappiness. All my inner actions tend to prevent satori, since they aim at the 'on high' whereas satori awaits me 'beneath'. And so Zen is right in saying that 'satori falls upon us unexpectedly when we have exhausted all the resources of our being'.

These considerations seem to indicate humility to us as the 'way'. It is true in a sense. Let us see, however, in what respect humility is not a 'way' if by this word we understand a systematic discipline. In my actual condition I cannot make any effort which, directly or indirectly, is not an effort towards 'on high'. Every effort to conquer humility can only result in a false humility in which I again exalt myself egotistically by means of the idol that I have created for myself. *It is strictly impossible for me to abase myself, that is for me to reduce the intensity of my claim to 'be'.* All that I can and should do, if I wish to escape definitively from distress, is less and less to resist the instruction of concrete reality, and to let myself be abased by the evidence of the cosmic order. Even then, there is nothing that I can *do* or *cease to do* directly. I will cease to oppose myself to the constructive and harmonising benefits of humiliation in the measure in which I have understood that my true well-being is to be found, paradoxically, where until now I have situated my pain. As long as I have not understood, I am turned towards 'on high'; when I have understood I am not turned towards 'beneath'—for, once again, it is impossible for me to be turned towards 'beneath' and every effort in that direction would transform the 'beneath' into a 'on high'—but my aspiration stretched towards 'on high' decreases in intensity and, in this measure, I benefit from my humiliations. When I have understood, I resist less and, on account of that, I see more and more often that I am humiliated; I see that all my negative states are at bottom humiliations, and that I have taken steps up to the present to give them other names. I am capable then of feeling myself humiliated, vexed, without any other image in me than the image of this state, and of remaining there motionless, my understanding having wiped out my reflex attempts at flight. From the moment at which I succeed in no longer moving in my humiliated state, I discover with surprise that there is the 'asylum of rest', the unique harbour of safety, the only place in the world in which I can find perfect security. My adhesion to *this* state, placed face to face with my natural refusal, obtains the intervention of the Conciliating Principle; the opposites neutralise one another; my suffering fades away and one part of my fundamental pretension fades away at the same time. I feel myself nearer to the ground, to the 'beneath', to real humility (humility which is not acceptance of inferiority, but abandonment of the vertical conception in which I saw myself always above or below). These inner phenomena are accompanied by a sentiment of sadness, of 'night'; and this sentiment is very different from distress because a great calm reigns therein. In this moment of nightly calm and of relaxation are elaborated the processes of what we have called the inner alchemy. The 'old' man breaks up for the benefit of the gestation of the 'new' man. The individual dies for the sake of the birth of the universal.

The conquest of humility, impossible directly, supposes then the use of humiliation. All suffering, by humiliating us, modifies us. But this modification can be of two sorts that are radically opposed. If I struggle against humiliation, it destroys me and it increases my inner disharmony; if I let it alone without opposing it, it builds up my inner harmony. To let humiliation alone simply consists in recognising to oneself that one is humiliated.

The Being, in our actual perspective, appears to us the unconciliated couple of zero and the infinite. Our nature urges us at first to identify it with the infinite and to try to reach it under this form, by incessantly rising. But this attempt is hopeless; no ascent in the finite can reach the infinite. The way towards the Being is not infinity but zero which, besides, being nothing, is not a way.

This idea that humility is not a 'way' is so important that we would like to come back to it for the last time. If I don't understand that, I shall inevitably withdraw such and such manifestations of my pretension in practical life, confine myself in a mediocre social rank, etc. I shall avoid humiliations instead of using them; imitations of humility are never anything but imitations. It is not a question of modifying the action of my fundamental pretension, but of utilising the evidences which come to me in the course of this action, owing to the humiliating defeats in which it necessarily results. If I cease artificially to fight against the Not-Self, I deprive myself of indispensable knowledge which comes to me from my defeats.

Without always saying so in an explicit manner, Zen is centred on the idea of humility. Throughout the whole of Zen literature we see how the masters, in their ingenious goodness, intensely humiliate their pupils at the moment which they judge to be propitious. In any case, whether humiliation comes from a master or from the ultimate defeat experienced in oneself, satori is always released in an instant in which the humility of the man fulfils itself in face of the absurdity, at last evident, of all his pretentious efforts. Let us recall that the 'nature of things' is for us the best, the most affectionate, and the most humiliating of masters; it surrounds us with its vigilant assistance. The only task incumbent upon us is to understand reality and to let ourselves be transformed by it.

EPILOGUE

CERTAIN readers of this work have wondered about the exact origin of the thoughts which they have found therein. They were presented with precise and often paradoxical notions concerning the state of man; one can understand that they asked themselves: 'Who has conceived this manner of looking at things? To what degree does the thought which is offered to us belong to the Zen Masters and in what degree to the author of the book?'

This reaction did not astonish me when I heard it, but I had not foreseen it. I want to explain this, and to propose certain ideas, in accordance with Zen doctrine, on the relations which exist between an intellectual truth and the individuality of the man who conceives it.

Let us first of all recollect the profound distinction that the Vedânta makes between Reality and truths. There is only one Reality, the Principle of all manifestation, embracing everything (intellectual and otherwise), unlimited and in consequence impossible to include in any formula, that is to say inexpressible. There is, on the contrary, an indefinite multitude of truths, aspects correctly perceived by our mind of refractions of Reality on the human intellectual plane. Each expressible truth is only an intellectual aspect of Reality, which in nowise excludes other aspects that are equally valid; for each expressible truth carries a limit within which it exists and outside which it ceases to exist. Within its limit a truth manifests Reality; outside its limit it fails. Every truth should then be seen as a duality: in so far as it manifests Reality—that is in so far as it is valid—and in so far as it does not manifest Reality—that is in so far as it is valueless. This distinction will allow us to connect the notion of truth with notions of the individual and the universal.

What takes place in me when I discover a truth, when there appears to me suddenly a relation uniting intellectual elements until then separated? I see clearly that I have not fabricated this new truth with old material; I have not fabricated it, I have received it, it has appeared in my consciousness in a moment of inner relaxation. Whence has it come to me? From a source within me, the source of all the organic and mental phenomena which constitute me, the Principle of which I am an individual manifestation, from the Principle which creates the whole Universe as it creates me. My truth has come to me from 'something' universal. From the universal my truth has taken on, in my individual consciousness, a form, a limitation; it has 'enformed' itself in my mind in accordance with my particular structure, in conformity with my personal style of thinking. In acquiring this form my truth has acquired the possibility of being conceived and expressed, but it has also acquired, beside the aspect which manifests the original Reality and which therefore is valid, the aspect which does not manifest Reality and which, in consequence, is valueless. The truth that I have expressed, in so far as it manifests Reality, is of a universal nature; it is, on the contrary, of an individual nature in so far as it does not manifest Reality and is valueless. In other words that which is valid, worthy of consideration, in the truth that I express does not belong to me-as-a-distinct-individual, and has not properly speaking any connexion with my particular person.

If I have understood that, I am altogether indifferent to the particular brain in which such a truth has taken shape; that particular brain is only the receiving-apparatus which has caught the message. If there exists an evident relation between the form of thoughts expressed and the particular structure of the man who expresses them there is no relation between this structure and the truth of the thoughts, with what the thoughts manifest of Reality. The formal aspect of my book is certainly mine, but the informal truth that it contains in the network of words and which may perhaps awaken in your mind unformed thoughts in accordance with your structure, this truth is not mine, or the property of any other man in particular; it is universal. A claim to the paternity of any idea is absurd; it comes from the egotistical fiction of divinity which, lurking at the bottom of our psychology, pretends that we are the First Cause of the Universe. In reality the individual never creates anything; if man creates it is as

244

universal man, anonymous, and as manifestation of the Principle. In the ages of truer wisdom artists, scholars and thinkers, did not dream of attaching their names to the works which took form through them.

The curiosity that we may feel about the paternity of a doctrine is in relation with a lack of confidence in our own intellectual intuition. If I seek a belief to which to adhere without the impression of internal evidence, without my intelligence exacting that it shall ring true, then indeed I look for private sources, for the authorities that are responsible for this doctrine. But why search thus? Such beliefs might have the most imposing origins but they will remain nevertheless, in my mind, unassimilated inclusions, not reconstituted in accordance with my structure, and in consequence useless for the accomplishment of my being. They will be spokes in the wheels of my machine. If, on the contrary, I wish to build up by degrees an authentic understanding, through intellectual nourishment which I can decompose and recompose in my own way, I shall seek everywhere without prejudice, with a complete absence of consideration for the person to whom I am listening or whose words I am reading. I am ready perhaps to find nothing in a certain famous teaching and to receive veritable revelations from an obscure source. The individual man whose thought I tackle matters little; I am only interested in that which, in this thought, might awaken my own truth which is still asleep. The Gospels interest me because I find there with evidence a profound doctrine, but discussions concerning the historicity of the personage of Jesus leave me indifferent.

If I have written *Zen and the Psychology of Transformation* as I have, without references, without precise documentation, without tracing anywhere the limit between the thoughts which took form in the brains of the Zen masters and those which took form in my own brain, that is because I am myself incapable of making these distinctions. After having read part of Zen literature and received from it, with an impression of evidence, a vivid revelation, I allowed my mind to work on its own. When we let it function without preconceived ideas the mind only asks to be allowed to construct; it establishes, by intuitive bursts, ever richer relations between the ideas already understood, and assembles them like the pieces of a puzzle. This work of co-ordination, of integration, results in a whole which is more and more harmonic and in which it becomes strictly impossible for us to determine what has been brought to us and what is created in us. And besides, once again, this discrimination is of no interest. The adhesion given by the reader to such and such a thought expressed in a book should not depend upon the fact that this thought has been conceived by such and such a man or by such and such another, but upon that inner resonance that we must learn to recognise and to use as our only guide.

Preoccupations concerning the individual who has conceived such a doctrinal exposition are in relation with our illusory need to find the Absolute in an aspect of the multiple. We wish to find the Absolute incarnated in a form. When we read a text expressing an ensemble of ideas we are tempted to adhere to it as a whole or to reject it altogether; that should be easier and should save us the personal trouble of reflection. From that moment we are led necessarily to envisage the author of the text as an entity whose individual value intrigues us: does he deserve our respect or our disdain? This way of reading, sound if a documentary text is in question, is no longer suitable when we wish to form our thought and discover our truth (that is, our own intellectual view of Reality). When I seek for my truth I know that I shall not find it outside myself; what is outside me—which I am going to use in order to find the truth in myself—can appear as a coherent whole; but I must not let myself be impressed by this appearance, otherwise I shall never succeed in effecting the analytical process which thereafter conditions my personal synthesis, my intellectual assimilation.

If I regard my book as a whole, I believe that the ancient Zen masters would have given me their *imprimatur*. But that matters little; above all they would have approved the detachment whereby I struggle to maintain my thought in the face of all other personal thought. One remembers that Zen master who, seeing one of his pupils poring over a Sutra, said to him: 'Do not let yourself be upset by the Sutra, upset the Sutra yourself instead.' For only thus can there be established between the pupil and the Sutra a real understanding.

INDEX

INDEX